AF600612

COMPANY TOWNS

Corporate Order and Community

NEIL WHITE

Company Towns

Corporate Order and Community

UNIVERSITY OF TORONTO PRESS
Toronto Buffalo London

Toronto Buffalo London
www.utppublishing.com

ISBN 978-1-4426-4327-7

Library and Archives Canada Cataloguing in Publication

White, Neil, 1976–
Company towns : corporate order and community / Neil White.

Includes bibliographical references and index.
ISBN 978-1-4426-4327-7

1. Corner Brook (N.L.) – Economic conditions. 2. Corner Brook (N.L.) – Social conditions. 3. Corner Brook (N.L.) – History. 4. Mount Isa (Qld.) – Economic conditions. 5. Mount Isa (Qld.) – Social conditions. 6. Mount Isa (Qld.) – History. 7. Company towns – Case studies. 8. Corporations – Social aspects – Case studies. 9. Community life – Case studies. I. Title.

FC2199.C67W45 2012 971.8 C2012-901553-9

University of Toronto Press acknowledges the financial assistance to its publishing program of the Canada Council for the Arts and the Ontario Arts Council.

Canada Council for the Arts
Conseil des Arts du Canada

ONTARIO ARTS COUNCIL
CONSEIL DES ARTS DE L'ONTARIO

University of Toronto Press acknowledges the financial support of the Government of Canada through the Canada Book Fund for its publishing activities.

This book has been published with the help of a grant from the Canadian Federation for the Humanities and Social Sciences, through the Aid to Scholarly Publications Program, using funds provided by the Social Sciences and Humanities Research Council of Canada.

To my parents, Lewis and Elizabeth White, who instilled in me a love of the past and of a good argument, to James Greenlee and Olaf Janzen of Sir Wilfred Grenfell College who taught me 'how to read' and write history, and to my lost brother, David Dearlove. You are missed.

Contents

Illustrations

Acknowledgments

This comparison would have been impossible without the invaluable support and always incisive advice of John Weaver and H.V. Nelles. The faculty and staff of the History Department assisted me in countless ways during my time at McMaster University.

In Corner Brook, the staff of the Ferriss Hodgett Library at Sir Wilfred Grenfell College has helped me since the late 1990s. George French and Kathy Elliott at the Corner Brook Museum and Archives opened their collections to me without hesitation. In St John's, the staff of the Rooms Provincial Archives and the staff of the Centre for Newfoundland Studies at Memorial University helped me locate crucial documents. I owe a debt of gratitude to Andy den Otter of Memorial University for supervising my master's work and to Chris Youe who gave me a place to stay and watch footy on Saturdays while doing research in St John's.

In Mount Isa, Stephanie McDonald and the staff of the Mount Isa City Council Library were always eager to assist my research, and Ailsa Bray of the Mount Isa Family History Society put me in touch with a number of local contacts. Les Darcy, one of those contacts, took the time to discuss his recollections about early Mount Isa and then give me an informal tour of the city in his car. In Brisbane, staff and friends at the Queensland State Archives, the John Oxley Library at the Queensland State Library, and the Fryer Research Library at the University of Queensland provided consistently invaluable aid to my studies. I must single out the staff of the QSA, the place where I spent most of my time, for their knowledge, professionalism, and friendliness. Jonathan Richards' detailed knowledge of all things Queensland assisted me inestimably.

The History Department at McMaster, the Social Sciences and Humanities Research Council of Canada, the Government of Ontario, and the Government of Newfoundland through Memorial University provided generous financial assistance for this project.

Finally, Karen Dearlove and Malcolm Dearlove-Stefan have my deepest thanks for helping me focus on the things that are most important in life and for keeping me relatively sane throughout this often maddening process. Any failure to acknowledge assistance on my part is inadvertent. Any errors or omissions in this study are my own.

Abbreviations

ALP	Australian Labor Party
ANDCO	Anglo-Newfoundland Development Company
Armstrong	Armstrong, Whitworth and Company Limited
ASARCO	American Smelting and Refining Company
AWU	Australian Workers' Union
Board	Woods Labour Board
BOHP	Bowater Oral History Project
BPPN	Bowater Newfoundland Pulp and Paper Mills Limited
CBMA	Corner Brook Museum and Archives
CMC	Committee for Membership Control (an AWU splinter group)
CNS	Centre for Newfoundland Studies, Memorial University
Commission	Newfoundland Commission of Government
IBP	International Brotherhood of Papermakers
IBPSPMW	International Brotherhood of Pulp, Sulphite and Paper Mill Workers
IP	International Paper
IPPN	International Power and Paper Company of Newfoundland
IWA	International Woodworkers of America
MICCL	Mount Isa City Council Library
MIM	Mount Isa Mines Limited
Mineside	The company-planned portion of Mount Isa
NP&P	Newfoundland Power and Paper Company
QHC	Queensland Housing Commission
QSA	Queensland State Archives

RNC	Reid Newfoundland Company
Rooms	Rooms Provincial Archives
Russo-Asiatic	Russo-Asiatic Consolidated Limited
TFAAC	Trade Facilities Act Advisory Committee
TLC	Mount Isa Trades and Labor Council
Townside	Mount Isa fringe community
Townsite	The company-planned portion of Corner Brook
Xstrata	Xstrata PLC, current owners of the Mount Isa mine

COMPANY TOWNS

Corporate Order and Community

Introduction

Since machines first sputtered to life in England over two centuries ago, company towns have existed on the world's resource and manufacturing frontiers. Capitalists of all stripes have, to paraphrase Marx, nestled, settled, and established connections 'everywhere' in their quest for 'constantly expanding markets.'[1] The need for growth has pushed firms seeking competitive advantages in controlling resources and dictating development from cities outward to geographic peripheries. Founded to extract resources or manufacture finished products for sale, company towns are vital early links in the commodity chains of global capitalism.

The pursuit of economic control fosters the desire among company officials to manage, to varying degrees, residents' social lives. Capital has power over community because of the single company's local economic dominance. The general fact of life for the residents of company towns, then, has been dependence: dependence on the company for the creation of the town; dependence on the company for livelihood; and dependence on the company for the survival of the community as a whole. Since the heyday of structuralism in the social sciences in the 1970s, this three-part typology of capitalist expansion, corporate control, and resident dependence has been the last word on company towns.[2] Researchers rarely have cast their gaze beyond type to ask whether other parts of the company town experience are worth exploring.

Similarly, little effort has been made to tally the total number of company towns. Searching Wikipedia for 'company towns' displays a list of 69 towns, none of them resource towns. Searching 'U.S. company towns' provides a slightly longer list of 113 towns, but towns in states with long histories of resource extraction, like Missouri, are absent from the list. In the Pacific Northwest region of the United States alone, historian Linda Carlson documented 94 and speculated about thousands of company settlements. The Australia Mines Atlas lists roughly three hundred mines operating today in Australia as well as several hundred historic mines. Searching Wikipedia for 'Australia' returns the vague statement that the remnants of company towns 'are spread throughout the country and are located in every state and territory.'[3]

For Canada, sociologist Rex Lucas arrived at the exact figure of 636 company towns in his seminal 1971 work *Minetown, Milltown, Railtown*. A decade earlier a federal government–sponsored survey found 161 resource-based towns in Canada. The online Canadian Encyclopedia's current entry on company towns refers to roughly 1,000 'resource towns.'[4] For these three countries alone we can extrapolate a conservative estimate of several thousand company towns. Studying the industrial geography of other countries would reveal hundreds and thousands of similar settlements. There is no estimate of how many millions of people have lived in company towns.

Further clouding the issue is the variety of forms that company towns have taken. From the utopian company towns of Port Sunlight and Letchworth Garden City in England through the corporate- and government-built 'instant towns' like Pullman, Illinois, and those studied here, to the export-processing zones of Juarez, Mexico, and China's Guangdong province, dependent settlements have grown up alongside various types of industry across different stages of capitalism. These settlements have experienced different levels of corporate paternalism.[5] Some companies have tried to control the lives of workers in minute detail while others have opted for a mixed level of paternalism and individual initiative. Some town-builders, like those companies that operate 'fly-in' resource sites with a rotating employee population, have to implement comprehensive employee welfare schemes by dint of the way work time is structured and scheduled, while other companies, such as those who operate the scores of assembly plants in places like El Norte along the Mexican-American border, feel no obligation or pressure to provide for the well-being of their poor, uneducated workers. Classifying company towns and levels of paternalism raises questions of empiricism and specificity.

Such poor and fragmentary accounting for a type of human settlement that is both global and fundamental to the existence of capitalist society suggests that the places represented by the notches in the tallies do not matter. Popular depictions of the company town reinforce this 'cookie cutter' image. Images of grim male faces, plant closures, isolation, loneliness, and frustration spring to mind in word association games. The muscular, self-righteous paternalism of Major Barbara in the eponymous George Bernard Shaw play, the coal loader who owes his soul to the company store in Tennessee Ernie Ford's classic tune 'Sixteen Tons,' and the simple, God-fearing townsfolk pushed past the breaking point by company thugs in John Sayles's film *Matewan* provide a more concrete sense of the simple binaries by which we have come to understand company towns. Rex Lucas captured the conventional wisdom best. 'Community identification,' he said, 'is immaterial, for the patterns are similar; differences are local variations on the major themes.'[6]

The structuralist definition of the company town pre-empts a deeper engagement with the scores of manufactured, time-bound, and historically relevant settlements obscured by the term. This core problem fosters a stereotyped view of company towns. *Company Towns: Corporate Order and Community* re-evaluates and complicates this notion by analysing the unique internal processes and moments that made two company towns: the western Newfoundland paper-making town Corner Brook, Newfoundland, Canada, and the outback mining town Mount Isa, Queensland, Australia.

I grew up in Corner Brook. It was my home for more than twenty years. I experienced dependence firsthand. Union politics, mill production, and the state of the company were sources of frequent local speculation. My grandfather worked in the mill and so did the parents of my friends and relatives. Corner Brook's company-built district – called Townsite – was planned and picturesque compared to the unplanned neighbourhoods that I grew up in. The company was omnipresent, but my life in Corner Brook was more than paper thin.

My family instilled in me an abiding interest in history and my friends nurtured a playful but critical eye for the ironies and absurdities of daily life. I honed those qualities at Sir Wilfred Grenfell College with the help of two stellar history professors who encouraged my study of the built environment of company towns. Through planning and chance, that kernel of an idea morphed into a doctoral thesis. My atypical life story suggested to me that others in Corner Brook had experiences that defied type as well. When first reading the literature on company towns I asked intuitively, 'Is the structuralist account correct? Are X, Y, and Z company towns the same? Are they the same as Corner Brook?' I wanted to understand why the definition overlooked the fundamental variety of social life, but to do that I had to find a methodological and interpretive vocabulary that could insert difference into a subfield where similarity reigned.

I decided that the most expedient way to test the structuralist hypothesis was to compare two towns[7] – to look at, as anthropologist Clifford Geertz's work suggests, 'and see the variousness of things, of thrones and dominations and powers,' to 'bring into uneasy compatibility the tides of globalization and the little harbours we build to accommodate them,' to unsettle rigidity and complacency.[8] A two-case evaluation promised to add new dimensions to the understanding of power and resistance, negotiation and hegemony in company towns.

Comparing two towns fulfilled three core criteria. It allowed for a broad *and* deep engagement with the history of each place. Limiting the number of towns also amounted to an intrinsic methodological challenge to conventional studies that lump company towns into large groups, presupposing similarities instead of uncovering and explaining difference. In addition, two towns were as much as I could handle in a deep, layered analysis. Because I knew its history and where the evidence could be found, Corner Brook would be one of the towns.

In order to challenge type, the choice of the other town needed to satisfy broad typological similarities. It had to be built around a resource extractive industry and situated on a resource frontier – the most typical version of a company town. It needed to have had some measure of physical and social planning undertaken by the company. Finally, so that I could observe town life firsthand as I had in Corner Brook, the comparator had to still exist. Being interested in re-evaluating and reorienting the study of company towns, I also hoped my methodology would help to pinpoint differences. If broad typological similarities existed, but environments, societies, and industries differed, then I would be able to steer analysis toward issues of local divergence faster. I chose the Australian base metal mining town of Mount Isa to compare to Corner Brook because it met all of these criteria. Mount Isa's location on the other side of the planet recognized the international scope of company towns, which most studies, focused as they are on a single nation, fail to consider.

Broad historical similarities between Mount Isa and Corner Brook suggest a comparative approach, too. Australia and Canada have resource-exporting economies with historical ties to Great Britain. Mount Isa and Corner Brook have provided raw materials to two world powers – metals to China and newsprint to the United States – and thus both industrial enclaves are plugged into similar global economic relationships. Both towns sprang up shortly after the First World War in the early 1920s, when comprehensive company planning on resource frontiers was at its peak. Both companies implemented wide-ranging paternalist schemes for their employees. Socio-spatial hierarchy in the form of sprawling unplanned fringe towns accompanied industrial development at Mount Isa and Corner Brook, too. But comparable trends do not communities make. The structuralist definition is woefully silent on the human agents and the social processes that created community in company towns.

I recognize that my methodology is unorthodox. An international two-town, two-industry comparison of company towns does not exist. There is no accepted methodology to follow, so I pieced one together from various sources. The kinds of evidence available for Mount Isa and Corner Brook do not always correspond perfectly, either. Anyone who engages in comparative study understands this basic research truth. But these limits also point to the fact that, despite best efforts to sort them into neat categories, human societies are fundamentally dynamic, elastic, and adaptable. My research methods highlight the messiness of human agency and social order, the 'grey areas' of human existence. I began my research believing that a deep comparison of two locales would disclose more about each than a study of one. The following chapters confirm that intuitive premise.

To understand the histories of Mount Isa and Corner Brook we must examine the experiences of the residents whose actions filled in the vast gaps between wilderness and industry to create local societies. In stark contrast to the steady authority of Major Barbara stands Glyn West, chairman of the first operating company at Corner Brook. West's failure to accept the dire peril his company was in put the Newfoundland venture in jeopardy from day one. In place of Tennessee Ernie Ford's anonymous miner we see John Noah, a Corner Brook merchant whose experiences with bigotry at the hands of local mill managers fostered in him an entrepreneurial spirit that helped him become a successful shopkeeper, landlord, and civic leader. Or in exchange for the reluctant strikers in *Matewan* we see the mercurial Pat Mackie, an ex-wrestler, longshoreman, and militant union man who became a national celebrity when he led the miners of Mount Isa in one of the bitterest labour disputes in the nation's history. The deeper we go, the more we are compelled to exchange ideas of control and resignation with examples of agency and complex societies. West's, Noah's, and Mackie's unique stories counsel caution against the structuralist definition.

Company Towns: Corporate Order and Community compares levels of local history – corporate, political, industrial, urban, labour, civic, and social – to pinpoint important differences between company towns, and it shows that towns like Mount Isa and Corner Brook differ from one another, not just in eras of origination and local timelines but also in the processes that fuelled industrial and community development. It takes the analysis several levels deeper than do the existing accounts and by doing so shows the sorely neglected but central roles unintended consequence, human agency, and adaptation play in making company towns distinct from one another. Peeling back the intersecting layers of history to view the totality of social relations shows that the companies maintained their authority mainly through shifting rounds of negotiation with subordinates, rather than through domination or control. It tells a story of deep divergence rather than broad convergence, of power and agency rather than faceless historical forces, of hegemonies rather than control, of uncertainties and missteps rather than relentless progress and triumphalism. It shows the variability of places that the received wisdom assures us are all the same.

The chapters work their way down through the layers of agency in Corner Brook and Mount Isa, beginning with corporate power and concluding with the autonomies town residents carved out for themselves in their daily lives. Each chapter compares a broad theme in town history: business-industrial history, town and social planning, the role of labour, the growth and impact of civic organizations, and the social dispositions or structures of feeling that grew out of daily experience in each town. Chapters 1 and 2 open the study at the recognized sites of power in company towns: the company. They complicate the stale story of corporate triumphalism, however, by showing how managerial mistakes shaped local history. Chapter 3 focuses on the built environments of Corner Brook and Mount Isa, in particular the unique relations between planned towns and unplanned fringes that developed at each place. Chapter 4 explains the contrasting labour histories of the towns. Class politics fuelled local issues in Mount Isa, while community-based 'localism' prompted collective action in Corner Brook. Chapters 5 and 6 are social histories of civic and daily life – a dimension of company town development that other studies tend to ignore. They compare residents' navigation of local hegemonies. Thousands of personal dispositions and experiences defined the ways residents negotiated their lives. For a variety of reasons, Mount Isa's local hegemony had a more antagonistic tone than that of Corner Brook.

In theory, the histories of Corner Brook and Mount Isa should be strikingly similar, but they are not. They should yield firm simple lessons about dependency, but they do not. Their developments have little in common except for broad corporate-economic trends. Upon closer examination, even these similarities dissolve into complex place-specific processes that generated different outcomes. The same distinct, living histories exist in other communities of single industry that we see simply as the products of dependence on external forces. On the contrary, each notch in the company town tally has a unique story whose import reaches beyond isolated industrial hamlets to shake old certainties about the past.

Chapter One

'The Old Order Changeth': Industrial Development at Corner Brook

There is no way around the fundamental fact that company towns are creations of capital. To achieve a deep reassessment of the structuralist definition of company towns, it is necessary then to start in this familiar interpretive territory. I begin with the business and industrial histories of Corner Brook and Mount Isa. Testing the tautology of corporate power against the evidence reveals a jagged gap in our understanding of company towns: we know very little about the specific form and content of development and social relations in different company towns.

The plans that the companies drew up for Corner Brook and Mount Isa either failed or had to be altered for a multitude of reasons. No all-powerful captains of industry liberated isolated resources for productive use, as the structuralist interpretation would have us believe. In western Newfoundland in this chapter, and in outback Queensland in the next, we see the opposite: confused managers of imperilled businesses struggling desperately to achieve financial stability while scrambling to direct events. The companies' varied responses to the demands of each unfolding situation established contrasting local dynamics in each settlement.

The first decade and a half of the Corner Brook operation was perilous for companies and for the crisis-prone Newfoundland government. Building and operating a capital- and labour-intensive plant on an isolated resource frontier was difficult, even when companies felt no need to provide amenities for employees. The task was far more challenging when companies built towns. In Corner Brook, as with many single-industry projects in the early twentieth century, the founding company wedded industrial development to town planning intended to attract and hold skilled workers. The legacy of the founding company, Armstrong, Whitworth and Company Limited (Armstrong) cast a long shadow over the history of Corner Brook, and the fate of Armstrong foreshadowed and resembled closely that of the Dominion of Newfoundland.

In his 1915 address to shareholders, Armstrong's new chairman Meade Faulkner offered a prescient opinion: 'The old order changeth.'[1] Faulkner's comment dealt specifically with government control over the producers of British arms, but it applied equally well to the socio-economic changes that took place during the First World War. Certainties that underpinned global European dominance for nearly a century were called into question. Between 1914 and 1918, established European powers were swept away, liberal free trade and imperial adventurism were dealt crushing blows, and an aggressive opposing form of economic and political organization surfaced during the Russian Revolution. A speculative economic bubble in the post-war years insulated the United States during the Roaring Twenties but bypassed Britain and its colonies. The changes mounted.

The global economy shifted from one that comprised a collection of small-scale, family-run firms to a more concentrated economy of vertically integrated corporations operating within a monopoly capitalist framework.[2] Businesses had to adapt to increased competition for skilled workers and shrinking markets as well as to pressure from governments that assumed increasing responsibility for their citizens' well-being. Those shifts, exacerbated by the global economic depression of the 1930s, forced industrial managers into a bind: they had to cut costs and retrench while providing an expected level of care for employees. Many companies went bankrupt, disappeared, or merged. A decade after his address, Faulkner's forecast applied to his own company.

Armstrong was the top armourer in Britain.[3] At the turn of the century, only Germany's Friedrich Krupp AG rivalled Armstrong in weapons-making. A year into the First World War, the British government assumed control over the price of arms and who would receive weapons contracts. Soon rival British armourer Vickers surpassed Armstrong. By 1918 Armstrong was in a precarious position. On one hand, the armaments boom expanded the productive capacity of the company.[4] On the other hand, greater capacity compelled the company to find something profitable to produce in peacetime.

Armstrong did not suffer the contraction in the post-war weapons trade alone. Excess capacity, coupled with lingering government controls on production and profits, put all British armourers into a state of disarray. The companies had borrowed greatly to increase capacity. Vickers historian J.D. Scott observed that company accounts were muddled.[5] The rapid onset of an economic depression in Britain in 1920 exacerbated internal company difficulties, while the Washington Naval Treaty of 1922 limited arms production further by curtailing warship production. Vickers sought diversification into peacetime engineering projects 'centred round electric power, traction and transportation.'[6] Armstrong followed suit.

With 'boldness ... the keynote, and thorough the watchword' Faulkner switched Armstrong's production from weapons to locomotives, automobiles, and merchant ships.[7] However, entering new markets during an economic downturn was not easy. Vickers tapped into British demand for urban electrification, but established auto and rail companies outmanoeuvred Armstrong's attempts to diversify in those directions. By 1920 the promise of a speedy post-war recovery had vanished.

Glyn West, formerly of the Ministry of Munitions, succeeded Faulkner as Armstrong's chairman in 1920 and instituted a bolder plan of expansion. If national markets were closed to Armstrong, it would seek engineering contracts abroad, particularly in Britain's developing dominions and colonies.[8] The booming North American pulp and paper industry of the early 1920s seemed an especially attractive opportunity, because it required considerable expertise in hydroelectric generation and shipping – two of Armstrong's specialities. More caution was justified.

Armstrong was ill-prepared to adapt to the ultra-competitive and highly speculative newsprint market. Deeply rooted but ignored management flaws conspired against the company's transition to a peacetime industrial engineering firm. Stuart Rendel, a long-time member of the Armstrong cadre, called Armstrong's management style a 'family compact' that concentrated decision-making in the hands of the chairman and left little room for the opinions of outside experts and shareholders.[9]

The company arranged financial deals and accounting in a slipshod manner. On many occasions accountants wrote off 'easily avoidable losses' by 'turning the bulk of these bad debts into so-called investments. The losses were then written off in the form of provisions for depreciation.' Glyn West stepped into 'a position which was ready-made for dictatorship.'[10] In the Corner Brook venture, West and his associates produced a stunning example of hubris in early-twentieth-century capitalism.

To the supremely confident West, conditions on the late-industrializing island of Newfoundland must have seemed the ideal setting for grand industrial development. The west coast is covered in a dense fir, pine, and spruce forest and has numerous waterways to drive logs to nearby shore-hugging settlements. From the late nineteenth century on, businessmen with links to Nova Scotia and New Brunswick built sawmills that produced building materials for export to Atlantic Canada, the United States, and the West Indies.[11] The western Newfoundland forests also offered pulpwood – the primary ingredient in the manufacture of chemical paper. In the early twentieth century, promoters in the pulp and paper industry touted the region around the Humber River as a prime site for a paper mill.

The Humber region is an undulating, mountainous, and tree-covered valley on the west coast of Newfoundland. The valley extends for 100 kilometres in a southern arc from the northeast tip of Deer Lake to the Bay of Islands in the northwest. Deer Lake empties into the Humber River, and the valley soon pinches into a narrow waterway that flows finally into the Humber Arm of the Bay of Islands. At the Humber Arm the valley continues from the southeast to the northwest for another 30 kilometres as a much-weathered fjord. Corner Brook is on the far southeastern shore of the Humber Arm, next to the outlet of the Humber River. It is located in a semi-circular bowl, with a small inclined coastal plain surrounded to the south by steep hills.

The region's climate is coastal subarctic. Short, warm summers give way to cool, wet autumns. Winter arrives abruptly and is the defining season in Corner Brook, lasting five or six months, with January and February the coldest months and the period of most precipitation. Winter temperatures average –15°C and snowfall averages between 1.25 and 1.5 metres annually.

Before the advent of the paper company, Corner Brook consisted of a small collection of villages whose residents fished and worked at the local sawmill. After 1923 NP&P built its planned townsite just east of the original village of Corner Brook, while the unplanned fringe community of Corner Brook West enveloped the adjacent heights. Three kilometres west of Corner Brook, where the Humber Arm begins to widen, was Curling, the largest community in the area before the mill. In 1920 Curling was a small regional administrative and merchant centre with its own sawmill and extensive fishing wharves.

Armstrong entered into contract work for hydroelectric and pulp-and-paper plant development in the Humber Valley between July 1920

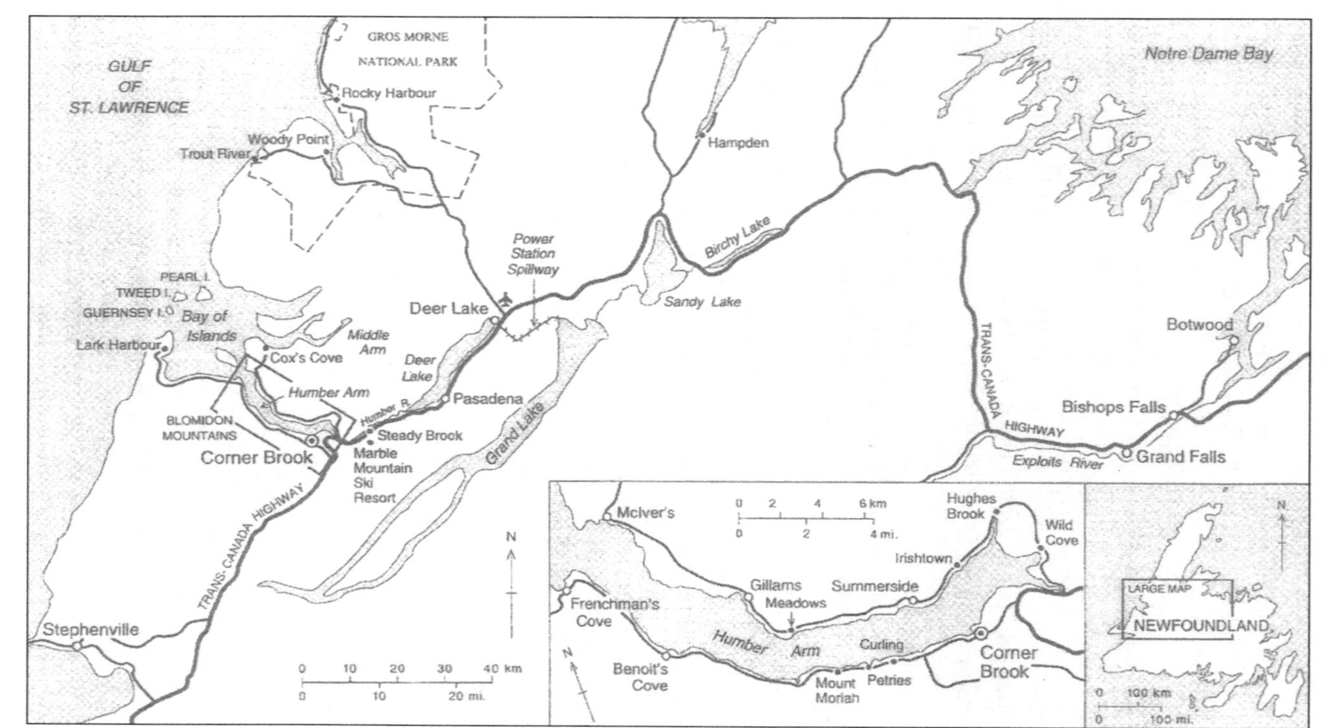

Humber–Bay of Islands region, Newfoundland. (Glen Norcliffe, *Global Game, Local Arena*, 43)

and April 1921 through agents of Newfoundland railway barons, the Reid Newfoundland Company (RNC). In October 1921 West committed Armstrong's agents to raise capital in London for executing contracts on a massive project conceived by RNC.[12] Unbeknownst to the English contractors, RNC faced its own suite of serious financial and political difficulties. For the Reid family empire, industrial development in western Newfoundland in the early 1920s was more chimera than sound business proposition.

Successive Newfoundland administrations since the late nineteenth century had tried to diversify the economy and reduce dependency on an outmoded cod fishery. From the 1870s on, Newfoundland officials aimed at boosting settlement through scientific agriculture and the creation of local manufacturing, but plans foundered on the reality of shallow, acidic topsoil, under-capitalization, and a small domestic market. The fishing merchants' vested interest in maintaining a fragmented fishing industry, and the island's scattered coastal settlements prevented a central administration from overseeing industrial development by local capital. The fishery persisted. Diversification came to be envisioned as mega-projects funded by foreign capital and government officials increasingly courted wealthy foreign developers.[13]

Ultimately, none of these development strategies could save Newfoundland from economic ruin and political collapse. In less than two decades between the early 1930s and late 1949, Newfoundland went from being a semi-autonomous dominion akin to Canada or Australia, back to a colony ruled by a handful of appointed commissioners. Finally, in 1949, following two very close referenda, Newfoundlanders surrendered their national aspirations to Canada in exchange for greater stability within a wider federation and provincial status.

The foreign direct investment approach achieved a measure of early success with the iron mine at Bell Island and the paper mill at Grand Falls – important precedents for the series of massive concessions made in the Humber Valley. Foreign direct investment was the only way to make a pulp-and-paper enterprise on the west coast of the island work. Weak and poor, Newfoundland governments could not impose substantive restrictions on foreign companies. In fact, the government behaved as a pleading supplicant.

The Reid deals of 1898 and 1901 cemented RNC's ownership of the island's transportation and communications network. For $1 million the government awarded Reid a fifty-year contract to administer the railway, and a two-million-hectare land grant that included mineral and water rights.[14] The gargantuan land grant placed a number of potentially valuable natural resources under RNC stewardship. RNC could develop the land or lease it to second parties, while workers and the products of industry would be transported on Reid trains and steamships. At the turn of the century, RNC oversaw a sizeable private transportation and communications empire.

The small-scale development of RNC's Humber properties highlighted the firm's difficulties, though. In 1902 the company leased land around the mouth of the Humber River for a small sawmill to Nova Scotian Christopher Fisher. The island's spruce and fir forests were not a suitable source for ship timber, and sawmills like Fisher's concentrated on making low-grade timber for home construction.[15] The Fisher deal exemplified a pattern of land and resource development confined to small, under-capitalized ventures that could not spur large-scale economic and demographic expansion. The improvement of the Reid lots proved more sluggish than expected.

RNC was enamoured particularly with the hydroelectric and timber potential of its western Newfoundland lots, but political resistance to an expanded Reid monopoly foiled a development scheme in 1900. RNC shelved the project for nearly fifteen years. Another west coast development plan foundered between 1915 and 1917.[16] By 1919, Harry Reid chaired a deeply troubled company. The railroad lost money continually, its upkeep neglected for years. The company seemed headed for collapse. RNC embarked on a plan to either renegotiate the agreement with the government or divest itself of the unprofitable railway and concentrate on developing its land holdings.[17]

Potential foreign investors should have paid greater attention to the troubled state of the Dominion of Newfoundland after the war, too. Serious financial problems compounded a depression in the fishery. The treasury paid $1.75 million annually to service its war debts, and government paid $1.3 million a year in subsidies to the RNC railroad. To meet its obligations, the government continued to borrow.[18] Post-war Newfoundland governments were frustrated by an empty treasury and presumed natural riches.[19] In his 1920 budget speech Finance Minister H.J. Brownrigg complained that valuable resources lay 'dormant and depreciating awaiting for the investment of capital to convert it to gold for our people.'[20] The government of Newfoundland was at least as desperate as RNC for an industrial panacea.

By 1920 Harry Reid had established a separate company, the Newfoundland Banking and Trust Company (Trust), to control his land

and water rights while RNC concentrated on the troublesome railway. Trust agents sought investors for Reid's battered Humber industrial scheme.[21] Desperate capitalists sought other desperate capitalists in a transatlantic courtship.

In March of that year Reid agents in Britain initiated talks with Norwegian hydroelectric and forestry developer Ragnvald Blakstad. A complex round of negotiations followed, involving the Reids, Blakstad, the Newfoundland government, British political and financial representatives, and Armstrong. In July Douglas Spencer, manager of Armstrong's hydroelectric department, expressed to a representative of the Trust his company's interest in building a hydro plant and other engineering projects in Newfoundland.[22]

Early in the spring of 1921 Reid and Blakstad hired an Armstrong engineer to evaluate the Humber proposition, and the survey proved 'most satisfactory.' In April Blakstad entered negotiations with Armstrong for a ten-thousand-horsepower hydroelectric plant and pulp and paper mill near the mouth of the Humber River.[23] One month later Blakstad began negotiations with the Newfoundland government, but talks fell apart because the government would not guarantee enough of the bond necessary to launch the project. In the summer of 1921 Harry Reid severed his partnership with Blakstad and concentrated on bringing Armstrong fully on board.[24]

But Armstrong officials had doubts about working with Reid. In early July 1921 Sir Walter Preston of Armstrong warned Reid that Armstrong was a contract engineering firm that avoided promoting or administering new industrial concerns.[25] Armstrong directors were interested only in the lucrative engineering contracts. In October, Reid settled a tentative construction contract with Armstrong and agreed to an offer by the English company to raise capital for the project if the Newfoundland government guaranteed the bond.

During the winter of 1921–2 Armstrong slid into the exact position of promoter and owner its executives had hoped to avoid. Early in 1922 Reid and Armstrong's officials were optimistic that the Newfoundland government would guarantee a $15 million bond issue, but in February the deal fell through. At that point, Armstrong sought the aid of the British Trade Facilities Act Advisory Committee (TFAAC), an agency established to reduce unemployment in Britain. Armstrong's reputation as a top engineering firm likely moved the committee to act in its favour. In March TFAAC agreed to guarantee half of the $15 million bond if the Newfoundland government would back the other half.[26]

TFAAC applied two critical conditions. First, Armstrong had to agree to a lump sum construction contract. Company officials had to submit a plan by October 1922 and it had to be comprehensive. Because of Armstrong's reliance on Reid construction estimates and shifting site plans, the scheme was becoming risky. Second, the committee made the guarantee contingent upon Armstrong's acceptance of majority control of the project.[27] The company that wanted only construction contracts faced the prospect of operating the mill and hydro plant. Armstrong and the Reids accepted the terms and formed a new company under Armstrong's control in July 1922.[28] All parties needed a success desperately and this led them to roll the dice.

After it accepted TFAAC's conditions, Armstrong secured the Newfoundland government's guarantee on the bond. The final agreement betrayed a patchwork of interests. The company's name changed to the Newfoundland Power and Paper Company, and 'the share capital was reorganized to give Armstrong 52 per cent' ownership. The Newfoundland government and the British treasury had representatives on the company's board.[29] Early in November 1922, Armstrong began work on the dam and canal that would divert water to Deer Lake's generators.[30]

From the outset, structural contingencies and human miscalculations combined to infuse the Humber development with a distinct character. Glyn West and Armstrong's directors were committed now to constructing and operating a sprawling industrial network in western Newfoundland. The first development plan proposed a power plant and mill at Corner Brook at the mouth of the Humber River; however, by the close of 1921 RNC surveyors had shifted the site of the mill and power plant from Corner Brook to Deer Lake, where the Reid railway could carry newsprint to port.

Between October 1922 and May 1923, the shifting site plans were finally settled. At a provisional meeting of the board of directors in October 1922, Harry Reid suggested Corner Brook as the site for the mill. The proposed location allowed for the creation of a deep water port where the paper could be shipped directly to market. When Glyn West pointed out the increased cost of such a move and the 'unfavourable reports of Armstrong's engineers on the Humbermouth site,' Reid dropped the idea. Two weeks later the board authorized Major D. Jennings to 'employ an expert to draw up a complete town scheme.' At that point the site for the entire NP&P project was still Deer Lake.

At the 29 December meeting, Armstrong's representatives R.P. Tod and W. Adamson argued to shift the mill site from Deer Lake to Corner

Brook to save on freight charges and in response to concerns about the carrying capacity of the narrow-gauge Newfoundland railway. After 'very careful consideration' the directors decided that a mill at Corner Brook would be more efficient and profitable, despite 'additional heavy expenditure.'[31] Part of the enlarged overhead would come from having to house approximately thirteen hundred temporary construction workers at Corner Brook as well as to provide permanent housing for skilled mill workers, all in addition to the existing construction camp for the dam and powerhouse at Deer Lake.

With political and financial roadblocks apparently behind them by mid-1923, the company appeared to be headed toward an industrial bonanza. North American newsprint had fallen from nearly $112 per ton in 1920–1 to $81 in 1923–4, but the price was still almost double what it had been at the outset of the First World War.[32] NP&P estimated that the Corner Brook mill would produce up to 400 tons of newsprint per day, at lower delivery, labour, and electrical power costs than its North American competitors could achieve.[33] It was driven to avoid delay.

The additional construction projects NP&P undertook pushed up expenditures. The company suffered cost overruns from port construction, the erection of a power line from Deer Lake to Corner Brook, and the laying out of a townsite. The board agreed to concentrate its marketing efforts in the United States because of the great demand for newsprint. Paper marketer Eric Bowater was on the NP&P board of directors from its inception. In spring 1923 Bowater made a tentative deal with NP&P to act as its North American marketing agent.[34] NP&P commissioned the construction of two ships to assist him with transporting newsprint to the mainland, but those costs had not figured in the original estimates either.

The planned Townsite was the most paradoxical of all the costly projects that sprang from the site change. It contributed greatly to NP&P's financial problems but became the basis for a burgeoning community. Armstrong's original plan was to construct only temporary dwellings for the workers. It assumed that mill workers would eventually build their own homes. Managers, papermakers, and mechanics, however, were in short supply in Newfoundland. British and Canadian skilled workers required housing and community amenities before they would commit to working in isolated western Newfoundland. In early 1923 the realization that the company needed lodging for over one hundred skilled workers led to the costly decision to build a permanent townsite. Apparently without regard for the extra cost, the board hired renowned town planner Thomas Adams to lay out what became known as Townsite and architect Andrew Cobb to design the buildings. A smaller planned settlement for power plant workers emerged at Deer Lake. No expense was spared for materials, civic amenities, or prompt completion.[35]

Reid lawyer Charles Conroy criticized the excessive civil engineering. In March 1924 G. Carpenter, superintendent of town building in Corner Brook, warned that the construction estimates he received from Canadian company townsites were outdated and did not reflect conditions in Corner Brook. In response Conroy complained that the project's scope was overblown. 'An unnecessary amount of money is being spent on building,' he said, and 'the type of construction will be far beyond what is reasonably suitable to the climate and conditions in Newfoundland.'[36] Local manager John Stadler, unaware of Armstrong's precarious financial situation, maintained the expensive building program into 1925 and 'considered that only what was best in design and equipment could possibly be good enough for the Armstrongs.'[37] Personal taste and incomplete individual understanding played a critical role in the planning of Corner Brook.

Socio-economic and climatic factors compounded the company's difficulties. By May 1923 over four thousand unskilled men looking for construction jobs had converged on Corner Brook and Deer Lake.[38] They posed a major problem for NP&P because it had to assign and supervise the army of labour as well as provide for its upkeep. In addition to permanent Townsite dwellings, NP&P erected temporary quarters close to the mill to house construction workers, but this stopgap proved insufficient. Worker resentment over wages and the blistering pace of work simmered until strikes paralyzed construction at both building sites in 1924. Unpredictable snowstorms, plunging temperatures, variable freezes and thaws, spring runoff, and mud churned by thousands of boots and hooves slowed work. Facing cost overruns, NP&P directors fell back on an old Armstrong accounting trick: in 1924 they transferred the debt to an in-house subsidiary 'utilities' corporation.

NP&P and its ghost utilities corporation continued construction on a massive scale with the best materials. The Glynmill Inn, the company's lavish staff and guest hotel, neared completion, and workers laid the foundations for houses at the rate of one per day.[39] Near the close of the 1924 construction season, manager John Stadler told local media that the project had exceeded its budget, while an NP&P lawyer warned Newfoundland's prime minister that the company had problems financing the utilities 'without injurying [*sic*] the security of the Debenture Stockholders.' London's financial press sensed trouble. In late December the *Economist* warned, 'Unless the Newfoundland venture yields a steady return within a comparatively short period [it will] be something in the nature of a burden for shareholders.'[40]

Glyn West tried to stem the criticism. At the 1925 general stockholder's meeting, an outwardly confident West reported profits, adding, 'I need not trouble you to go through the figures of the balance-sheet in detail.'[41] He set the opening of the mill for August. Pessimistic officials at the Bank of England, meanwhile, rightly attributed the cause of the parent company's 'tangled position' to the Humber project. The bank appointed J.A. Frater Taylor, well known in Canadian industrial circles as a 'company doctor,' to investigate.

Taylor arrived in the summer of 1925 and found 'a very unsatisfactory and dangerous situation.'[42] He estimated that the mill needed at least another £1 million to reach capacity. By 1926 Armstrong's total debt had reached $45 million. Most of the debt – approximately $39 million – came from the Corner Brook project. A ton of newsprint now made a profit of only $22.50.[43] Taylor and the Bank of England's solicitor, Lord Southborough, insisted on removing West as chairman of Armstrong in June 1926.

Southborough publicized Taylor's initial findings days later in a revelatory speech at Armstrong's annual general meeting.

> In 1923 it was contemplated that the pulp and paper mill and power development should be constructed together on practically adjoining sites. Some time after work had been started on the dam and water power development, it became evident to our engineers that it would be unwise to build the pulp plant and newsprint mill at Deer Lake, and it would be more economical for future working to construct works at deep water, so that the newsprint when manufactured could be shipped direct from Newfoundland to the United States and other ports without the intervention of a railway haul. But this change, so wise structurally and economically, necessitated a large increase of the initial capital outlay. The original capital had been provided on the basis of a complete scheme at Deer Lake which was much less costly. Apart from the increased expenditure involved in the change of the original plan it became apparent that certain auxiliary works and utilities, such as an adequate scheme for housing the

Corner Brook before industry. (Corner Brook Pulp and Paper Limited Photographic Collection courtesy of the Corner Brook Museum and Archives)

> company's employees, would be required, and a utilities company was formed to finance these additional works.

Taylor's report attributed Armstrong's difficulties 'to the Newfoundland enterprise, in which millions of capital [had] been locked up and losses sustained.'[44]

Taylor instituted a five-year moratorium on debentures, and Armstrong's stock plummeted. He finished his report in December, which found that 'some matters' were 'worse than expected.' He concluded that it would be a 'considerable time' before shareholders saw returns on the Humber venture. The bank forced Armstrong and NP&P to restructure. The new Armstrong board entered into negotiations for a merger with rival Vickers, and the once world-leading weapons manufacturer became the armaments branch of Vickers. The Humber development fell outside the deal.[45]

London financiers and Newfoundland leaders could not allow the Corner Brook paper mill to founder. Taylor's original plan was to

Corner Brook after industry. (Corner Brook Pulp and Paper Limited Photographic Collection courtesy of the Corner Brook Museum and Archives)

avoid receivership by vesting complete control of NP&P in qualified managers 'resident on the spot.' Taylor secured additional capital for NP&P with the caveat that the Bank of England gain a seat on NP&P's reorganized board of directors.[46] Local Managing Director Stadler resigned, and the director responsible for commissioning Thomas Adams to lay out the town was asked to step down.[47] The Newfoundland government, a shareholder and guarantor of the project, retained a nominal seat on the board but accepted the changes because of the dominion's own precarious economic position. The Reid family lost heavily. Creditors forced the firm into receivership in 1931.[48]

This tale of business collapse is instructive because it shows that Corner Brook's first corporate hegemon was not governed by an inherent capitalist rationality. By 1927 Armstrong directors' 'only satisfaction' was a high standard of work carried out in a timely fashion.[49] In varying degrees, the knot of business and government relations that the Humber project created contributed to the end of a world-leading armaments and engineering firm, the business receivership of Newfoundland's primary transportation and land developers, and, ultimately, the slide of Newfoundland into political receivership.

With both parent companies forced out of NP&P, the development entered a transitional phase that the new directors hoped would yield profits. Their expectations had foundation, because in 1926 local production costs were an acceptable $44 per ton, with newsprint selling for nearly $72 a ton in New York. Wages for unskilled mill workers at Corner Brook were among the lowest in North America, and the mill averaged a 16 per cent higher operating capacity than mainland competitors.[50] NP&P, however, did not have the market connections of established papermakers. That was only part of the problem.

NP&P emerged from the local disaster of the early 1920s into the bursting bubble of the North American newsprint industry. Shortly before the First World War, the American government overturned its longstanding tariff on Canadian newsprint, allowing free access to U.S. markets, and by 1919 Canadian pulp and paper exports reached nearly $100 million. By 1921 a ton of newsprint sold for between $112 and $137.[51] Canadian mill construction accelerated throughout the 1920s. According to industry historian Barry Boothman, this reckless expansion 'reinforced a drift toward disaster – not the elaboration of rational bureaucratic systems.'[52] Over-production caused newsprint prices to plummet. From its 1921 peak, the price in New York dropped to $82 per ton in 1923, to $77 in 1925, and to $72 in 1927.[53] It made little difference how much money NP&P saved in production, because NP&P officials could not generate enough in sales to pay its debts. The mill's London backers escaped further losses by selling the company to International Paper (IP) of New York a year after the reorganization.[54]

IP was a massive paper conglomerate centred in the depleted forests of the northeastern United States. The removal of the U.S. tariff on Canadian newsprint in 1913 fostered an intense competition between IP and smaller companies. IP's mills experienced erratic supply because they could not easily import wood from Canada in the face of smaller, more flexible companies that built mills in the forests of northern Ontario, Quebec, and New Brunswick. IP's President P.T. Dodge undertook a policy of aggressive expansion after the First World War.[55] IP expanded into Canada during the 1920s.

In 1924 A.R. Graustein became president of IP, and he pushed his predecessor's strategy further.[56] In 1927 news of the coming sale of NP&P reached New York, and Graustein jumped at the opportunity to acquire the modern mill, hydroelectric plant, and possibly even the right to harvest Labrador timber to supply his northeastern U.S. mills. According to local industrial promoter H.J. Crowe, Armstrong was a company of 'battleship builders' compared to the 'practical operators and paper manufacturers' of IP.[57] Between the spring and fall of 1927, IP's representatives negotiated with Bank of England officials and a Newfoundland government desperate to avoid a shutdown on the Humber. In mid-August 1927 the Newfoundland government gave speedy assent to the sale of NP&P to American paper barons.

IP called its Newfoundland acquisition the International Power and Paper Company of Newfoundland (IPPN). It gained major concessions in the takeover. In its survey of expansion during 1927, IP boasted that production from Corner Brook's four paper machines could be 'economically increased' and that the timber rights to an area larger than the state of Delaware cost only a small annual payment with no stumpage fees. The mill's location and modern design made it 'one of the lowest cost producers in North America.'[58]

IP hired E.A. Charlton as managing director of IPPN. He increased production at the Corner Brook mill and Deer Lake power plant and more than doubled its timber rights.[59] The company began to sell electricity to small power companies and new resource industries like the mine owned by American Smelting and Refining Company in central Newfoundland. Strategic location, high efficiency, and low-cost production combined to make the company an average of just over $700,000 a year between 1928 and 1932. Profits began to drop after 1930 when the U.S. price per ton of newsprint sagged from $62 to $48.[60]

IPPN's buoyant economic position until 1932 spurred the physical expansion of Corner Brook. Industrial and planned town growth led to the spread of fringe communities on Townsite's eastern and western flanks. Populated by unskilled mill workers, and the owners and employees of small businesses, unplanned Corner Brook East and West were characterized by a vibrant independent community ethos as opposed to the more rigid social hierarchy existing 'in Town.'

Between 1921 and 1935 the population of the Humber District more than tripled from 4,745 to over 15,000. Corner Brook – the census designation for Townsite and Corner Brook West at that time – grew from 411 residents in 1921 to 6,374 in 1935, and Corner Brook East from 369 to 1,248. Curling's population nearly doubled as well.[61] By the early 1930s, IPPN directly and indirectly administered several large 'instant' Newfoundland towns. However, IP was not able to enjoy the precarious stability.

The Great Depression hit Newfoundland's resource exporting economy with ferocity. By 1930 the volatile fishery accounted for 43 per cent of the dominion's exports while 55 per cent came from foreign-owned mining and forestry ventures. The government borrowed heavily to service its debt. Given the export focus of the island's underdeveloped economy and the general economic chaos of the period, the government simply could not maintain its meagre social spending.[62] In the Humber Valley, the crisis translated into spiralling losses for IPPN.

The bottom fell out of IPPN's Corner Brook operation in 1932. Newsprint prices in major U.S. markets fell below pre-war levels. Prices did not significantly rebound until the onset of the Second World War. IPPN responded by exporting more newsprint to the United Kingdom, but the measure did not stanch its capital haemorrhage. Revenue at Corner Brook dropped by over $500,000 between 1932 and 1933. In the following five years IPPN lost an average of $317,000 per annum.[63] These losses cut the revenues of the 1928–32 period nearly in half, and IPPN still carried a substantial outstanding debt from the takeover.

From 1932 onward the company instituted local cost-cutting measures. In July it cut wages by 10 per cent for all employees. In the following years, IPPN cut wages further and introduced short time at the mill.[64] Yet residents of Townsite could have their low rents deferred and supplement food purchases by growing their own vegetables. Loggers bore the brunt of IPPN's cutbacks.

Starting in 1930 IPPN reduced or suspended annual log drives. This meant the complete shutdown of many harvesting divisions. Pay per cord of wood dropped from $2.50 in 1931 to between $1.10 and $1.35 over the next seven years. Unemployed loggers received the pitiful dole at six cents per day for each family member while working loggers made an average net income of $20.25 a month – less than 30 per cent of the minimum income needed to sustain an outport family.[65] The unrecognized local logger's unions formed the most vocal resistance to IPPN's cuts, initiating over a dozen large and sometimes violent strikes during the 1930s.

The American parent company did not fare much better than its Newfoundland subsidiary. IP was the primary price-setter in the North American newsprint industry in the 1920s.[66] The American conglomerate was over-extended and under-diversified. IP sustained $20 million in net losses. Its Canadian companies did not make a profit until 1940.[67] In January 1936 Graustein resigned. The problems IP encountered at its Corner Brook subsidiary illustrate the common pitfalls of early-twentieth-century resource extraction, but with distinct roots and particular local consequences.

Newfoundland politicians could offer little assistance to the flailing company and its workers. In the early 1930s the government contemplated bankruptcy before being bailed out by British, American, and Canadian loans. After avoiding default by way of another joint British-Canadian loan in mid-December 1932, the guarantors compelled the prime minister to accept a royal commission into Newfoundland's finances. The commission found that Newfoundlanders were incapable of governing themselves and recommended the dominion take 'a rest from politics.' In February 1934 the elected government of Newfoundland officially surrendered democracy to a British-appointed six-member commission.[68] The so-called Commission of Government lasted for nearly sixteen years to 1949, after which Newfoundland entered confederation with Canada.

The Commission focused on country-wide problems. It could not deal with the specific difficulties of a company whose mill workers escaped the gloomy circumstances endured by the majority of Newfoundlanders. IP gained the benefit of a malleable local administration early on, but it had to deal with the consequences of political crisis in later years. Newfoundland's weak government was welcomed when companies sought generous contract terms, but proved a curse during economic collapse.

In 1937, Taylor and the Bank of England, backed by IP and Newfoundland's Commission government, sought a buyer for Corner Brook's newsprint network. The Bank of England remained Corner Brook's principle guarantor, while officials highly sympathetic to the Bank's interests now directed the minority guarantor, Newfoundland's government. Bowater emerged as the prime potential buyer in late 1937. It weathered the Depression better than most competitors, was English-owned, had past connections to the venture, and owned substantial shares in the Corner Brook mill.[69]

After nearly six months of talks, Bowater purchased the Corner Brook enterprise between May and June 1938, creating the subsidiary Bowater Newfoundland Pulp and Paper Mills Limited (BNPP). Eric Bowater envisioned Corner Brook as his bridgehead for entering the lucrative North American newsprint market. He got a bargain. Bowater paid IP $5.5 million for the Newfoundland venture – a far cry from the $20 million IP paid a decade earlier.[70] BNPP assumed IPPN's nearly $25 million debt. The harried Commission awarded Bowater concessions in the operating contract.[71] For Corner Brook, the deal signified expanded capacity, more jobs, a stable British administrator for the mill and Townsite, and increased prosperity for the region. BNPP operated the mill until 1984.

BNPP took over as the global Depression ended. The Second World War boosted the demand for newsprint and ushered in the first sustained period of prosperity in the history of the Corner Brook enterprise. In 1939 the Corner Brook operation enjoyed its first profit in seven years. BNPP consistently made its debt payments during the war and managed to buy all of the Bank of England's shares in the Corner Brook enterprise for only $6.5 million. The bank's directors had little faith in the profitability of the mill and sold when Eric Bowater made an offer. In December 1942 Bowater became majority owner of the mill. Increasing post-war demand for newsprint validated the older arguments about Corner Brook's low overhead and efficiency. As long as a favourable market climate prevailed, profits surged.[72]

In 1946, the company announced a large-scale expansion to the Corner Brook mill that would see the installation of a seventh paper machine. The expansion increased employment at the mill. By this time the settled community produced its own group of new employees.[73] When Number Seven began regular production in 1952, BNPP's Corner Brook mill had the highest-rated capacity in the world.

BNPP undertook new community planning early in its administration. New manager H. Montgomery 'Monty' Lewin undertook a town beautification scheme. After the Second World War, BNPP contributed to new residential construction on the immediate outskirts of Townsite and veteran's housing on the West Side hills.[74] Civic improvements represented the commanding presence of 'the company' in Corner Brook. But management intended to abandon direct paternalism.

Bowater aimed to be a top North American producer of paper products. In that wider corporate vision, the Newfoundland newsprint mill amounted to a stepping stone. Bowater began negotiations for a new United States paper mill in the early 1950s.[75] Bowater bought another mill in Liverpool, Nova Scotia, around the same time. A decade after war's end, the parent corporation achieved its objective with production nodes along the eastern seaboard and market linkages across the continent. The company's westward expansion marginalized Corner Brook. The Newfoundland enterprise went from the springboard of expansion to a reliable but increasingly neglected source of development

Corner Brook, ca. 1955. (Corner Brook Pulp and Paper Limited Photographic Collection courtesy of the Corner Brook Museum and Archives)

capital for other projects. Costly forms of company paternalism were first to go.

BNPP began to divest its non-industrial assets in the 1940s. The most potent symbol of BNPP's new direction was its sale of Townsite homes. By the mid-1950s the paper company sold most of its homes to company employees and allowed the building of private homes on the outskirts of Townsite. The sale of company services was a clear retreat from direct paternalism but was usually explained by stressing the importance of competition to community development and the maturation of Corner Brook. 'There comes a stage when, having become well-established,' said one company official, 'it is in the best interests, not only of the main business but also of the community as a whole, that such ancillary businesses should be entirely segregated from and operated quite independently of the principal business.'[76] BNPP did not discuss with residents the savings and the capital it gained from selling services.

Residents' demands for greater local self-government and amalgamation grew throughout the late 1940s. The union of Newfoundland's 'second city' was achieved as the result of a combination of company policy, public support for a greater say in the future course of the region, and a new Canadian provincial government with greater means to promote urbanization and economic diversity in Newfoundland. BNPP was obliged only to pay Corner Brook a small annual grant in lieu of municipal taxes.

Viewed from a critical empirical perspective, the early corporate history of Corner Brook depicts everything but powerful companies in control of events. Success, failure, or stagnation resulted from agents with imperfect understanding of events negotiating particular contingencies, not when the forces of capital said so. Social processes made company towns, and made them distinct from one another. Though it began as a company town at the same time, Mount Isa's corporate history presents significant contrasts to Corner Brook's.

Chapter Two

'Worth Dominating?' Industrial Development at Mount Isa

The corporate developers of Mount Isa faced their own suite of obstacles and opportunities that shaped local history. To compare briefly, the characteristics of the resources that base-metal and paper companies dealt with led to contrasting modes of extraction and different industrial and economic rhythms. A mineral discovery entailed risk while a paper mill could be a relative 'sure thing.' The metals of Queensland's hilly subtropical Cloncurry region lay buried where timber and water resources are visible above ground. The small exposed veins of lead on the spinifex-covered hills along the Leichhardt River offered prospectors only tantalizing clues to the actual amount of ore underground. The differences extended to industrial and corporate arrangements.

The low-grade ore deposits at Mount Isa required the newest flotation and smelting technologies to separate the metals from the mass of useless rock in which they were fused. The technology for turning timber into paper, on the other hand, was set by the early 1920s. In the 1920s and 1930s machinery for extracting marketable ore from low-grade deposits was in its infancy. Mount Isa Mine's (MIM) staff had to grapple with adapting costly new technology to its environment, even as it dealt with the uncertainties of base-metal mining. Finally, global price fluctuations for metals and paper differed. Different market trends shaped industry-specific periods of growth and decline.

The mine at Mount Isa did not arise out of a plan to develop the Queensland outback. An independent prospector discovered the lead and copper deposit at Mount Isa during a period of industry-wide decline and heavy government regulation. Queensland's extensive high-grade ore deposits, those that drew the most foreign capital, were already established or exhausted by the 1920s, and low-grade fields did not interest companies that could find less expensive and more immediately profitable ventures elsewhere.

Capital was footloose in the Australian base-metal mining sector. The mines that small companies attempted tended to be at small high-grade deposits that would require minimal capitalization. They lasted for a short period of time. These archetypical boom-and-bust enterprises left dispersed tailings dumps, rusting mills, and ghost towns in their wake. A concurrent program of increased social spending undertaken by Queensland's governing Australian Labor Party (ALP) discouraged foreign investment by adding a political constraint on companies' ability to freely exploit the region's resources.

The early result at Mount Isa was a speculative rush by local capital that accomplished little physical construction. The impetus for development proceeded from a loose collection of local interests, through one large local company, to large-scale investment by foreign corporations. Queensland's political culture shaped these developments from the beginning. That level of analysis serves as the best entry point to Mount Isa's corporate history.

An important difference between Australia and the rest of the British Empire was that labour had a significant political voice before the First World War. At the beginning of the war, one third of Australian wage-earners were unionized, and the parliamentary wing of the labour movement, the ALP, held seats in every state parliament. Federally, voters first elected a majority labour government in 1910, years before the first such administration in Britain. In 1915, Theodore Ryan's ALP swept to power in Queensland. The Queensland ALP had strong ties to the administration of the state's other main labour organization, the Australian Worker's Union (AWU), and its huge rank-and-file membership. The Labourite plan was straightforward:

> Capital, particularly when supported by the state, possessed vastly superior resources than Labor in any industrial confrontation. It was vital, therefore, for Labor to hold government in order both to deny employers access to state power in disputes, and to develop and maintain a process whereby disputes could be resolved in a way which did not depend on the relative power of the contending parties.[1]

Ryan introduced numerous bills aimed at enshrining the place of labour in state society and politics. From 1915 on, an increasingly centralized Labor bureaucracy implemented a number of social welfare programs and sought to control the vagaries of Queensland's resource exporting economy for the benefit of Queensland workers. The state owned herds, abattoirs, and butcher shops, and established a State Insurance Office to compete with private insurance companies. Labor implemented controls on the state's private sugar and steel producers and in 1916 enacted an industrial arbitration system whereby the state's Industrial Court was given the power to impose binding agreements in disputes between capital and labour. Those initiatives made the Queensland ALP the most socially progressive government in Australia.[2] Labor's social progressivism did not endear Queensland to investors, as was evident particularly in Queensland's mining industry. The state underwent a mining boom in the late nineteenth century when gold discoveries and abundant coal, silver, and tin deposits were buoyed by high metal prices. High wages for unskilled miners led to the establishment of dozens of boom towns just inland from the state's northeast coast and across the interior. By the second year of the First World War, however, foreign investment had dried up. When the ALP took office in 1915, gold production had slipped 33 per cent from 1900, tin output was down, and the state's silver mines produced 20 per cent less than they had in 1908.[3]

In keeping with the ALP strategy of regional economic development through increased industrial regulation, the Ryan government began during the 1910s to nationalize the state's mines. The government installed mines officers on nearly every field in the state and charged them with reporting on all developments in the industry. Ryan and his successors also introduced worker's compensation, minimum wages, and safety legislation that placed costly overhead charges on private companies attempting to get a foothold in the Queensland mining industry.[4] By the early 1920s, knowledgeable financiers and industrialists shunned mineral extraction in Queensland as an overly risky bet.

Fundamental problems with the state government's conception of the mining process made the industry volatile as well. The Ryan administration maintained a late-nineteenth-century preoccupation with the small-scale development of mines in which local prospectors and capitalists should develop mines on shallow, high-grade deposits and gradually develop a low-capitalized native industry. The ALP's early attempts to curb the power and land holdings of the large pastoral companies that leased extensive tracts of state land predisposed the government to favour a mining industry composed of numerous small concerns.[5] Successful mineral extraction along these lines was virtually impossible after the First World War. The global pursuit of resources and international finance capital's quest for investment opportunities had rendered the ALP economic vision anachronistic.

The discovery of high-grade surface or 'alluvial' gold and silver deposits initiated the first mining booms in Queensland. The company type that grew out of the relations between the characteristics of the resource and the Victorian liberal development policies of the time was usually a small-scale family-based partnership that sought quick profit for minimal capital outlay. From this stemmed extensive boom developments of ramshackle communities and their equally rapid shutdown and abandonment when the quick money dried up. By the turn of the century this mode of operation was antiquated because high-grade surface deposits throughout Queensland had become exhausted. A considerable amount of ore remained, but it was buried deep, and extraction yielded a high ratio of valueless rock to ore. Ore in these 'refractory' deposits was more tightly bound to the surrounding rock and necessitated more exacting and expensive separation technology.

The old order of fly-by-night mining on high-grade, shallow deposits was waning, but established mining companies in Queensland often failed to respond to the dictates of refractory deposits. Owners were reluctant to fund research and development, adopt new technologies, and replace aging machinery.[6] 'Companies, rather than partnerships,' argues one mining historian, 'became the norm.'[7] Linked to the necessity of greater capitalization for mines and mills was the need for industry to confront the challenge of providing some form of community for its essential skilled workers. With considerable difficulty, what emerged was a reliance on large-scale, capital-intensive, and usually foreign corporations. The corporate history of Mount Isa experienced all of these upheavals.

Queensland depended for revenue on resource rents from the pastoral, mining, and sugar industries. Officials were concerned about sluggish development in the northern and western regions of the state, and the general lack of a thriving manufacturing sector, but Queensland's economy was relatively resilient. Queensland's bureaucracy was pervasive. Though the government in Brisbane did not always control events, it observed and sought to influence developments in even the most remote parts of the state. The ALP had considerable support from the AWU and its widespread membership, and once the ALP inherited the state apparatus it increased its surveillance of the population. During the period of nationalization and welfare regulation in the 1920s, the ALP controlled a burgeoning panoptic state. Over the next four decades the state's ability to observe and direct events grew.

Cloncurry, a savannah region directly south of the Gulf of Carpentaria, benefited from successive governments' commitment to development in the first decades of the twentieth century. Before the base metals boom of the early twentieth century, Cloncurry's major industry was cattle grazing, and settlement was sparse. Uncertainty was a fact of life. The region's alternating wet and dry seasons made it a desert for much of the year and a scene of tropical deluges during the summer months. Cloncurry's main river systems, the Cloncurry and the Leichhardt, provided an inconsistent water supply, becoming raging torrents during 'the wet' and then drying up into a series of brackish mud holes during the winter.

Nearly seven hundred white pastoralists lived near the Cloncurry River in the late 1860s, but a series of clashes with the local Indigenous Kalkadoon people and the difficulties of dealing with drought, scarcity, and isolation convinced settlers to abandon the area.[8] The late 1870s and 1880s witnessed a flurry of copper discoveries that precipitated a brief period of land speculation, but actual industrial development foundered on the realities of isolation and capital requirements beyond the means of local developers. The first large-scale mining operation in the area opened in the mid-1880s and closed by the end of the decade, and further mine development did not occur until the price of copper rose in 1906. By that point, years of fighting had broken the back of the Kalkadoons' resistance to white settlement. Aboriginals became a cheap source of local labour for pastoralists and a source of complaint for many white 'pioneers.' One Queensland writer euphemistically called the marginalization of Aboriginals and the violent land seizures accompanying it 'detribalization.'[9] Marginalized in 'white Australia,' they had little impact on the industrial settlements of the interior. That there is no evidence of Aboriginal employees at the Mount Isa mine reinforces this point.

Without capital and aid, large settlements were untenable. Industrial development failed due to difficulties beyond the means of local developers. The first large-scale mining operation in the area had opened in the mid-1880s but closed by the end of the decade because of high overhead, low output, and slumping copper prices. Spurred by a later boom in copper prices between 1906 and 1907, the British-financed Duchess copper mine was one of the first opened in the new century.[10] Following the rising price of copper and developments on the Cloncurry field, the Queensland government in 1908 completed a nearly six-hundred-kilometre railway to Cloncurry, linking the remote town to the markets of the east coast. The continued profitability of copper into the next decade led to increasing consolidation by larger corporate entities like London's Mount Elliott Limited, which purchased most of the mineral leases on the Cloncurry field between 1912 and 1915. A short distance away, Hampden Cloncurry Copper Mines Limited consolidated the Hampden and Duchess deposits.[11] These first successful capital-intensive companies showed that development in this environment required a willingness to spend in the short term to earn more later.

During the First World War, metal prices boomed, but by 1920 the demand for war materials collapsed and copper suffered. The companies around Cloncurry experienced serious financial difficulties. On top of the decline in prices, mining in Queensland required a significant shift in technology in order to make low-grade deposits profitable. The flotation process for separating refractory ore from rock was pioneered at Broken Hill in New South Wales, but it was an expensive technology. The companies that benefited from the years of prosperity had neither the wherewithal nor financial patience to make such investments. Residents deserted the mining towns of Cloncurry when the operating companies pulled out of the ventures, leaving scattered ranching stations and ghost towns across the region.[12]

Unsurprisingly there were no serious expressions of interest from foreign developers when prospector John Campbell Miles discovered what he believed to be a massive silver-lead deposit in the unsettled Leichhardt River Valley. The several works that chronicle Miles's 1923 journey through northwestern Queensland searching for gold, and his 'stunning' discovery of the rich deposit at Mount Isa exaggerate its significance.[13] The more prosaic reality was that the region rose and fell on copper mining. Foreign investors did not consider a lead mine a worthy risk in the early 1920s. Miles extracted ore for assaying throughout 1923, and a glowing estimate from the Queensland Government Geologist at year's end induced a speculative flurry.

By January 1924 approximately thirty men worked a patchwork of over a hundred leases that ran north to south along the Leichhardt for eight kilometres.[14] Miles's discovery first interested local speculators who hoped to profit from selling leases to more-established mining companies. The Labor government's promotion of local gouger's rights corresponded well with the speculators' intentions, but it did not cor-

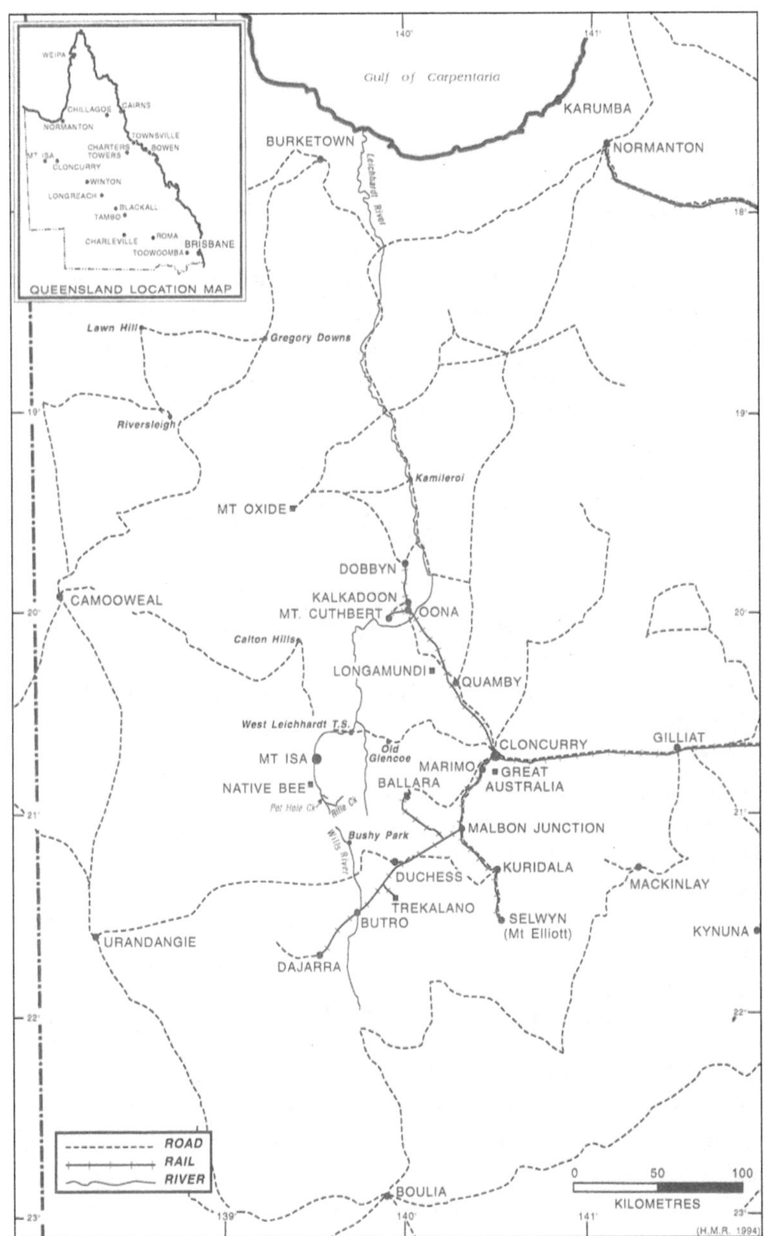

Cloncurry region, Queensland. (Don Berkman, *Making The Mount Isa Mine*, 2.)

respond to the realities of the low-grade deposits around Mount Isa. In the first years of the discovery, the question surrounding the Mount Isa silver-lead field was not who would dominate but whether it was worth dominating.[15]

The most persistent of the early local leaseholders was Mount Isa Mines Limited. Registered in Sydney in January 1924, MIM was a partnership between mineral speculator Douglas MacGillivray and W.H. Corbould, the former general manager of Cloncurry's Mount Elliott copper mines. MacGillivray possessed mineral leases for the richest deposits on the Mount Isa field. MIM's Australian directors named Corbould chairman of the new company, and he appointed MacGillivray the project's local director. Yet the only mining that MIM carried out was small-scale and exploratory. Several other Australian investors floated companies on the field in quick succession and began surface mining,[16] but none could undertake the extensive and capital-intensive industrial and infrastructural development necessary for a sustainable low-grade base-metal mining operation. Instead, the companies spent much of 1924 and 1925 buying each other's leases.

Early settlement, based not so much on a mineral boom as the possibility of one, grew modestly during 1923 and 1924. The earliest settlement was an instant town on the western shore or 'Mineside' of the Leichhardt River. By mid-1924 there were roughly 350 inhabitants in crude tents and shacks made of tree boughs and slabs.[17] The legacy of the fly-by-night mining fields throughout the region predisposed people to an itinerant existence. In the first three years of development, the lease-holding companies needed money to buy out competitors. Only after the field was controlled by one company could the directors begin large-scale construction.

But early on, uncertainty prevailed. MIM wanted the entire western 'Mineside' of the Leichhardt for industrial development and the space to build company houses. State officials in 1924 surveyed the government settlement on the eastern shore of the Leichhardt, opposite the area of the first squatter settlement. It became known as 'Townside.' Between 1926 and 1928, Mineside residents moved grudgingly across the river to the surveyed town.[18] Residents set up rough homes and businesses in the hope of a prosperous mine, company officials proposed industrial and civic schemes before their place on the field was secure, and the state government surveyed lots, laid out streets, and encouraged already settled inhabitants to move to the government half of the settlement to aid an unproven mine.

Corbould engineered the greatest boost to Mount Isa's fortunes by convincing the state government to build a branch railway from Duchess to Mount Isa in mid-1925. He knew that MIM needed capital and that the best source was Britain. However, no company would touch an isolated, low-grade, silver-lead deposit without a reliable link between it and ports. MIM's chairman struck a deal with the government whereby top government officials obtained thousands of shares in MIM in return for a government-built branch line. Feeling secure in the project's future, Corbould bought out Mount Isa Silver-Lead Proprietary in November 1925 to give MIM a monopoly on the field.[19]

Historian Geoffrey Blainey contends that Mount Isa 'was the first great field in Australia which was controlled from the inception of large-scale mining, by one company.'[20] Blainey's statement leaves an inflated impression of the scope of the development in the mid-1920s, for it was hardly a large-scale operation. Corbould's experience with refractory ore deposits made him conscious of the need to plan for permanent settlement, but structural impediments limited his ability to realize that vision.

Then there were local difficulties. Railway construction lagged and MIM did not interest foreign investors. Between 1926 and mid-1927 MIM had no capital to spend.[21] Corbould's plan to run the operation with a strong local management was a prescient stroke. A similar ground-level management style benefited the later incarnation of MIM, but in the mid-1920s MIM suffered. In 1927 MIM directors first sought a financier and ultimately accepted a buyer.

A range of complex and inconclusive negotiations took place between Corbould and various groups between mid-1926 and mid-1927. A tentative agreement with a London financier fell through early in 1927. Next Corbould tried to interest the Anglo-American Corporation, a South African mining conglomerate. In April that company failed to exercise its option on 550,000 Mount Isa shares because of delays in the completion of the railway and concern over its projected high freight rates. Yet the field had potential, and on that point the various consulting companies that Corbould brought to Mount Isa agreed. The Guggenheim-owned American Smelting and Refining Company, in a survey of northwestern Queensland mines, commented on the field's potential but were put off by the poor state of MIM's finances. Anglo-American's withdrawal left MIM with no capital. In June a last-minute deal with British mining magnate Leslie Urquhart gave his company, Russo-Asiatic Consolidated Limited (Russo-Asiatic), a controlling interest in the mine and buoyed hopes.[22] The Russo-Asiatic deal brought the first large foreign investment to Mount Isa and 'the first major capital input into the Queensland mining industry for nearly twenty years.'[23]

Like that of Glyn West and Armstrong in Newfoundland, Urquhart's involvement in Queensland mining was indirectly linked to the events of the First World War. Until 1917 he was one of Russia's great industrialists. After Russia's failed 1905 revolution, Urquhart bought several mines in the Urals and Siberia.[24] A hatred of labour unions led him to the conclusion that company planning for employee welfare, while initially expensive, could curb labour unrest. In his Russian operations he provided company-built housing, a range of civic amenities, and wages unheard of in the semi-feudal eastern empire. Unlike Armstrong's reliance on expert planners and onsite architects, Urquhart tried to manage his businesses personally. Until the war, his paternalistic turn proved a success. Midway through the war, conservative estimates placed his Russian assets at £56 million, making his mines some of the largest private enterprises in the country.[25]

The 1917 Bolshevik revolution wiped out Urquhart's Russian possessions. Shortly after the Bolsheviks staged a successful coup in St Petersburg in October 1917, the new Soviet government expropriated all private industrial property. Renewed worker unrest in the last months of Urquhart's tenure in Russia reinforced his hatred of unions, and the Bolshevik expropriation of his mines set him on a quest to receive compensation. He became one of the primary British advocates of counterrevolution and advised British prime ministers in negotiations with the new Soviet government at the Genoa (1922) and Hague (1929) Conferences.[26] But Bolshevik victory in the civil war and the tacit international acceptance of the regime that followed meant that nationalized industries would never return to their original owners. Urquhart continued his quest for restitution into the late 1920s but failed at every turn.[27]

Urquhart consolidated his depleted assets and finances into Russo-Asiatic and searched for attractive developments in other countries, but by 1926 the company was in dire financial straits. When an Anglo-American official leaked an assessment of the Mount Isa deposit, Urquhart outmanoeuvred ASARCO's more reticent chairman, H.A. Guess, by capitalizing on MIM officials' preference for a British buyer.[28] Corbould and senior MIM board members resigned their seats to Russo-Asiatic personnel, and the Sydney office became little more than a rubber stamp for the London board.[29] In the distant and unproven

Mount Isa venture, Urquhart envisioned a last chance for industrial success, but state mining officials were not so sure. In February 1928, one agent remarked, 'Mount Isa is a low-grade proposition, and will need to be worked on a very large scale to return a reasonable profit on the large capital necessary for its development.'[30]

Urquhart's experience in Russia combined with his determination to avoid labour disputes in Queensland – a state known for its vocal and militant unions – led Russo-Asiatic to focus on comprehensive planning and the installation of the most up-to-date mine machinery. In a letter to his wife in January 1928 he stated his purpose: 'I am going to take no risks,' he confided, 'and will use labour saving machinery whenever it is possible ... to so arrange matters as not to be dependent on conscienceless skulking loafers.'[31] Local considerations such as the size and type of deposit, the availability of construction and mine workers, and the necessity of providing the workforce with a steady supply of clean drinking water made planning necessary as well. Urquhart made a fully planned company town and onsite processing facilities the twin pillars of the project. The program was expensive. By mid-August 1929 observers described Urquhart as 'anxious and obsessive,'[32] And he had good reason to be.

Under Russo-Asiatic, development at Mount Isa was certainly bold but not very successful. Urquhart and company did not comprehend the unique processing requirements of Mount Isa's low-grade ore until after they purchased the field, and then they had to install and adapt costly separation technology.[33] Construction workers rushed the Rifle Creek dam to completion to supply water to a ballooning population sustained by speculative development money, not mine profits. Even had Russo-Asiatic been able to extract and process the ore, there was no means of transporting the product to market because the state government did not complete the Duchess–Mount Isa railway until April 1929, nearly two years after Urquhart bought MIM. In 1928 the General Engineering Company of America, the mine construction contractors, warned that the mine was perilously behind schedule.[34] Urquhart's will to develop on a comprehensive scale overrode local difficulties.

The situation worsened as the Depression set in. In mid-1929 Urquhart, defying protests from shareholders, split his company into Russo-Asiatic and the Mining Trust Limited. He created the latter to deal with the particular problems of Mount Isa and to float more shares for the troubled enterprise, but Mining Trust debentures were undersubscribed from the beginning, leaving it dangerously undercapitalized.[35] That November, Urquhart reported that the mine would 'enter the profit-earning stage' in August 1930. However, in April 1930 mine excavators struck water, flooding the shafts and causing yet another expensive delay. Three months before Urquhart's projected date of profit, the mine was not even open. The treatment plant could smelt lead carbonate, but the company had not completed the zinc refinery.[36] To make matters worse, world metal prices plunged in the deepening global financial panic.

Throughout the accumulating crises, Urquhart fell back on lauding his company's foresight in planning for workers' well-being. At the November 1929 general meeting of the Mining Trust, Urquhart commented on the 'difficult labour conditions' but assured shareholders that the 'considerable capital cost' expended on 'housing and other civilized amenities on a scale hitherto unknown in any mining enterprise in Australia' would 'more than satisfy any good Australian workman.' The expense was 'fully justified.'[37] Meanwhile, in May 1930 there were 3,500 residents of Mount Isa, but the industrial, and only, reason for the settlement remained unfinished.[38]

Urquhart represented the vanishing pre-war capitalist who maintained a personal paternalistic style of management in the face of increasingly complex financial arrangements. That style called for steady professional onsite and head-office direction, and constant communication between the two. Instead, desperation drove Urquhart's boldness. He was determined to renew his lost industrial empire and had an uncompromising vision of what Mount Isa would be. Urquhart and his directors must be assigned the lion's share of the blame for rushing the construction of a planned town instead of focusing on their main objective: building and operating a mine. That the planned communities turned out to be a boon to later companies and residents hardly exonerates the founders from mismanagement. This fascinating error in capitalist judgment shows that the grand resource projects of the time grew out of the vagaries of personal impulses, clever sales pitches, development manias, and chance, as much as they were the products of a prudent stewardship of investors' funds and bankers' loans.

Midway through 1930, the directors of the Mining Trust sought significant investment, and an attentive Premier Arthur Moore secured a guarantee on the needed £500,000 debenture in order to convince outside interests to aid the venture.[39] Moore's coalition Country Progressive-National Party ousted the Labor government in 1929. The Moore administration spent only one term in office, but coalition officials immediately began to overhaul the laws that restricted investment and industrial development. The favourable reports of the deposit and the massive amounts of sunk capital made Mount Isa the primary hope for mineral wealth in an otherwise declining regional industry. That commitment endured through the succeeding decades, despite changes in government.

Despite the debenture guarantee, extra money from London financiers was out of the question. The project guzzled successive infusions of capital with no earnings in sight.[40] Sources portray Urquhart at this time as confident in the success of the venture, but he may privately have rued the day he became involved in Mount Isa. Urquhart turned to the American Smelting and Refining Company. ASARCO's Chairman H.A. Guess, who earlier had expressed a mild interest in the mine, bought two of the six seats on the Mining Trust board of directors for £500,000 and gained an advisory capacity in the company. In September Urquhart removed the 'no foreign (non-British) owner clause' from the Trust's Mount Isa contract, paving the way for the New York mining giant's rapid takeover of the mine and town.[41]

Guess bought a third seat in November 1930 with the added provision that ASARCO be allowed to select a local general manager. The company chose Julius Kruttschnitt, the former general manager of ASARCO's operations in the southwestern United States and Mexico and a proven fixer of troublesome mines. Kruttschnitt arrived in Mount Isa in late December to find flooding an ongoing problem and the mine still not fully operational.[42] By October of the following year, ASARCO had gained full technical control of the project. Urquhart's Mining Trust endured only as the nominal owner.

The purchase of Mount Isa was part of ASARCO's program of relentless expansion. As its name implies, the company originated as a smelting and refining business, processing ore for mining companies. After 1903, under the leadership of Daniel Guggenheim, ASARCO purchased mines in the United States to feed its network of processing plants. The company pursued low-grade deposits because such properties were cheaper, and the company's background in processing gave it a technological advantage in the separation process. ASARCO weathered the downturn in the base-metals market after the First World War, and by 1925 it was expanding its network of mines.[43] Canadian-born chairman H.A. Guess was intrigued at the prospects of mining in Australia as well. After 1927, ASARCO directors continued to monitor progress at Mount Isa through Urquhart's American engineers. By late 1930 Guess felt confident about purchasing the mine. The completed company town at Mount Isa represented a bargain, and Julius Kruttschnitt was a trusted onsite manager.

ASARCO's administration differed significantly from Russo-Asiatic's. Where Urquhart centralized control in his own hands, Guess favoured strong local management.[44] ASARCO's management resembled Corbould's desire for local decision making for the original MIM, but in ASARCO's case Kruttschnitt was backed by the New York office's considerable influence, deep pockets, and vital technological acumen. The regional MIM board of directors became little more than a symbol of Australian influence.[45] Board meetings were under-attended or not attended at all. ASARCO was in charge.

The first local MIM managers came from North America and embodied ASARCO's wise preference for education, experience, and an industrial ethos stressing rational production and principles of scientific management.[46] ASARCO introduced a radically modern corporate regime to Mount Isa and, for that matter, to Australia. It was a highly capitalized and diversified organization that stressed training, research and development, and industrial efficiency. ASARCO focused know-how on the profitability of the industry more than on running a model community. Kruttschnitt reflected the ubiquity of the North American mining expert on the Mount Isa field in the 1930s. In a later interview he said, 'I was a graduate mining engineer so I knew enough about ore deposits to realize that a deposit of that size and that potential would have to succeed sometime.'[47]

Immediately after arriving in Mount Isa, Kruttschnitt pushed the development program ahead 'with utmost speed.' Yet problems persisted at the mine and in the town. ASARCO supplied workers with the pumps necessary to remove the water from flooded shafts. Local managers also installed expensive 'selective separation' technology to treat the extracted low-grade ore.[48] Selective separation opened one production gate, but MIM experienced serious difficulties smelting the lead carbonate. The ore's low melting point made the top layer of lead fuse over the smelter's intake grates, blocking airflow and the loading of more ore. The dangerous fumes that escaped from the clogged machinery caused nearly three hundred workers to be lead poisoned between 1931 and 1933 and led to a government investigation. Kruttschnitt brought in expert metallurgists from Australia, the United States, and even one from Newfoundland, but it was MIM's own mill superintendent who solved the problem by mixing the lead with sulphide ore to increase the melting point.[49]

The main mining, separation, and smelting problems were solved by 1933, but Kruttschnitt's ambition to get in the black by operating at capacity in an unpleasant and dangerous environment created what one state mining official mildly referred to as 'a feeling of antagonism between the workers and the management.'[50] ASARCO's speed up caused several work stoppages and threats of strikes in the early 1930s.

Tensions came to a head in late 1933 when Kruttschnitt locked out all workers for two months. Kruttschnitt reminisced, 'Something had to be done because of the low metal prices and the low productivity and the constant interruption by the constant downing of tools. It upset the operation to such an extent that I asked the chairman of the company if I could just close it down for a while, let things cool off.' When a shocked local magistrate asked Kruttschnitt for an arbitration hearing to determine the position of management and employees, he replied, 'We haven't any employees.' MIM had paid them and then laid them off.[51] Management felt justified in its heavy-handed treatment. 'There were plenty of men outside the gate ... during the Depression,' Kruttschnitt stated candidly. 'It kept those on the job on their toes.'[52] Compliant state officials and the state's major union bureaucracies hardly objected.

The 1930s were extremely difficult years for MIM, its American parent company, and employees. Between 1931 and 1932 the market price for a ton of lead dropped from £18 to a historical low of just over £9 and stayed below the 1931 price for several years.[53] To MIM's detriment, the negative effects of an economic system in tatters reinforced ongoing local difficulties. Kruttschnitt's authoritarian local management and ASARCO's continued belief in the potential of the mine were factors in its survival. The support of the government comprised an essential third plank.

The state government supported MIM by defusing the lead poisoning issue and by establishing a long-running productivity incentive called the 'Lead Bonus' that paid miners extra for every ton of ore extracted. The government also lowered the high freight rates on the Mount Isa–Duchess railroad. Government arbitrators granted MIM a small wage reduction after the two-month lockout in 1933 and assisted the company with negotiating loans.[54]

Thanks to its alliance with state administrations, MIM extended its local operations and prospered for the first time during the Depression. After the trying first half of the 1930s, MIM declared its first-ever net profit. MIM was not yet a success, but ASARCO and Kruttschnitt had weathered local and global storms. In 1937, ASARCO promoted Kruttschnitt from local general manager to chairman of MIM, giving him greater local control.[55]

When war came to Australia, the shrewd onsite chairman was well placed to take advantage of economic opportunities arising from resource scarcity and mobilization for total war. War helped make MIM profitable. When Britain declared war on Nazi Germany in 1939, Australia joined. In late 1941, the Japanese overran Singapore and bombed Darwin. To combat the expansionist threat, Prime Minister John Curtin placed some of the relatively small Australian military under command of the American General Douglas MacArthur. Domestically, the Commonwealth government instituted price, wage, and rent controls. Two of the main results of Australia's involvement were greater post-war state centralization and an increased willingness to engage in Keynesian social spending.[56]

Mount Isa became a major garrison for thousands of Australian and American troops engaged in the construction of a road north to the coast.[57] Militarization influenced community life at the same time that the mining company underwent major shifts in its extractive process and workforce composition. At the onset of the war, the primary consumer of Mount Isa zinc was Japan. The company's market for lead to Britain dried up because Japanese and German forces threatened oceanic shipping routes. Meanwhile, Australian industry – now coordinated by the Commonwealth government – had little use for Mount Isa's ore because it could obtain as much as it needed from Broken Hill. In March 1941, E.J. Muir, assistant inspector of mines, reported, 'Large stocks of lead bullion are accumulating at the smelter, due to the difficulty of obtaining transport to an overseas market.'[58]

Two months later the company received promising news when the Commonwealth government provided economic stimulus to the production of copper by raising its purchase price by £8 to a lucrative £86 per ton. MIM switched to copper mining and processing in late 1941.[59] Kruttschnitt obtained the necessary copper-processing equipment from the abandoned and underused machinery throughout the Cloncurry region and then adapted it to local vagaries. This considerable saving was reinforced by ASARCO's expertise in copper mining and smelting. As Kruttschnitt put it, 'We could operate on copper with half the force that [we] required for lead.'[60] A reduced workforce and military enlistments among Mount Isa miners caused the town's population to decline and create social turmoil just as the Isa was on the cusp of a boom.

By August 1943, MIM processed 500 tons of copper per day compared to the 500 tons per week it had produced the previous year.[61] Four years later the formerly hapless outback mine made a profit of over £3 million and applied it to paying interest on loans and retiring debentures. The company then decided to reintroduce lead and zinc production in 1947, and that led to MIM's most successful year to date. In that same year, MIM paid its first stock dividend. Thus, from the perspective of shareholders, the first profitable year came twenty-four years after construction at the site began – hardly an overnight success. The company resurrected a comprehensive program of community planning and welfare.[62] By 1951 MIM's ASARCO backers finally bought out and liquidated Urquhart's Mining Trust and cemented their ownership. MIM was doing better than ever.

Newfound prosperity contributed to a post-war population boom. In 1946 MIM increased its workforce from 850 to a stunning 1,800 employees and stated its commitment to 'increase and improve amenities' for its workers. Yet later that year MIM reported employee turnover at 113 per cent. Throughout the rest of the decade turnover averaged nearly 50 per cent a year, and this instability became MIM's main problem for the next decade.[63] Census statistics for the numbers of married and single residents in Mount Isa are unreliable throughout this period, but population data come from an array of unofficial sources. All sources indicate that up to 1970 the town's largest population cohort was single males.

There were approximately 3,500 permanent residents in Mount Isa in 1947, and population grew rapidly thereafter. Seven years later the population doubled to over 7,400 residents, 98 per cent of them directly or indirectly dependent on the mine for their livelihood.[64] New arrivals built lodging on the Townside, but town services lagged behind sprawling residential growth. In 1949, the company magazine, *MIMag*, reported that local officials were endeavouring to build new cottages to replace outdated steel and tent houses, but the demand for shelter far outstripped MIM's housing program.[65] At a time when company town administrators like Bowater were retreating from paternalism, MIM increased company planning on a grand scale.

The 1950s and 1960s were the period of greatest company and community growth since the founding of Mount Isa, and MIM profits showed annual increases throughout the period. In 1953 MIM became the largest mining company in Australia, and Kruttschnitt ceded his position as MIM chairman to George R. Fisher,[66] who became the first Australian to hold the position since Corbould in the mid-1920s. The managerial switch demonstrated ASARCO's confidence in the mine, but also Australians' capability to run a lucrative foreign-funded venture. Three years into Fisher's rule, MIM accounted for 60 per cent of Queensland's copper output and employed half of the state's mining employees, despite a turnover rate that averaged nearly 50 per cent of its workforce.[67] All of this corresponded to an extensive industrial expansion program. MIM paid for a new dam and reservoir at Lake Moondarra to provide water to the mill, smelter, and town, added a new power plant, and accelerated the mine's expansion. It also purchased a copper refinery at coastal Townsville.[68] In order to provide housing for a workforce that in 1953 had ballooned to over two thousand, Fisher and General Manager K.B. Gross instituted another housing program to supplement Kruttschnitt's post-war town expansion.

Kruttschnitt's and Fisher's town plans went a long way toward increasing Mount Isa's ability to accommodate thousands of miners and cut the turnover rate. High wages and the state's lead bonus combined to make MIM employees' pay packets some of the best industrial incomes in Australia. By the end of the 1950s Mount Isa's population doubled once again to nearly fourteen thousand. Many of the new arrivals were 'New Australians,' part of the larger post-war emigration from northern, southern, and eastern Europe.[69] The company encouraged immigrants to take up positions at Mount Isa because of its preference for inexperienced and malleable workers.

In 1959, MIM closed the company store it had run since the early 1930s, citing the need to improve competition among small businesses in the community, and by 1964 the company had removed and demolished Urquhart's original planned town, to make room for an open-pit expansion to its valuable copper mining operation.[70] Retreat from paternalism and a sizeable, relatively affluent population opened the town to greater investment. A range of retail businesses opened outlets in the town in the 1960s and in 1963 the state government made Mount Isa the seat for its own shire council.[71] MIM regularly publicized its pleasure at the growth of self-government and the shift in residential construction to community and state authorities. Belief in democracy and individual initiative was the public face of its concern, although those beliefs had not moved the company to promote such qualities in the past. MIM could retreat from paternalism because turnover had decreased and it was making record profits.

But overall security and progress were deceptive. The company's underground workforce grew increasingly disillusioned with MIM management, and major labour disputes paralyzed the industry twice in the early 1960s. In 1961 miners protested scientific management techniques that eroded their control over the work process.[72] They worried, too, about the high cost of living in northwest Queensland. In March, Queensland introduced the Industrial Arbitration Amendment Act to stem labour militancy. The act shifted the settlement of the lead bonus from the purview of the third-party Industrial Commission to direct negotiations between company and workers[73] – a deliberate provocation to organized labour – and Queensland workers responded with a series of strikes. For the miners of Mount Isa, the act exposed state politicians' alliance with big business.

Miners went on strike for six weeks between September and November, with the result that the Queensland government declared a state of emergency in late November that suspended civil liberties and allowed police to arrest recalcitrant strikers, and a settlement of the strike followed immediately. Government involvement had only increased tensions.[74]

A far more intense and drawn-out strike erupted three years later. The original issue centred on wages, but it escalated to encompass grievances with company influence in the town – problems with ossified union bureaucracies in Brisbane, and a critique of the longstanding MIM–government alliance. The labour action – at first a work-to-rule slowdown or 'go slow' – began in September 1964 when workers agreed to switch from piecework to a wage rate in light of another refusal by the Industrial Commission to raise pay. MIM responded by locking its gates. Shortly thereafter, miners seceded from the AWU and formed a local they claimed was more representative of their wishes. The union responded with claims of communist subversion.

In December 1964 the government declared another state of emergency, but this time local miners refused by a massive margin to return to work. The government responded with an astounding Order in Council that allowed police to search houses and arrest anyone aiding strikers. In February 1965 MIM offered to 'let the strikers back.' By early March, roughly 230 of the company's 2,000 employees had returned. Over the next month, MIM's workers went back to work, but the town took longer to recover. Enmity lingered for years.

The strike had a more positive effect on MIM's profit margin. Company intransigence and government repression broke labour militancy, and MIM was free to determine wages and work conditions. 'During the dispute the price of copper rose from £340 to £560 per ton, as Australia changed from an exporter to an importer ... ASARCO interests outside Australia actually profited from the dispute.'[75] The MIM boom continued. With high global copper prices, ASARCO held a strong hand.

The hand of the state grew stronger in the following years as well. Under the rule of Johannes 'Joh' Bjelke-Petersen from 1968 and 1987, the state government, always aspiring to blanket surveillance and rigid control in the interests of 'development,' took extraordinary steps to cement authoritarian control and introduce a brand of homemade corporatism to Queensland. Social historian Raymond Evans sums up in angry detail the depths to which Queensland's democracy – eroded for decades by petty autocrats on all sides of the political spectrum – sank under the 'philistinism' of Bjelke-Petersen:

> This was a period when democratic principles were trammelled to privilege the interests of a select and powerful minority ... Bjelke-Peterson was not the first premier to behave despotically, erratically or vaingloriously in office ... Yet he was arguably the most unpredictable, grandiose and headstrong leader since [Thomas] McIlwraith. Nor were the Bjelke-Petersen governments ... the first in Australia to toy cynically with voters, hoodwink the press, ride roughshod over democratic forms ... or generally behave in exceedingly autocratic ways. Yet they were the first to carry out all such tendencies, as a complete package, so far in the direction of outright tyranny and ultimately over the brink of public tolerability.[76]

Petersen and his followers were highly attuned to potential disruptions in the economy-leading minerals industry. To deal with the subversives who he imagined were lurking everywhere, Petersen perfected the use of sensationalist scare tactics like the spectre of Communism to polarize and divide Queensland society – unskilled from skilled workers, rank-and-file from union heads, city from country, as on down the line – so that his government, and the wealthy interests like MIM that it represented, would prosper.[77] The culmination of years of neglect and abuse of democracy was reinforced by the elite's stubborn refusal to listen to labour and civil groups who envisioned a more progressive state. Some of that pressure came from below, from the workers and residents of Mount Isa, but those groups faced nearly insurmountable obstacles to reforming Joh's Queensland.

In 1968 the state government granted Mount Isa city status and an elected municipal council. The city had 16,000 residents. MIM directly employed over 4,300, and the new city was still a company town. In 1979 MIM Chairman J.W. Foots commented on the company's need to 'walk the fine line' in the community 'between actively involved ... and not appearing to try to control [town] organizations.'[78] That year a company newsletter stressed that 'the city is developing an identity separate from the Mine.'[79] Statements of this type illustrate the difficulties Isans encountered in surmounting dependence on a single industry, particularly within the political-industrial climate that prevailed in Queensland after 1960.

Between the world wars, the corporate culture of the Western world shifted. Companies based on personal, familial-type relations and free-wheeling development schemes were replaced by increasingly vertically integrated corporate networks whose experts tried to analyse and direct all aspects of ventures. The transformation was the great business trend of the period, and it hears echoes in Mount Isa and Corner Brook. War's contrasting effects lured companies to the resource frontiers of outback Queensland and western Newfoundland. Russo-Asiatic was desperate to develop a mine after the loss of its Russian properties while Armstrong needed to diversify out of wartime production. Directors' mistakes and the systemic problems in corporate chains-of-command resulted in strict micromanagement at Mount Isa and the board's stubborn refusal to curb excessive spending at Corner Brook. The immediate result in both cases was financial disaster, but from there business paths diverged once more and to ever greater degrees.

The companies' successful and failed adaptations to structural constraints and local contingencies in a series of specific historical moments created local corporate orders. Abstraction and over-generalization obscure these critical developments just as they omit the vital social processes that shaped Mount Isa and Corner Brook's built environments, labour, and community histories.

Chapter Three

'Praying for a Conflagration': Planned and Fringe Towns

Moving from the corporate histories to a comparison of the built environments of Corner Brook and Mount Isa pinpoints deeper differences between company towns. A built environment is the frame of daily life in any settlement: the structures, utility and transportation infrastructure, and layouts that characterize a place. Social relations are expressed in the wood, metal, and bitumen that make the physical outlines of a town. These differences go far beyond surface judgments of placement and aesthetics, though, into histories of power relations and social processes. Nowhere is this function of creating a built environment more apparent than in locations where a single industry plays a pivotal role in defining a space. Yet a structural approach, in the rush to classify and envelope, downplays the variety of forms that capital assumes as well as the myriad ways residents participate in the spatial dialogue between company and community.

The foreign companies at Corner Brook and Mount Isa designed communities to provide workers with comfortable and stable social lives. Executives believed that stability would nurture workforces free of the inefficiencies that plagued earlier frontier industries and create steadier corporate earnings. Despite this shared motivation, the socio-spatial relations in Corner Brook and Mount Isa diverged strikingly. In Townsite, Corner Brook, the company instantly designed a rigid scheme of house types for skilled workers and management only. MIM's intense workforce turnover problems, on the other hand, compelled it to build hundreds of shelters over four decades in Mineside, where MIM rented dwellings to all employees. Simple power relations in the planned settlements got complicated in the sprawling fringe towns that sprang up on the borders of company authority. The companies rescaled unequal relationships between capital and labour, between corporate centres and resource peripheries, to the relationships between planned and fringe towns in each place. But ordinary residents shaped the fringes to considerable degrees as well. Fringe settlements often functioned as free-wheeling complements to the regulation of the planned towns. But more than this, the fringe settlements at Corner Brook and Mount Isa differed in their relationships to corporate paternalism.

The town plan for Corner Brook that NP&P officials agreed on finally in 1923–4 was appealing. London clerk Ebenezer Howard created the style near the turn of the century as a remedy for the ills of industrialization and urban slum growth in Britain. His ideas were a utopian call for Britain's evolution from the selfishness of capitalism to communal living, but industrialists saw Howard's Garden City as a way to standardize town planning and promote industrial efficiency.[1] By the mid-1910s Garden City proponents continued to revere Howard's designs while they downplayed his ideas of grand social change. Planning became an end in itself for planners who promised profits for their capitalist patrons.

Howard's efforts established a popular style and a coterie of loosely aligned planning experts who popularized planning throughout the West. Thomas Adams, the secretary of the original Garden City Association, was the most prominent member of the group, but dozens of itinerant planners travelled the globe at this time, lecturing on the benefits of directed residential design.[2] Not all adhered to Garden City precepts, but by the early 1920s town planners represented an expanding profession, an epistemic community whose work could be found around the world.

Private enterprise sustained the planning profession up to the 1950s. Industrialists saw in town planning methods like the Garden City the forum through which 'capitalism could be most easily preserved,'[3] and the alliance between expert planners and companies was a fruitful one.[4] By the early 1920s planners regularly received contracts to design comprehensive company towns for extractive and manufacturing firms. The opportunity for planners to create instant towns was a real-world laboratory for urban design, but for corporate patrons the form of the plan was subordinate to its function as a spur to efficiency and profit.

Corporate town planning in Newfoundland reflected wider North American trends. The instant pulp-and-paper and mining towns of Grand Falls and Wabana, Bell Island, confirmed the interest in corporate planning between 1905 and 1909.[5] Comprehensive planning in the paper industry was possible from the beginning because forest surveys could estimate the amount of available pulpwood and, thus, the size of the processing plant and related infrastructure. The Grand Falls mill town included elements of the Garden City style.[6] Planning for resource industries in Newfoundland began at roughly the same time as those on the mainland.

Armstrong received a broad mandate from the Newfoundland government for planning the Humber venture. Operating contracts stressed the company's authority and obligation to build or grant land 'for the purposes of road ways, canals, watercourses, gardens, churches, chapels, schools, places of amusement, places of recreation, and other purposes of public or private whether of the Company or otherwise which may seem expedient.'[7] Terms also included the responsibility for housing and waste disposal, and control over business hours within the new town.

'Expediency' proved difficult. A major problem was that the NP&P board could not decide where to build the paper plant and its adjoining town. It even began to clear brush for a townsite at Deer Lake before relocating the site to Corner Brook in early 1923. The board set the location for the mill at the opening of the Humber Arm. The main residential area would be built on a forested, marshy incline to the northwest of the mill site.

In 1921 the population of Corner Brook barely exceeded four hundred. Most residents logged or fished seasonally or worked for wages at the local sawmill. The hamlet had no permanent clergy, doctors, or teachers, and relied on the neighbouring merchant centre of Curling for its minimal services.[8] NP&P surveyors found that most of the undeveloped land was leased to the Fisher and Gushue families.[9] The firm bought their leases and gave the former landholders concessions in the new town. The Fishers received company houses and the opportunity to run businesses in the planned town. The company bought large quantities of building lumber from the Fisher sawmill too. It gave the Gushue families company-built houses on Main Street on the site of their original residences and hired the men to work at the mill.[10]

In November 1922 the NP&P board hired a planner to 'draw up a complete town scheme.' They procured the services of a town planner of 'high authority,' Thomas Adams, to lay out the settlement. In hiring Adams and Fraser, Brace and Company – a construction firm well-experienced with power projects at a number of Canadian company towns – to realize the Humber scheme, NP&P joined the epistemic planning community that was slowly altering social, political, and industrial relationships around the world.[11] The project placed the peripheral Dominion of Newfoundland at the confluence of major global trends.

Adams, however, would not draw up a plan because the site was covered in snow. The board ordered the erection of temporary accommodations for construction workers and staff to begin 'at once' and awaited a complete plan. With the unanticipated flood of nearly four thousand unskilled workers by May 1923, shack-towns sprang up near the mill site and in Deer Lake. The ramshackle Corner Brook sprawl became more permanent than the company anticipated.[12]

Adams submitted a plan for Townsite in the spring of 1923, placing the site on a plateau hemmed in to the east and north by 'high, forest-clad hills' and to the west by the Corner Brook valley. A narrower plateau led southeast to a third flat area overlooking the Humber Arm and mill site. According to Adams 'the site ... had great natural attractions but made an economic layout very difficult to secure.'[13] His design contained all the elements of the Garden City style but was condensed for the workforce of a single industry. The main residential area consisted of a grid of rectangular lots fronting three parallel streets, but Adams otherwise followed topography. He planned a residential addition curving northwest of the principle settlement and implemented a measure of zoning previously unknown in Newfoundland, separating the residential area from the narrower southwest plateau – slated to be the town's commercial district – by an open green area subdivided by angled and curving streets.[14] Relying on the contours of the land to determine the street layout was a primary Garden City motif. So too was the segregation of residential, commercial, and industrial zones by parks, farms, or forests.

Adams separated the bulk of the housing stock from a view of the mill in order to preserve a sense of rural living. He planned a commercial district on a single street that led to the civic centre overlooking the mill. The town square provided a scenic view of the rugged Humber Arm but also directed viewers to the NP&P paper mill. Adams included some residences in the commercial and civic sectors in order to downplay the appearance of strict exclusionary zoning in a rigid plan. Like the other Garden City themes that Adams included in the plan, he used mixed zones to create a sense of natural organic growth, but with a clear subtext of 'order within irregularity.'[15]

The names that mill officials chose for streets and buildings asserted corporate ownership. The head office created Armstrong Avenue, West Street for Chairman Glyn West, and Reid Street to credit the Newfoundland partner. The company's lavish executive staff hotel, the Glynmill Inn, evinced corporate pretensions as well. Corporate tributes were a common practice in company towns where instant development precluded locally designated place names.[16] At Corner Brook, however, place names became memorials to the town's failed founding firm, a twist perhaps on what historians understand as post-colonial legacies of outside control.

The company hired Andrew Cobb to design the town's buildings.[17] Cobb's specialty was the Craftsman home, an architectural style that could be easily incorporated into Adam's wider plan. The style affirmed 'beauty through elimination,' shedding ostentatious design in favour of simple but attractive structures, and compact cottage-style houses made from native materials.[18] Harried NP&P officials accepted a simple design because it promised low-cost, durable structures. Most of the building materials were local.[19] NP&P consulted no Newfoundlanders on questions of planning or style.

Cobb's houses reinforced the company's hope for order and harmony among skilled workers. Cobb designed four basic dwelling types, each incorporating minor variations to downplay repetition.[20] The homes were all two-storey and wood-clad. Single detached houses and duplexes were the primary forms. Most dwellings had steep-pitched shingled roofs, dormer windows, and large verandas sheltered by overhanging roofs. Cobb planned difference by 'reversing' houses to make each house a mirror image of its neighbour, turning them sideways, or adding minor decorative flourishes, but the houses within each type were virtually identical. Ephemeral diversity masked 'fundamental homogeneity.'[21]

Housing assignments depended on the resident's occupation at the mill. Type-4s were the smallest and most numerous and were meant to house skilled tradesmen like mechanics and paper machine operators, as well as clerical staff. Type-3s, built on West Valley Road – apart from the main residential area – were considerably larger than Type-4s and had more decorative interiors. Type-3s were for middle management like department superintendents and the company treasurer, as well as professionals such as doctors and school administrators. The company assigned Type-2s to lower management like shop-floor foremen. Cobb mixed Type-2s with the more common Type-4s in the main residential area to encourage social ties among occupational groups.

Company brass, like the mill's local director, lived in the most commodious and extravagant of the four types. A tree-lined rock outcropping that reinforced management's special status separated the executive dwellings from the view of the rest of Townsite.[22] NP&P rewarded Cobb's work by naming its exclusive street Cobb Lane. The rules of occupancy imposed by the company on top of the already segregated zones of Townsite and hierarchy of dwelling types comprised the physical embodiment of its ideology that planning led to a happy, efficient workforce and, thus, a lucrative venture.

Astonishingly, by November 1925, NP&P's managing director reported that most of the plan was complete. Construction teams had got the mill up and running, having completed 170 houses with electrical and telephone connections, opened the company store, and nearly finished a school, hockey rink, and stables.[23] But, despite apparent success, local contingencies intruded to compromise the plan and hasten NP&P's collapse.

A serious communication breakdown between the head office and the local manager compromised the project at its source.[24] The weather undermined construction schedules and stressed the massive construction force, making it difficult to deal with.[25] Resident Marian Oxford's enduring images of the construction phase were mud 'up to the axles,' electrical blackouts, and waiting lists.[26] Skilled workers had to register on a wait list and live in boarding houses or temporary barracks, or rent rooms in the fringe towns. Some still waited for the company to call their number when IP took over in 1927. Other skilled workers decided the 'model' town was not worth it and built private dwellings beyond company control. To soothe tensions, the company paid for quality schools, refurbished temporary quarters, donated land for churches, and sponsored all manner of recreation. Each palliative spilled red ink over the company's balance sheet.

In June 1926 interim NP&P chairman Lord Southborough subverted the superlatives of harmony and perfection that Glyn West had used to describe Townsite, complaining that 'the only satisfaction' was the high standard of construction.[27] Southborough was shocked at what he considered frivolous spending. Thomas Adams also distanced himself from the company's final interpretation of his plan.[28] NP&P nevertheless implemented a lasting industrial-residential hierarchy in Corner Brook. Company-defined hierarchies survived long after NP&P disappeared, shaping community life in Townsite and throughout Corner Brook.

Central Street, Townsite, Corner Brook under construction, 1924. (Corner Brook Pulp and Paper Limited Photographic Collection courtesy of the Corner Brook Museum and Archives)

'Cobb's Quads,' Townsite, Corner Brook. (Corner Brook Pulp and Paper Limited Photographic Collection courtesy of the Corner Brook Museum and Archives)

Townsite, Corner Brook completed, 1934. (Corner Brook Pulp and Paper Limited Photographic Collection courtesy of the Corner Brook Museum and Archives)

When IPPN took over the enterprise in 1927, its increased paper production brought more skilled workers who required more company houses. It retained Cobb's designs for employee housing.[29] IPPN commissioned additional dwellings on Reid Street in the main residential area as well as a series of 'Cobb's Quads,' or four-apartment row houses, on the lower end of West Street, adding over a hundred structures.[30]

By 1927 residents and company alike expected planning, and the mill's American manager E.A. Charlton expressed those sentiments in his earliest interview with local reporters, saying he intended to improve Townsite to make it 'the brightest light in this old country.'[31]

By 1930 planning in Townsite neared completion. The company town now had all the amenities of other urban centres in Newfoundland including a hospital, company-run and independent businesses, a large school, churches, recreation facilities, and full telephone service, and the soaring population increase of the construction phase had relaxed into slightly more manageable growth. In 1935 the population of Townsite was over 6,300, up from 411 in 1921.[32] In the future, the company expected to limit town planning to modest beautification projects. The housing construction phase had occurred in a short intense burst.

Industrial and demographic expansion also led the American firm to streamline welfare policies in Townsite. IPPN converted NP&P's unwieldy utilities subsidiary into a Town Department. From his office on Fisher's Hill – overlooking not the town but the mill – the town manager administered most aspects of Townsite life. Rents and service bills went through the town wing of the mill company, employee committees coordinated recreation, and Town Department employees delivered meat, dairy products, and seeds for backyard gardens to town residents. In winter, employees knocked icicles from the eaves of company houses, and every few years they painted the houses inside and out. Homes for skilled workers had a set colour scheme while middle and upper managers could choose their own colours for their houses.[33] Including town administration in an industrial management framework fit IPPN's general philosophy of 'functional management' whereby local managers stayed in close contact with the New York head office.[34] IPPN cemented NP&P's industrial-residential hierarchy, expanding construction and corporate paternalism and, in the process, presided over the mill's first profits.

Shortly after Bowater took over the Corner Brook operation, Morley Richards, a correspondent for London's *Daily Express*, reported in 1939 that he had not seen a 'better organized,' 'more cheerfully communal' industrial town outside of Bourneville or Port Sunlight.[35] Bowater officials maintained the Town Department and company paternalism. The Bowater contract, like IP's a decade before, reinforced company control over town administration by enshrining its responsibility to make and enforce laws for building, sewerage, streets, lighting, water, fire protection, closing hours, general public health, and other requests when affirmed by the government.[36] Townsite remained a company town. Local manager 'Monty' Lewin kept pre-existing programs running into the early 1940s.

Yet, to Eric Bowater, the Corner Brook mill represented a mere step toward a North American paper empire. By 1945, the expense of running a town of 8,700 people did not jibe with his corporate vision.[37] Bowater's plan to use Corner Brook to finance the construction of mills in central market locations on the mainland precluded ongoing paternalism on the periphery. By the late 1940s, Bowater and Lewin also were confident that Corner Brook had enough amenities to reproduce a skilled workforce.[38] BNPP preferred to sell costly Townsite assets at the earliest opportunity and cede town administration to inhabitants.[39] Under Bowater, Townsite was supplementary to industrial efficiency and increasingly an unwanted investment. The new hegemon saw itself as an expanding multinational corporation, not a mill town administrator.

Near the end of the Second World War, BNPP took its first step towards ending town administration by selling company houses to residents. Houses went for $3,000 to $6,000, depending on type and location. Current occupants and company employees received preference, and the monthly mortgage usually equalled twice the former rent.[40] Workers received a sturdy, attractive home for a relatively small price, but the company no longer had to spend money on upkeep. By the mid-1950s the company had sold most of its houses and allowed ever greater private home construction on the outskirts of Townsite. Lewen limited the company's direct imprint in Townsite to beautification projects like tree planting and lending technicians to community groups.[41]

BNPP sold its subsidiary businesses in 1948. It closed the company store, sold its laundry facilities to a local operator, sold the newspaper to a Newfoundland publisher, and transferred other assets like the port and construction operations into a temporary subsidiary Western Newfoundland Investment Company, a holding company with a mandate to sell assets.[42] In early 1950, experienced municipal government consultant H. Carl Goldenberg released his report on municipal administration in the greater Corner Brook area. BNPP partially commissioned the report. Goldenberg recommended that the company institute a Townsite council of elected residents instead of relying on a company-appointed town manager. The next year the company followed his suggestion by creating a six-member council with three company-appointed and three elected members.[43] It lasted until 1955 when residents of Corner Brook's four towns voted to amalgamate into a single municipality.[44]

With amalgamation BNPP achieved its goal of ending financial responsibility for non-industrial assets. It also arranged an exemption from municipal taxation in the new city. Before amalgamation, BNPP reputedly paid $250,000 per annum for the upkeep of Townsite. After amalgamation, the company paid an annual grant in lieu of taxes, deciding the grant amount with non-binding input from the town council, which hovered around $120,000. In 1956 the majority of Corner Brook's 23,200 residents depended, directly or indirectly, on the paper company, but Bowater had negotiated a deal that allowed it to operate in the city essentially for free.[45] The third foreign company gained the most from the stability of the planned town and cast it aside when the economic climate was favourable.

Bowater's retreat from paternalism meant also an enlarged arena for resident control over civic matters, but this was not a simple either/or proposition. The company maintained considerable informal influence over municipal affairs after amalgamation, and many residents of Townsite preferred company paternalism over local democracy. Similar to the ways colonial powers' relationships with the colonized carried influence into the post-colonial age, complex and flexible corporate hegemony in Corner Brook echoed through the post-company era.

The planning history of the company town at Corner Brook – indeed the history of most company towns – is incomplete without addressing the make-up of unplanned fringe towns. The planned and unplanned settlements that arose from a single reliance on one company formed a spatial dialectic at the base of town life. The boom towns of Corner Brook West and East that bordered Townsite emerge as foils and remedies to life in the ordered industrial hamlet. The fringe exposed the contradictions of the companies profit-centred planning for employee welfare and prompted changes in local society.

There was no systematic planning in Newfoundland outports. The astonishing feature of Townsite was how completely it contrasted with the traditional Newfoundland communities. Before the advent of NP&P, Corner Brook and Curling were fairly typical outports. Residents built houses and businesses in a strip along the shoreline and otherwise as close to the water as geography or their leases permitted. Settlement in Curling hugged the waterfront. At Corner Brook, a crude main road travelled west along the narrow plateau overlooking the Humber Arm, dipped into the Corner Brook valley where Fisher's sawmill was located, and continued onto another plateau on the west side hills. Individual homesteaders' properties abutted dirt roads and formed a patchwork of uneven leases based on longstanding familial relations.[46] Lots like those owned by Stanley Lewis and the Buckle family typically had space for a house, subsistence garden, or a small farm. Patterns of settlement in pre-industrial Corner Brook were based on access to the sea for local fishing and seasonal trips to Labrador and eastern Quebec; the woods providing hunting, firewood, and logs for milling.[47] Small populations kept pressure on land and real-estate speculation to an absolute minimum. The Crown imposed few rules about development, and settlements grew organically in small waves of family growth and new arrivals.

The industrial boom flooded the site with thousands of Newfoundland men looking for construction work. Single men found lodging in the company's shack-town in the valley until they found rental space or land. In 1925, NP&P's local manager had to change the temporary quarters into semi-permanent structures because many employees could not find shelter anywhere else in Corner Brook. The 'temporary' shack-town lasted into the late 1930s.[48]

Imposed divisions between skilled and unskilled workers were evident from the outset. Foreign skilled and Newfoundland unskilled workers and their families made up the bulk of Corner Brook's population.[49] Townsite resident Arthur Scott recalled 'a tendency to stick with your own crowd.' A manager envisioned a day when unskilled male labourers would settle down and stop their 'rude remarks.'[50] Further segregation occurred across the company's extractive network. The industry did not require extractive and manufacturing functions on one site, so loggers had to fend for themselves to secure lodging in the outlying villages that depended on seasonal forest work. Just as NP&P rescaled imperial centre–colonial periphery and management–skilled worker hierarchies within Townsite, it imposed a wider division between skilled and unskilled employees through its industrial network.

To the east and west of Townsite, intense demand for housing led to land speculation and unregulated sprawl. On the west side, property owners like John Noah subdivided and sold their lots to individual homebuilders and, more frequently, land speculators who then leased property to new arrivals or built structures to rent to residents or businesses.[51] Speculation combined with the traditionally lax enforcement of land-tenure regulations to form a classic boom town with inadequate services and cramped living conditions.

With level land at a premium, speculators and residents built as many structures on a given lot as possible. They thought little of ordered growth and had scant knowledge of surveying or advanced building standards. Rough dwellings and businesses with narrow frontages sat at odd angles lining the winding dirt roads. The main street – named Broadway – quickly became the centre of Corner Brook West. When settlers exhausted Broadway's fairly level land, they carved out narrow streets crammed with owner-built homes and rental units radiating off Broadway, twisting up and down the slopes of the plateau. It was the outport form writ large and adapted informally to incorporate a large number of year-round industrial workers. The ad hoc inclusion of modern elements within a traditional form was the reverse image of the modern form with pseudo-traditional elements imposed by company-hired expert planners in Townsite.

Summary statistics illustrate the sustained fringe growth in Corner Brook West and East. In October 1924, the local paper reported that over 40 businesses had 'sprung up' outside of Townsite since the previous fall. By March 1925 the erection of homes on the fringe surpassed the blistering pace of home construction in Townsite, and the trend continued. In 1950, 480 Townsite houses and a dozen or so businesses compared to 510 houses and 60 businesses on the East Side, and an amazing 980 dwellings and 110 businesses on the West Side. Population figures show similar uneven growth. In 1935 approximately 2,000 people lived in Townsite and the East Side, and 3,500 in Corner Brook West. A decade and a half later, Townsite's population was virtually unchanged, while 3,500 and 7,500 people lived on the East and West Sides respectively.[52]

Life on the fringe was less regimented than in Townsite. The fringes were centres for small business development and the locus of several kinds of subsistence work – like personal logging, domestic labour, and seasonal fishing. With two movie theatres, soda shops, and numerous bars, Corner Brook West was a physical and social amalgam of outport and urban life, contrasting particularly to the staid orderly rounds of work, home, and leisure in the company town across the brook in Townsite.

Real physical problems resulted from the lack of central authority. Neither fringe town had a municipal authority capable of collecting taxes, lobbying for improvements, or singling out trouble areas. Congested muddy and dusty roads and substandard architecture brought criticism from all quarters, including the absentee Newfoundland government, the body normally responsible for such matters in lieu of municipal authority. Sanitation and public health suffered. Residents dumped household waste in local cesspits. When it rained, drinking water from West Side wells often became fouled by the runoff from small rubbish dumps and hundreds of outhouses. The local paper reported annual outbreaks of typhoid and other preventable ailments,

Broadway, Corner Brook West, late 1920s. (Corner Brook Pulp and Paper Limited Photographic Collection courtesy of the Corner Brook Museum and Archives)

some of which were fatal.[53] Unlike Townsite residents, whose sewerage systems protected against such outbreaks and whose privileged position in the industrial hierarchy guaranteed free medical service, fringe dwellers had to pay for treatment at the company hospital.[54] Even the precarious position of houses was dangerous. Heavy snowfall dislodged poorly built homes from their foundations, and in one case an avalanche on the West Side killed a mother and child and seriously injured two other children.[55] Authorities responded to the poor state of Corner Brook West with a sustained public flogging of the fringe community and its residents.

The preconditions for sprawl were established during NP&P's brief tenure, and the next two companies had to find ways to deal with their untidy neighbours. IPPN responded by building duplexes in Townsite for 'workmen requiring a cheaper grade of dwelling, and to accommodate employees of the paper mill ... living in unsuitable quarters outside the Townsite limits,'[56] but the morally satisfying gesture of new housing did little to relieve the population pressure on the outskirts. The New York company sold electricity to Curling and the West Side while Townsite residents got their electricity for free.[57]

The Bowater takeover in 1938 had no remedial impact. Morley Richards congratulated Bowater for realizing the 'cheerfully communal' Townsite where 'masters and men' worked toward a common purpose, making only passing reference to the considerable 'poverty' on the outskirts. He remarked derisively, 'Anyway, perfection is so dull.'[58] At about the same time, BNPP commissioned two of its engineers to survey Corner Brook West and provide a cost assessment for improvements. The engineers reported that residents had improved water provision and roads over the previous decade, but that 'the town as a whole presents a fire hazard.' They also complained about the town's poor location, jumbled layout, and filth. They claimed the fringe town needed at least $200,000 just to install a decent sewer system. The authors blamed the original residents' rush to buy land and lack of proper surveying.[59]

The Newfoundland government provided little help throughout the 1920s and 1930s. Agents of the Commission periodically bemoaned the poor conditions but rarely consulted residents or funded improvements. In response to residents' call for the formation of a municipal council in Corner Brook West in 1935, Justice Commissioner W.R. Howley said the commission would consider the matter when it 'got 'round to it.'[60] It did so in 1942. Charters for Curling and Corner Brook East followed in 1947 and 1948. In a case of bureaucratic circular logic, the fringe towns were ineligible for assistance from the government in the interim because they were not municipalities.

By the early 1950s, Canadians joined the critics of Corner Brook's fringe towns. In a 1952 article for the urban affairs journal *Civic Administration*, Robert Campbell, vice-president of a Toronto advertising agency, said that in contrast to the order of Townsite, its filthy 'sister community across the brook' was 'praying for a conflagration' that could wipe it out in order to start anew.[61] Campbell's modest proposal nearly became reality a few months later when a massive fire – the fifth fire in two years – ripped through the west end of Broadway, razing seventeen buildings and causing an estimated $1,325,000 in damages.[62]

After Confederation, Corner Brook became a minor cause célèbre. Articles appeared in journals like the *Community Planning Review*, and the federal government's 1953 study of Canadian company towns mentioned Corner Brook prominently. Canadian municipal expert H. Carl Goldenberg carried out the first large-scale study of Corner Brook's problems. To Goldenberg, Townsite was, not surprisingly, the best-administered community. Residents had the amenities of a large urban area, and most houses were mortgaged to private owners. Corner Brook West and East contrasted in every respect with the planned town. The West Side had water and sewer connections to only 250 of the over 1,000 structures. Most utilities clustered around the Broadway business area. The East Side had no water, sewer, or street lights. Conflicting local taxation policies and reliance on provincial government grants had created an inconsistent revenue stream for the fringe towns. Meanwhile, other commentators like William Wonders mistakenly attributed the problems to Newfoundlanders' 'cultural aversion' to taxes instead of highlighting the unpalatable realities of neglect and dependence.[63]

Goldenberg urged the fringe councils to increase 'organized community effort,' with the strongest suggestion in the report for all four communities to amalgamate to provide a centralized authority that could rationalize the tax base and direct city development better than four separate towns. As for Bowater, Goldenberg recommended that it end company administration of Townsite as early as it could.[64] Goldenberg's professional analysis jibed quite remarkably with Bowater's own opinion of the situation.

Corner Brook's city council commissioned several urban renewal studies after amalgamation. Most concentrated on improving Corner Brook East and West through a combination of stricter zoning laws and

Broadway, Corner Brook West, 1953. (Corner Brook Pulp and Paper Limited Photographic Collection courtesy of the Corner Brook Museum and Archives)

the creation of new neighbourhoods on the surrounding hills. Money came from increased local taxation, provincial grants, and loans. The council never tried to force Bowater to pay municipal taxes. City administrators soon realized that making subdivisions on Corner Brook's steep hills was extremely costly. Most of the schemes languished because dreams of development were bigger than the public purse. Local efforts accomplished significant improvements after 1955, but they came at a high cost. Former town councillor William Brown said that by the early 1960s the city was $9.2 million in debt.[65]

Ordinary fringe residents had little say in discussions on the necessity of improving their towns. Instead, they criticized company control in Townsite in informal ways. Fringe residents asserted a measure of autonomy by refusing to patronize Townsite businesses. They spoke openly about Townsite residents' 'superiority' complex and sometimes avoided socializing with their neighbours in the planned town.[66] More positively, residents endeavoured to improve the quality of life in the fringe towns. Contrary to the general impression given by officials and civic boosters, the West and East Siders were not as a group passive or fatalistic.

Despite a public discourse that 'blamed the victims' of structured underdevelopment, the fringes were attractive for a variety of practical reasons. Some skilled workers decided to build houses where they did not have to accept company regulations. Others opened businesses and lived comfortably on money made from a rapidly expanding retail sector. Lebanese business owner John Noah says the company refused him work and denied him a house in Townsite, but he maintained that 'the best thing that ever happened' to him 'was not getting a job at the mill.'[67] Meanwhile, most residents of Townsite patronized fringe businesses to a greater extent than company-sanctioned stores. Even those who accepted corporate order in Townsite routinely escaped it by crossing the bridge to Corner Brook West.

The Corner Brook fringe towns grew out of industrial development like the planned company town. But the fringe remained an ad hoc mixture of outport and urban life largely as the result of conscious neglect from company and government officials whose mixed message of massive industrial development and exclusive housing policies on the one hand, and their corresponding failure to aid the fringes financially and administratively on the other, made sprawl unavoidable.

The agents who created the company town of Mineside, Mount Isa, improvised their plans with far greater frequency than those who built

Humpies. (Courtesy Jonathan Richards)

Townsite, Corner Brook. Where Corner Brook moved fairly quickly from greater to lesser company rule, MIM reached a post-company atmosphere after wave upon wave of expanding paternalism. MIM bosses' recurring homilies to 'the real, honest-to-goodness pleasures' of the 'average guy' in company newsletters underscored the truth that industry and society at Mount Isa were not as settled as they were in other places.[68] Local town planning emerged as variable and chaotic.

The wildly fluctuating Liechhardt River is a fitting symbol of the obstacles that outback Queensland presented to would-be developers. Earlier mine-town residents of the Cloncurry region coped with extreme weather and boom-and-bust copper mines through mobility. If periodic drought struck or a mine fell on hard times, working residents packed up and left for the east coast or other mining towns. Easily disassembled tin and canvas dwellings called 'humpies' represented the fundamental impermanence of the outback.[69]

Government policies conspired against mega-projects too. By the early 1920s, Queensland's Labor government had nationalized a number of industries and was feeling the pinch of foreign capitalists' wariness to invest. Labor's very conception of mining – small, competing enterprises run by local capital – was unrealistic in the prevailing depressed metal markets and the industry's drift towards vertical integration.[70]

The low-grade silver-lead deposit at Mount Isa required a large, sustained construction effort to sink the deep shafts and build processing works. The company needed expensive, up-to-date technology to separate and smelt the ore, and all of this meant a sizeable and diversified workforce of managers, skilled technicians, and semi- and unskilled labourers. Finally, because of the need to retain skilled workers and legions of temperamental miners who were accustomed to fly-by-night operations, company officials had to plan housing as well. Corporate planning for mine towns was rare in Australia at the time.[71] MIM officials had to buck longstanding environmental, political, and industrial trends and plan for permanence.

The primary feature affecting settlement at Mount Isa was the Leichhardt River. Flowing north to south, the muddy waterway divided the settlement into western and eastern halves. The company built the mine, works, and company town west of the river. The unplanned fringe town, Townside, developed east of the river in response to industrial development. It remained highly reliant on the mine in later years as well. But in its earliest stage, this division did not exist. Between 1924 and 1928 a dusty mining camp made up of employees of small mining companies, independent prospectors, itinerant peddlers, and a small number of women and children sprang up between the ore-bearing hills and the west bank of the Leichhardt.

As in other Queensland mining settlements, residents built where they could and with the materials at hand. Haphazardly situated corrugated iron buildings transplanted from defunct ghost towns, thick canvas tents, and sheds or humpies composed of boughs and wooden or metal detritus made up early Mount Isa. The ad hoc hamlet had several boarding houses, supply stores, a saloon, and crude open air movie theatres.[72] The speedy establishment of a rough but relatively diversified service sector was characteristic of people used to moving around. In response to concerns about squatter growth and water provision from the temperamental Leichhardt, in March 1924 concerned residents formed a Progress Association to lobby government for a town survey,[73] and they got what they asked for, but not in the form they envisioned.

Two months later, the government surveyor, acting in the company's interests, surveyed the town on the river's east bank. Established residents did not want to transfer everything to the surveyed town because of its distance from the mines and because the Cloncurry Shire Council administered the east bank, charging higher taxes than the west bank's Barkly Tableland Shire. In September 1924 several residents and new arrivals bought surveyed lots in a speculative rush.[74] Many inhabitants lingered on the east bank for several more years, but the original boom town withered in the face of the government–industry alliance. In the following years, residents of Townside complained that state officials routinely ignored calls for town services like schools and post offices.[75]

The company centralized its authority over housing mine employees. Company officials hoped to avoid private residential land titles like those on Townside, arguing that the company needed the entire west bank to keep employee houses a suitable distance from the works and to control hotel construction and alcohol consumption.[76] While those were important considerations, the primary motive was to set the conditions for a closed town. MIM's onsite managers realized the importance of strict corporate control to overcome the field's drawbacks. The state government – several members of which held shares in MIM – was more than happy to help an Australian company that promised a Broken-Hill-size bonanza.

Despite bureaucratic recognition of MIM's control over Mineside, Corbould and company did not have free reign. Early settlers lingered on the river's west bank until 1928. MIM's legal authority on Mineside was flouted daily by the presence of squatters but there was little the company could do, depending as it did on some of these same townspeople for services. MIM set the stage for a comprehensive company town but it could not navigate the socio-political and funding obstacles of its time.

Corbould had envisioned town planning for employees but was never able to undertake more than piecemeal construction. Even so, it was more than that undertaken in average Australian mining towns, most of which were typical of boom towns that could be found at the time on resource frontiers around the globe, consisting of ramshackle houses and a handful of basic businesses, a bare minimum of services, and a pervasive feeling of uncertainty that gave rise to transient populations. Boom settlements adjoining surface fields rarely developed into sustainable and complex communities as a result of the inherent uncertainty about the deposits and because local services remained underdeveloped. All parties to mining were used to a quick build-up, quick profit-taking, and quick departures. In Queensland, Charters Towers was the largest of the mining boom towns, reaching a population of several thousand at its peak in 1890, but this boom town did not give way to comprehensive planning for stable populations until large low-grade deposits became economically feasible.[77] Mount Isa was to be the first well-planned mining town in Australia, but the new mode of development was extremely expensive.

Before Russo-Asiatic's purchase of the field in mid-1927, MIM had built only minimal community facilities on Mineside. The company managed a handful of simple, raised, wooden houses for managers, staff buildings, a failed experimental dam, and a couple of decent wells for drinking water.[78] It took an injection of foreign capital and the desperation-fuelled dreams of industrial revival to create a comprehensively planned industrial settlement at Mount Isa. Leslie Urquhart supplied a steady stream of capital and dreams.

Tsarist mining law obliged Urquhart to plan for the welfare of his Russian workforce. Between 1908 and 1912 in and around Kyshtim, a copper-rich region of Siberia, Urquhart's firm built hospitals, company stores, libraries, mosques and churches, thirty schools, and extensive housing, and he implemented similar measures at his other properties.[79] The relevant literature contains little discussion of the specific planning or architectural styles Urquhart employed in Russia. Urquhart's company planned the Russian structures, but considering the vastly different environments, the same structures would have been unsuitable for the Queensland outback. Unlike Corner Brook's clear links to the Garden City and Craftsman styles of the day, precursors to the chain of planning at Mount Isa are obscure.

What is certain is that Urquhart jumped head first into massive industrial and residential development with little regard for the deposits' specific qualities, depressed domestic and international metal markets, the environmental peculiarities of the outback, or the opinions of the majority of mine workers. In late 1927 he decided that in order to get the 'best men' for the mine he had to provide them with a comprehensive town. His February 1928 cost estimate was £100,000 each for the Rifle Creek dam and housing.[80] Between 1928 and 1929 Queensland town surveyors McInnes and Manning laid out the townsite while construction contractors Campbell and Sons, and Brown and Broad Newstead Homes Ltd designed the structures under Urquhart's watchful eye.

Russo-Asiatic situated the town west of the ore-bearing hills, which ensured an extra degree of separation from Townside. By slightly separating the houses from the mine works, the company hoped to create the impression that it did not control everything. Urquhart and his planners partially eschewed the rigid grid survey of earlier mining towns, deciding that the town centre should follow the valley's contours. Curvilinear streets led to an open rectangular town centre, and roads to Townside curved between the hills.[81]

Russo-Asiatic graded houses hierarchically. The size and quality of the house and lot increased, depending on the occupant's position in the company. It placed managers' houses slightly apart from the largely grid-bound workmen's cottages, and made them of the best material. They also included 'the best of furniture.' 'Electric light and power, water, garbage service, septic system, and laundry' were free. Top management paid no rent, and lower managers paid between 17s. 6d. and 25s. per week – a relatively small portion of their salaries. Workmen's cottages varied but were smaller and more elevated than staff houses. Ground floors were semi-enclosed, with kitchens, bathrooms, and toilets. Second floors had one to three bed/living rooms and large, fly-screened verandas. This configuration drew on the pattern of the traditional 'Queenslander' house, mounted on posts for ventilation. Rent ranged from 10s. 6d. to 17s. 6d. per week – again a reasonable fee. There were also multi-room dormitories and mess halls for single workers. Construction cost just over £84,000.[82]

Details of the numerous changes in housing types under Urquhart are not as important as the fact that the goal of town planning as a supplement to industry got away from him after 1929.[83] In 1930 the company discovered that in order to bring extractive and processing functions together on the same site, it needed roughly 350 more permanent workers. It also had to provide lodging for hundreds of construction workers. Ten extra dormitories and sixty simple canvas structures were erected, along with communal bath and toilet facilities. Urquhart even had sixty steel sheds – 'austere, steel framed houses, clad in iron and reminiscent of army huts' – cobbled together to relieve the housing pressure for married workers. Those units were added to the over 250 workmen's and staff houses, company clubhouse, company store, butcher shop, library, and sporting and entertainment facilities already in place. That year, town spending ballooned to £130,000.[84]

Urquhart's dictatorial but absentee leadership pushed construction forward, despite mounting costs and spiralling debt. The company lacked a capable onsite manager.[85] When issues requiring immediate pragmatic compromise between local development tactics and strategic business survival arose, Urquhart decided the course. With characteristic immodesty he recognized as much in a 1932 shareholders meeting, saying, 'I have been in close personal contact with every phase of every business [for twenty-five years] ... I have had ... practically my whole resources invested in it, and the burden which I have had to bear has at times seemed almost too much.'[86] Urquhart never halted or scaled back projects. He only expanded them, and the result was a company town for many workers, but an end for the company that planned it.

When ASARCO's Julius Kruttschnitt arrived in late 1930 to assume control of the project, Urquhart's town plan was complete. By that time, Mineside had already witnessed unplanned squatter growth, minimal company housing under Corbould's MIM, instant town construction, and ad hoc supplemental housing. Between 1928 and 1930 the planned town for staff and skilled workers evolved into a vast, chaotic, company housing project for *all* mine employees. Still hundreds of mine workers could not obtain company houses and rented rooms on Townside or squatted outside company control in what Kruttschnitt called 'impossible humpies and shacks' near the banks of the Leichhardt. Kruttschnitt was not fond of Urquhart's best houses either. He described his own dwelling as 'a house up on stilts which had harboured goats underneath ... it smelled to high heaven.'[87]

The first decade of development at Mount Isa provides instructive contrasts to that of Corner Brook. The newsprint and mining industries demanded different degrees and rates of planning. Mill companies knew the maximum number of skilled mill employees they needed and planned for it from the outset, whereas mining was far more speculative. Urquhart's comprehensive town could not house all the skilled and unskilled, extractive and secondary processing workers the venture demanded. Queensland's characteristically mobile workers required an incentive to stay. Though individuals were interchangeable from the perspective of management, bulk labour still was at a premium in the outback, so the need to maintain a workforce of various skill levels compelled Mount Isa's owners to undertake new waves of planning, even during the initial comprehensive planning phase. In comparison, Corner Brook was relatively stable.

From December 1930 Mount Isa's new American owners endeavoured to make the mine efficient and profitable.[88] Unlike Russo-Asiatic, ASARCO emphasized responsible onsite management. Kruttschnitt focused on fixing the one part of the project over which management could assume a degree of control – productive efficiency. In May 1931

Mineside, Mount Isa in the 1930s. (Courtesy Jonathan Richards)

Town square with band rotunda, Mineside, Mount Isa. (Courtesy Jonathan Richards)

workers hauled the first significant quantity of ore to the surface, and in mid-June the mine and works opened.[89]

ASARCO's experts made the mine more efficient, but they could not stop workers from leaving the site en masse.[90] Nor could the company cope with the constant flood of new recruits arriving to fill the vacant positions. Throughout the 1930s, labour turnover at Mount Isa fluctuated between 47 and 80 per cent.[91] In a given year, roughly half the employees left the site and were replaced with new employees who needed to be trained and integrated into company welfare schemes. The total workforce increased annually as well. In the Depression, the only answer for the cash-strapped company was to build cheap, semi-permanent quarters.

ASARCO was no stranger to town planning. The company planted towns on its properties in the southwestern United States and in Mexico, and built a closed town at Buchans in central Newfoundland in the late 1920s.[92] But similar planning was not feasible in Depression-era Mount Isa so Kruttschnitt attempted to convince workers to build their own dwellings with materials provided by the company on credit and paid off in small weekly instalments. The wooden, iron, and canvas 'tent houses' – modified versions of Urquhart's tents – were poor imitations of actual houses. The occupying families still relied on communal baths and toilets in 1938, and despite the novelty of the design, workers 'realize[d] they [were] better off in one of the rented cottages.' By 1935 MIM had given up its tent-ownership program and simply rented them out to workers. In that year MIM owned 121 tent structures on Mineside in addition to all the previous structures.

MIM even offered to partially fund a home-owning scheme on Townside in the late 1930s, but it foundered because the Cloncurry Council could not obtain its portion of the money.[93] The financial difficulties of the primary industry and the tendency of workers to leave the site meant that the local corporate authority could not afford grand permanent housing schemes and that, in any event, workers did not want to be tied to the town. The Isa companies had to undertake rounds of additive planning and housing provision to keep the outback mining venture at an acceptable level of production. MIM's 1939 *Annual Report* complained that the 'shortage on the field of suitable housing accommodation for married employees has continued to be an important factor in our problem of securing and retaining the services of skilled and efficient tradesmen.' Turnover was a comparatively low 48 per cent that year.[94]

The war brought complex new challenges. Isans enlisted in the armed forces, and mobilization for total war led to MIM's timely switch to state-subsidized copper production. Both factors reduced the workforce to well under a thousand men.[95] This reduction relieved local housing and turnover difficulties for a time, but the massive American and Australian military presence in the area led to yet another round of additive construction on Mineside. A Base Supply Depot sprang up overnight near the railway tracks to provide for the hundreds of Australian servicemen who built the tactical road to army camps in the Northern Territory and the thousands of Americans who travelled back and forth supplying those positions. In a stark example of the prejudice shared by Americans and Australians, Black American servicemen were segregated from their white counterparts and townspeople.[96] In an already highly stratified town, there was still room for new types of exclusion. After the war, MIM converted the military structures into dormitories, mess halls, and an open air theatre for employees.

The post-war return to mixed metal extraction resurrected the turnover problems that lay dormant during the war. Turnover was a stunning 113 per cent in 1945–6, 125 per cent in 1946–7, and 131 per cent in 1947–8.[97] Yet, for the first time in decades, a prosperous and stable international metal market prevailed. After the war, the company more than doubled the wartime workforce to 1,800 employees and improved Mineside amenities to hold workers. In a testament to the continued belief in the efficacy of town planning, ASARCO-MIM began its own comprehensive planning initiative. Kruttschnitt oversaw the erection of over one hundred new rental cottages in the area just south of Urquhart's company town. New houses came in various types, depending again on the position and marital status of the occupant. MIM laid out a grid-shaped suburb with some curvilinear streets, provided each resident with garden soil, and planted hundreds of trees.

Sustained post-war boom again nearly doubled the workforce to 2,600 employees by 1951, and MIM required temporary houses once more. Kruttschnitt had dormitories at the Base Supply Depot converted into single-worker apartments and even commissioned new tent houses to deal with the problem. Meanwhile, Kruttschnitt improved his own living conditions, commissioning a large mesa-style home for himself in the relatively posh 'executive' area of Mineside and immodestly naming it Casa Grande.[98]

MIM also expanded its welfare initiatives. In December 1947 the company published its first issue of *MIMag*, a monthly newsletter. *MIMag*

Various MIM worker's residences with 'humpies'. (Courtesy Jonathan Richards)

detailed the company's benevolence and constantly reminded Mineside residents to keep their gardens tidy – because 'a street of neatly kept cottages and gardens can be spoilt by Mr and Mrs Don't-Care' – to avoid political allegiances that disrupted local harmony, and take personal responsibility for safety at work.[99] In mid-1950 the company also hired E.W. Eley to take over administration of the town from the mine's general manager. Apart from the over two hundred houses it had built between 1947 and 1953, the Community Department paved Mineside's dusty streets and expanded Mineside services and recreation to include a day-care centre, slaughter yards, a ladies club, and an Olympic-sized swimming pool.[100] The unending paternalist project coincided with massive industrial expansion and annual profit growth.

Kruttschnitt's program failed to solve the turnover problem, which averaged 65 per cent in the early 1950s.[101] Building on the post-war trends of encouraging private home ownership, state assistance to homeowners, and increasing government reliance on town planning through organizations like the Queensland Housing Commission (QHC), new General Manager George Fisher decided to make individual home ownership a remedy to turnover, through a succession of cooperative housing societies. He took that step for two reasons: to end turnover by making occupants responsible for the considerable financial investment of a home and to gradually get away altogether from expensive company provision of houses. Starting with the Soldiers Hill cooperative housing scheme in 1954, MIM and QHC built houses for the specific purpose of giving miners their own property.[102] Other Mineside subdivisions schemes in the second half of the 1950s continued that partnership. The decade-long company and community expansion programs cost MIM roughly £100,000,000, which was a tremendous capital layout, considering the monies already sunk into home construction over the years.[103]

Fisher had most of Urquhart's original planned town and Kruttschnitt's tent houses demolished and planted several monotonous grid suburbs on the west bank of the Leichhardt. The main reason for the demolition of Urquhart's town was to make space for a massive new open-cut mine, but relocation played into the new ownership scheme as well. The company built the northernmost suburb – Soldiers Hill – as a memorial to the Australians who served in the New Guinea campaign of the Second World War. The suburb had modern, affordable houses designed by Brisbane architect Karl Langer. MIM staged contests for residents to name suburbs and streets, implemented a flexible home-ownership plan, and even developed a rent-to-buy program for household appliances – anything to foster a sense of permanence.[104] Fisher also closed the 'community' or company store in 1959 in order to stimulate private business growth.

The frequent paternalist initiatives on Mineside after the war were possible because the company had turned the corner from bare solvency to stellar profits in the buoyant post-war metals market, but they were necessary because of the demands of the local labour market. Since Urquhart, the mining company had established a precedent of providing for all employees. Workers expected it. Mine wages and the lead bonus were not enough to make Isa attractive. Workers wanted well-built homes, but until the 1950s the company could not provide the capital needed to build homes worth owning, so workers preferred to rent.

Company–government partnerships enabled the construction of several instant suburbs for MIM workers into the 1970s. With greater control over its own affairs and government aid, Townside officials approved the scheme. MIM and the QHC funded planned suburbs with 850 houses on Townside, and the company also extended housing in Soldiers Hill and other areas of Mineside.[105] After authorities quashed the labour revolt of the early 1960s, Fisher's home-ownership plans finally began to pay off. In its 1968 *Annual Report*, MIM reported a sizeable decline in labour turnover from 45.9 per cent in 1967 to 37.4 per cent, and that trend continued into the 1970s. By 1971 Mount Isa's population stabilized at around 26,000. MIM employed over 5,000 Isans directly, but private industries and services were growing and, most important to company officials, 3,100 of the town's 6,700 dwellings were privately owned.[106] By the early 1970s, MIM finally could focus on the main industry and influence – not directly administer – the town.

Company town planning at Mount Isa was an ongoing negotiation of physical space between the unique business rhythms of extracting and processing Mount Isa ore and the vagaries of the local labour market. The size of the deposit – only hinted at in the 1920s and 1930s – made the Mount Isa project worth pouring money into, even when global economics dictated otherwise. Workers did not consider high pay enough to stay in the Isa, so MIM planned constantly to provide for the social needs of the flow-through workforce. The oscillating rounds of spatial reorganization arose out of and reinforced local social tensions. De-colonization – or de-companyfication – proved to be a far more complicated process in Mount Isa than in other company towns, and in

Mineside looking east to Townside. (Courtesy Jonathan Richards)

the end, MIM had to build a series of new housing developments and tear down the older one, to set the conditions for a more stable local society and workforce.

The physical divide between Mineside and Townside – planned and fringe town – was arbitrary. MIM and the Queensland government coerced the original residents who squatted on the west bank of the Leichhardt into resettlement between 1924 and 1930. The state surveyor laid out a simple grid on the Leichhardt's east bank, and over the following years the government established a rudimentary civil structure with a bank, post office, school, churches, and police station. But it transplanted those basic structures from ghost mining towns in the region. The physical and architectural shape of Townside did not promote inhabitants' belief in stability or in the government's intention to nurture civil society.

Between 1928 and 1930, Mineside town and railway completion led to a population boom in Townside. The surveyed town grew from several hundred to several thousand. Throughout this period residents complained that the town's basic infrastructure – right-angled dirt roads and a community 'bore' or well water – could not accommodate the population, but authorities made few improvements. Delay and debt on the west side of Mount Isa preoccupied company officials and politicians.

Structures on Townside were either the rusted hand-me-downs from defunct mining towns or structures cobbled together with the materials at hand. As an example, officials transferred the police station from Ballara and the school from Kuridala. The mining warden complained in 1930 that 'most of the improvements on the allotments [consist] of tents and bag or canvas structures,' the best of which, he said, were valued at only £4. Others described 'houses' made of corrugated iron, wooden crates, and 'flattened out carbide drums.' The mining warden concluded, 'With its scores of unsightly temporary dwellings the [Townside] Esplanade is at present an eyesore.'[107]

That year Cloncurry's sub-inspector of Queensland Police reported 2,500 residents in Townside and 1,500 in Mineside. He classified approximately 500 Townside residents as unemployed transients seeking work in the mines, whose chances of gaining employment were slim. Mining Trust General-Superintendent Gray said the company employed 1,200 workers, while Police Constable Landy reported that 3,000 to 4,000 men showed up daily for work in the mines.[108] The completion of company town planning on Mineside disrupted the chaotic

Townside, Mount Isa, looking west. (Courtesy Jonathan Richards)

half-decade boom in what residents considered the legitimate town of Mount Isa. While state mining and law enforcement officials continued to file reports on the social climate of the town throughout the 1930s, they made little effort to remedy the problems they highlighted. Government enforcement of company demands located Townside, and the fringe sprawled in time with mine development. Townside also housed most of the mine's flow-through workers. This dependency made all of Mount Isa a company town, but from this structured dependency the fringe created its own local dynamic.

The state's hollow panopticism exposed itself in local residential disputes. Most were products of Mineside and Townside segregation and the favour shown by the government to the company settlement over its own surveyed town. Once Urquhart finished work on his comprehensive town, many of the company employees living in Townside left to live in better-serviced, rented company dwellings in Mineside. Between 1930 and 1935 Townside property-owners, speaking through the Progress Association, complained bitterly to state authorities about the exodus to Mineside and the resulting depreciation of property values for houses and businesses they felt had been purchased in good faith. At first, the criticisms dealt with company-sponsored social clubs and business activities that were 'killing commercial life on the eastern side of the town,' but they worsened into a panic for private-property owners.[109]

In December 1933, Progress Association Secretary Hector MacDonald related to the minister for mines how Townside landholders had to lower rents to keep tenants from moving to Mineside. A few months later the secretary claimed 90 per cent depreciation in the actual value of Townside allotments since the completion of Mineside, and the state mining warden confirmed the alarming claims, describing the situation as the product of 'extraordinary unforeseen circumstances,' and commented on the lack of interest in the auction of new allotments. When the Progress Association demanded a decrease in lease fees, the state government responded by lowering the leases on certain Townside properties but refused to lower payments overall.[110]

The decision did not please Townside residents. Complaints of favouritism and company monopoly cropped up time and again over the years. Townside residents defended the redundancy of two hospitals – one in Townside, one in Mineside – throughout the 1930s. Fringe residents believed Townside was the rightful location for state-administered social services.[111] In another case, Townside residents refused to

Townside shops, 1930s. (Courtesy Jonathan Richards)

implement the forty-five-minute daylight savings adopted by the company on Mineside, and the refusal resulted in Swiftian absurdity. 'At a meeting called for 9 am in the town, the Mines representatives were there before the others were actually out of bed. One can have dinner [midday] in the town and stroll over to the Mines in time for afternoon tea ... This scheme, however, has its drawbacks, for instance, leaving the town after a show finishing at 11 pm, means one is not in bed on the Mines side before the next day.'[112] While at first glance the situation seems ridiculous, it demonstrates the deep divisions between planned town and fringe, but such pettiness is understandable within the context of conscious neglect by authorities.

The regional authority for Townside – the Cloncurry Shire Council – also did little to improve living standards in the fringe town. During the property assessment dispute of the early 1930s, Cloncurry councillors were more concerned with collecting property taxes than aiding Townside. As Shire Clerk Mike O'Callaghan put it, 'If the drift from the town side to the Mines side not be stopped, it will result in very few ratepayers being left ... to pay the burden of interest and redemption on loans which have been borrowed from the [state] government for the purpose of the establishment of the town.'[113]

The Shire Council gained some minimal property taxes from MIM, but the company never paid much tax, and the shire in any event did not use the money to improve Townside. Near the end of the decade, Mount Isa's representative advocated a planned suburb on Townside. MIM agreed to end its housing program in the event of a council-sponsored suburb and said it would pay for part of the development.[114] The council vetoed the plans and postponed them indefinitely. Not only were Urquhart and state officials more concerned with events on the west bank of the Leichhardt, but the fate of Townside was decided by a body that was responsible primarily to taxpayers in Cloncurry, a town sixty-five kilometres away that did not even have a direct rail link to Mount Isa.

In the sequence of events beginning with Urquhart's industrial setbacks, company and government focused on the mine and company town and made the Townside into a fringe community. Local tensions in the following decades resulted from the decision to ensure the survival of the industry above all other considerations. American control of MIM increased the tensions, because ASARCO enticed its employees to Mineside with ever-expanding rental accommodations. That many new arrivals chose MIM's tent houses and steel huts rather than live in Townside demonstrated the fringe town's position at the bottom of the local hierarchy. Many who lived in Townside and experienced the marginalization considered it a betrayal of their rights as Australian citizens.

The influx of military personnel in the early 1940s brought significant new construction to Mineside, but Townside saw no such development. The impact of the war on Townside residents included public disturbances between Australians and Americans at downtown hotels.[115] The neglected fringe was not just the creation of the mine – it was the mine's whipping boy as well. During the post-war boom, company officials and Mineside residents complained frequently about the sub-par living conditions prevailing on the east side of the Leichhardt. In 1946 one company representative said, 'The mine is worthy of a better town than the settlement across the river,' and Fisher often commented on the need for Townside to 'keep pace' with the company town.[116] Visitors criticized the fringe town as well. R. Emerson Curtis, a correspondent for national lifestyle magazine *Walkabout*, captured the starkness of Townside in his 1947 travel article: 'At 1000 feet we swung back towards Mount Isa. The drab little township by the river was laid out in rows of houses that looked from above like tin boxes in the sun's glare. There were no trees to offer shade.'[117]

Local newspaper editorials blamed Townside residents for underdevelopment, arguing that they were not taking advantage of the great opportunities presented to them. In *MIMag*'s profiles of Mineside residents, the main complaints about the community as a whole were commodity shortages, isolation, and the poor state of Townside,[118] but the constant harangue against the fringe was a one-sided public discourse that rarely took the voices of fringe residents into account.

Three decades after MIM was founded, a 1955 study from the University of Queensland described Townside: 'The scene mirrors so vividly man's uncertainty and unpreparedness, the "slap happy" construction of the moment when quick riches beckon and anything will do for a home ... The landscape is thus one of contrast – on one side, the "Lease" with its planning and stability, on the other the "Township" with its heterogeneity and uncertainty.'[119] Another study in 1960 bemoaned the lack of green space on Townside, calling the town unfit 'for human habitation' and a 'blighted area.'[120] No language was too strong to condemn the fringe town.

Townside had serious housing, infrastructure, and aesthetic problems. Yet the idea that residents were the culprits was overstated. The

Cloncurry Shire Council consistently refused to take part in the creation of planned suburbs on Townside.[121] The ongoing neglect of an obstructive absentee government combined with the reality that Mineside was not a 'model' settlement. Urquhart's outdated planned town mixed with ad hoc structures like tent houses and converted military barracks, and none fostered feelings of permanence any more than did the crude Townside grid. Even later company suburbs like Soldiers Hill were laid out in unimaginative grid formations with street names like Carbonate and Oxide that intersected with Sunflower and Urquhart.[122] Proclamations from MIM that the new suburbs fostered markedly increased levels of stability among the population were wishful thinking. Turnover plagued the company and the entire community.

In his 1960 study of Mount Isa, Malcolm Cummings hinted that 'the disorder of the town reflects the apparent disorderly growth of the mine' but failed to assign greater responsibility for improvements to MIM or state and regional governments.[123] By the late 1950s company and state officials began to recognize that not all of the civic problems and workforce turnover originated on the fringe. A measure of transience was unavoidable in mining towns, but decades of planning on Mineside failed to create a stable, working, resident base for the company. The compromise solution was increased planned and resident-owned housing on Townside and a move away from divided planned and fringe settlements to local self-government for a combined Mount Isa.

Townside was something of a free space for the tensions that came with cramped industrial labour and corporate authority in wider society. Most small businesses were located on Townside. Many Mineside residents *decided* to shop and spend their leisure hours there. A number of miners preferred to live outside company jurisdiction as well, for not only could they own a house or rent from a small-property owner, but they had greater control over their own fate in the event of a market bust. MIM continued to compete with the township for a time but ultimately left such things to private enterprise. Retreat from comprehensive paternalism saved the company money, and it promoted the idea that Isans were taking care of their own community, instilling the very feeling of permanence the company had striven for. MIM officials finally achieved stability by recognizing and fostering residents' desires for personal autonomy.

From 1960 onward Townside experienced expanding private enterprise and planned housing. MIM and the QHC financed the construction of hundreds of mortgaged, resident-owned houses in the fringe town.[124] The grant of local self-government was a major factor. Expanded local control allowed a degree of orderly growth for the fringe. The 1968 declaration of Mount Isa's city status increased the community's ability to raise funds, direct local development, and diversify into a regional centre.[125] In the decade after 1963, Mount Isa's population surpassed 26,000, and much of the animosity between Mineside and Townside subsided.

Lest we assume that post-company life at Mount Isa was unconstrained and trouble-free after self-government, it is important to conclude with what MIM gained during the 1960s. The company gained the freedom from continued administration of community affairs. It still built houses, but in partnership with other groups, and it did not have to maintain them afterwards. When state government–aided home ownership began in 1963, Fisher expressed his relief that, after erecting 1,900 homes, 'a great burden' had been lifted from the company.[126] In the mid-1960s *MIMag* ceased to be a community newsletter. Instead it, like its parent company, focused on industrial matters. The company also gained a more stable workforce than it had ever had. By the early 1970s, turnover hovered at 25 per cent – a number beyond the wildest dreams of MIM management in earlier decades.[127] Lower turnover meant less time spent training workers and a more capable labour force. Finally, for its continued – if slightly diminished – authority in the community, MIM was freed from the kind of municipal taxation a corporation of similar size in a large city would be required to pay.

Mount Isa and Corner Brook followed different paths in the development of their built environments: despite a far more intrusive state government than in Newfoundland, Mount Isa did not achieve comparable self-government until the early 1970s, whereas Corner Brook's forest-based industry could establish itself quickly, but because of the difficulties of creating and keeping a massive workforce in the outback, it was not simple for MIM to end paternalism. In Mount Isa and Corner Brook, the companies were intimately involved in the move to self-government, but in different ways: the former through increased planning, the latter through a near-total retreat from paternalism.

This chapter separated the physical shape of communities from the social 'sentiment of community,' in order to highlight the different power relations inherent in the contrasting material conditions of existence in Mount Isa and Corner Brook.[128] Company planning and the response of fringe dwellers set the peculiar physical parameters of experience in each locale. Residents had to navigate their way to acquiring lodging and then through the social hierarchies embedded in the very shape of the towns. The spatial dynamics negotiated by corporations and residents generated specific inequalities and opportunities for agency from below at Mount Isa and Corner Brook.

Comparing built environments sets the stage for a better understanding of the labouring lives of residents. The local spatial context filtered residents' perceptions of work. Regimented hierarchical industrial employment also fed back into the reasons workers built fringe towns or accepted company paternalism.

Chapter Four

Collaborators, Communists, and Casanovas? Labour at Corner Brook and Mount Isa

Years had been spent cultivating employers and establishing the sober and responsible nature of the union; a plunge into the fiery cauldron of [labour militancy] at this point would impel organization in the opposite direction. Always the goal was to organize workers, to preserve and advance the union.

Robert Zeiger, Paper Mill Workers' Union historian

Who put the 'W' in AWU?
Was it men like you and I at the tail end of the queue,
Or was it Edgar Williams and his Dunston Palace crew?
Something's got to go and it won't be 'W.'

CMC rhyme, Mount Isa Strike, 1965

Political economies of industrialization and built environments set the outlines of town growth in Mount Isa and Corner Brook, but it was the actions of thousands of residents that filled in those spaces to create communities that defy type. It is to these critical social histories that we turn in the remaining chapters, beginning with a comparison of the labour histories of each town.

The inimical interests of capitalist and working classes define the structural terms of capitalist economies. It follows that class relations are central to the functioning of company towns. Working-class consciousness – the subjective understanding of belonging to an economic class and the collective responses that arise from this understanding – is another matter. The labour traditions of Queensland and Newfoundland combined with company and government reactions to worker demands and forged distinct work cultures in each locale. No workers in either company town acted as a movement culture to articulate Marxist theories of working-class revolution, but the miners of Mount Isa were more cognizant of class divisions than were the mill hands of Corner Brook. Labouring life at Mount Isa revolved around class to a greater extent than at Corner Brook, but the Isa's class sentiment remained localized.

The industrial production of paper from pulp wood was well established by the time Armstrong began building its Humber Valley mill. Company engineers installed debarking, pulping, and paper-making machinery with little need for local adaptation. Technological changes came slowly over the next four decades. Increasing mechanization eroded woods and mill-labour forces but did not change the basic form of wood extraction or paper production. The dispersal of pulpwood over vast swathes of forest also enabled the Corner Brook paper companies to segregate their workforce geographically into relatively privileged mill workers who lived in the company town and poor seasonal woods workers scattered across dozens of rural settlements. Sound methods of paper-making engendered settled relations of production.[1]

Labour in the Newfoundland paper mills where union organization followed the North American pattern was decidedly non-militant throughout this period. Essential skilled workers like papermakers established small, exclusive trade unions, and mill labourers organized larger industrial unions. In 1910, shortly after the Grand Falls mill opened, skilled papermakers – many recruited from mainland North American and British mills – organized a local chapter of the International Brotherhood of Papermakers (IBP). Three years later in 1913 the remainder of the Grand Falls mill workforce joined the North American industrial union, the International Brotherhood of Pulp, Sulphite, and Paper Mill Workers (IBPSPMW).[2]

The dedicated Victorian paternalist owners at Grand Falls, the Harmsworth family, refused to recognize the mill unions for decades, preferring instead to negotiate wages and work conditions with company-dominated employee committees while the IBP and IBPSPMW spoke informally to the company on behalf of workers. Newfoundland had no labour legislation that affirmed the rights of unions.[3] The combination of employers who were anti-union but generous on their own terms and a government dependent on a handful of resource industries for stability meant that labour had little bargaining power.

For their part, IBP and IBPSPMW were preoccupied with keeping inter-union jurisdictional peace in the 1910s. Tensions originated in the United States. In 1901 skilled and unskilled workers had combined in the International Brotherhood of Papermakers, Pulp, Sulphite, and Paper Mill Workers. Animosities between the two groups over rates of pay, hours, and the papermakers' desire to maintain their exclusive tradesmen status spilled into union politics. In 1906 the papermakers seceded and formed the IBP. Each union raided the other's members until 1909, when they reached a tentative peace. By 1920, the North American officials of the two unions had established a fairly cordial relationship in which they 'bargained in common with many large pulp and newsprint firms.' But that consensus was short lived. By 1925, paper companies across North America had set out to crush the unions.[4] Construction workers on the Humber project, however, were unfettered by considerations of organizational survival.

In 1924, construction workers – first at the Deer Lake hydroelectric site and later in Corner Brook – staged the area's first strikes. To Armstrong and its construction contractors, construction workers' utility consisted of hands and backs. Assisted by hundreds of company horse teams, armies of men levelled and cleared massive tracts of forest to make room for dams, canals, hydro and paper plants, power lines, and company houses. At both sites, men worked ten hours a day, six days a week for approximately twenty-five cents an hour. At day's end the workers crowded together in row after row of hot, poorly ventilated, temporary shacks – undoubtedly likened by the men to the company stables – with basic amenities and few diversions. Contractors deducted room and board of seventy-five to eighty-five cents a day. Managers lived for free in comparably commodious staff houses.[5]

The unorganized workers complained about being 'sweated' by foreign contractors.[6] Armstrong's split-second decision to build the paper plant and main settlement at Corner Brook instead of Deer Lake sowed further confusion, and the company's tight operational deadline resulted in the recruitment of hundreds more men and a disorganized speed-up. In March 1924, the Deer Lake project alone employed over fourteen hundred men rushing to complete Newfoundland's largest industrial network.

On 26 March, 400 Deer Lake workers walked off the job in protest of the improper handling of construction worker Thomas Hartery's dead body. They signed a petition demanding that Fraser, Brace Limited, the site contractors, 'put out' the doctors on the next train for their negligence in handling the man's corpse. Some shouted, 'Put them into the lake.' Site superintendent William Murray not only refused to discipline the doctors but said he would raise Fraser, Brace's eighty-five-cent board to a dollar a day. A quickly convened magisterial inquiry blunted the ill feelings about Hartery's death, but the men stayed off work to protest Murray's 'injudicious' rate hike. On 28 March, Armstrong requested police support. The government investigated the walkout.[7] There was no violence at the site.

The government's report favoured the construction workers, who complained that the contractor gave preferential treatment and pay to Canadian workers, that shacks were overcrowded, and that conditions at the temporary medical shacks were unacceptable. Government investigators found that after the cost of necessities for a family of five was subtracted from annual pay, a full time construction worker cleared only thirteen dollars a year, and that calculation did not even cover the price of coal. The report also stressed that Fraser, Brace's board charges were higher than that of Armstrong's in Corner Brook, and that increasing it by fifteen cents 'would be an outrage and should not be permitted by this government.' The government pressured Armstrong to intercede with its contractor, and the British owner, fearing more delays during the height of construction season, negotiated improvements in every area, including lowering board at Deer Lake to the Corner Brook level of seventy-five cents.[8] The walkout was the only major dispute at Deer Lake until the Depression.

Late in July 1924, workers walked off the job in Corner Brook demanding a daily pay raise from $2.50 to $3.00. The walkout began on 28 July among the permanent coal-loaders and spread to day labourers. By noon on the next day, 2,500 employees – both skilled and unskilled – had abandoned work.[9] To the company, the time wasted during the strike was bad enough, but strike leader Alfred Prince also enlisted the help of the head of the Fishermen's Protective Union and major force in Newfoundland politics, William Coaker, to bargain for the workers.

Armstrong refused to recognize unions. The July 1924 walkout was an early challenge to company prerogative. Construction ceased between 29 July and 2 August. Armstrong's Corner Brook Superintendent William Alexander engaged in an increasingly volatile exchange with Coaker and cabled St John's for police 'sufficient to preserve order' among 6,000 workers. Coaker pleaded with Alexander to accept him as the workers' negotiator. Alexander refused, arguing that a small number of agitators had caused the mass walkout, maintaining the company's policy of negotiating through the government. Coaker threatened to organize a formal union at Corner Brook and warned Alexander that if the company cut services, 'mob rule will result.'[10]

Armstrong kept its barracks and cafeterias open during the dispute but obstinately refused to deal with Coaker. The matter came to a swift conclusion on 1 August when the HMS *Valeria* – sailing on the orders of business-friendly Prime Minister William Monroe – arrived in the Humber Arm, discharged a large contingent of police, and waited ominously in port. According to the local magistrate, Monroe's gunboat politics 'had salutary effect.' Later that day, the men held a secret ballot and voted overwhelmingly to return to work. In a final frustrated appeal for fair dealing, Coaker threatened 'endless future trouble.'[11] Work resumed on Monday 4 August without a pay raise.

Company and government officials were perturbed by Coaker's 'most pernicious and dangerous interference.' In a telegram to Alexander, Armstrong Chairman Glyn West voiced his concern over 'the harsh feeling men have against company.' 'One match applied might destroy 1,000,000 dollars timber.'[12] Concern for financial stability explains the alarmism. The strikers had not committed 'a single breach of the peace' during the eight-day dispute, while the authorities threatened the unorganized strikers with violence if they refused to return to work on the company's terms.[13] There were no further labour disputes during the construction period and the company maintained a policy of opposing unions for another decade.

When production began, Corner Brook's mill workers did not press for union recognition. Corner Brook's residential boom limited class tensions. The population was instant. Few residents had lived there before 1923. New arrivals like the Scott and the Oxford families had to wait for company housing, obtain land and build a house, or find space to rent. Many of the town's renters and business owners were new arrivals as well. Corner Brook's socio-industrial relations were undeveloped and problems with the company threatened to shut down the mill and town growth with it. A work stoppage would imperil the town.

The first skilled workers had to wait extended periods for company houses and the men were frustrated. Yet skilled labourers in particular had prospects and ambitions. The case of the Pickering brothers provides insight into the way some early mill employees balanced annoyance with ambition. Originally from Minnesota, the two men worked as papermakers at the Grand Falls mill for several years. They travelled to Corner Brook to do better for themselves by 'getting in' early. Their experience got the Pickerings papermaking jobs, and their savings and company connections enabled them to open Townsite's first boarding house.

The Pickerings' story resembles that of many of the first skilled workers at Corner Brook.[14] They saw an opportunity for rapid career advancement at the new plant. Although waiting for housing was annoying to workers with wives and children, skilled workers favoured the benefits of company paternalism, the prospect of settling down, and company-conferred instant respectability. The formation of a skilled papermakers union seems to have been a secondary concern at the time.

Unskilled workers formed Corner Brook's first labour union. Most jobs at the mill required little training or experience. Hefting logs into the debarking 'tumblers,' stacking newsprint, loading rolls of newsprint onto ships, and clearing workstations of debris required coordination and strength, but none of the technical knowledge needed to run, maintain, or repair the massive paper machines. The company did not grant these labourers – the vast majority of whom were Newfoundlanders – the perquisites of its skilled labourers. Some were the sons of Corner Brook's original residents; others worked on mill construction and then moved into jobs at the mill; the remainder fled the poverty of the outports. Soon after the mill opened, Charles Ballam – a resident of Curling who had worked at Grand Falls and in mainland mills – organized non-papermakers with the help of a young labour organizer named Joseph Smallwood.[15]

Documents pertaining to the establishment of the union have not survived.[16] Ballam was associated with Pearce Fudge – one of the leaders of the 1924 construction strike – and with self-proclaimed socialist Smallwood.[17] With personal experience of unions at Grand Falls and on the mainland, it is not surprising that Ballam agitated for a union or that unskilled mill workers supported an organization that promised collective assistance. The Pickering brothers and other foreign tradesmen organized the skilled workers shortly thereafter.[18] The precise chronology is fuzzy, but by 1926–7 unskilled workers formed Local 64 of the IBPSPMW and papermakers Local 242 of the IBP.

From 1927 IPPN's anti-unionism sprang from parent company International Paper's war against organized labour in its North American mills. With paper prices high in the early 1920s, companies experimented with new ways of planning and controlling production. IP decided to push established unions out of their mills and declare open shops. Between 1921 and 1926 the IBP and IBPSPMW fought IP unsuccessfully to retain union shops. By the end of the decade the paper mill workers' union was nearly bankrupt, and only dues from Canada sustained it. But the papermakers fared no better. Prolonged unrest and 'the heavy burden of providing financial relief for the strikers' resulted in 'complete defeat' for the IBP and near bankruptcy.[19] That was the position of Corner Brook's parent unions when their foe, International Paper, took over the mill.

IPPN refused to recognize the Corner Brook mill unions until 1937. Up to that time negotiations for rates of pay, increased benefits, and improved safety were handled within a corporate framework. Ballam recalled that 'disputes were looked at by a committee of workers rather than the union, but all committee members were union members.'[20] According to IPPN's 1928 employee rulebook, grievances had to be filed by an individual employee or a committee of employees, not a union. In cases of victimization, individual employees could appeal to the mill manager, who was the ultimate arbiter of discipline.[21] The fact that the mill workers had unions meant little, because they could not openly represent workers and bargain on their behalf. Corner Brook's workers remembered the uncertainty of the NP&P period and the government's willingness to enforce company demands with the threat of violence. They accepted a bargaining system defined by the company.

An attempt by unions to form a cooperative store in 1927 expressed power relations similar to the bargaining processes operating on the shop floor. The co-op movement had a long pedigree in Britain and had migrated to North America around the turn of the century. Grand Falls had a co-op at that time. Corner Brook workers were influenced by developments in the neighbouring mill town. Mill management responded to the request by promising to build a company store with cheaper prices than those at the town's private shops, and workers accepted the conciliation.[22] Unionists did not approach management as members of the papermakers' or the mill workers' union but as employee-residents who wanted improved social conditions. Management's promise to set up a company equivalent satisfied workers for the time being.

As Townsite's early Catholic priest Desmond McGrath put it, the 'workers [were] familiar with the aspirations of management.' Arthur Scott, another long-time resident of Townsite and once president of the small Corner Brook branch of the International Brotherhood of Electrical Workers, maintained that the unions focused on 'modest demands.' As a result, 'change came gradually' and 'you took what you could get.' Even Charles Ballam downplayed union–management tensions.[23] In

Papermaking, 1944. (Corner Brook Pulp and Paper Limited Photographic Collection courtesy of the Corner Brook Museum and Archives)

early Corner Brook we encounter a curious situation where the company agreed informally to allow unions at the mill and the unions agreed to abjure collective action to gain concessions from management. The unions exercised no power apart from their organizational knowledge of the workforce and the ever-present but unused threat of collective unrest.

When the Great Depression hit the island in the early 1930s, IPPN dealt with low paper prices by reducing the wood cut, lowering wages, and slashing workers' hours at the mill. Mill workers and their families endured hardships. Wives of skilled workers suffered tight financial conditions. Marian Oxford 'had to cut everything very fine' and make her children's clothes to keep up with the mill managers' well-dressed children.[24] Emily Watson said that Townsite housewives were extremely busy with child-rearing, housekeeping, and maintaining small gardens. When not involved in one of those chores, 'every spare minute they had a needle in their hands.'[25]

Economic collapse hit unskilled mill workers in the fringe communities of Corner Brook West and East harder than the residents of the company town. All pay dropped in the 1930s, but wage decreases for unskilled workers were an extra blow because of their lower income. Townsite resident Arthur Scott recalled women from the fringe towns going door to door with their children begging for food. Younger women began to supplement male income by taking jobs as domestics, store clerks, and company secretaries. Scott said that, despite the loss of income, 'we were considered to be really fortunate.'[26]

The consensus among people who lived through the Depression in Corner Brook was that times were not as tough for mill workers as for most other Newfoundlanders. One of respondents' most common refrains was, 'We didn't want for anything.'[27] The company gave skilled mill workers credit at the company store and allowed tenants to defer rent payments. Even the unskilled always had jobs at the mill. IPPN slashed its wood quota and wages, but company officials soon realized that they needed ever stricter economies to weather the market collapse. Instead of the company sacking several hundred workers, the employee committees negotiated a short-time schedule at the mill, which spread reduced operating hours across the workforce, allowing all workers to remain on the payroll. As a result, the Humber District maintained one of the lowest levels of 'able-bodied relief' in Newfoundland during the Depression.[28] People in Corner Brook 'got by' better than most Newfoundlanders. Woods workers – the pulp and paper industry's most exploited employees – suffered more than most.

The logging arm of the pulp and paper industry relied on seasonal labour from the outport that was, according to logging historian Dufferin Sutherland, constrained by capital: 'The thousands of outport workers who toiled in the woods with bucksaws for crucial wages limited forest capital's accumulation of surplus. The highly capitalized and productive mills had to appropriate surplus from woods labour through continuous production and downward pressure on wages and living conditions. Otherwise, to make profits, capital would have to revolutionize production in the woods which they avoided as long as the social formation [of seasonal loggers working for supplemental income] provided them with a cheap and abundant labour supply.'[29] Loggers' isolation from the company towns enforced their social and economic distance from mill workers, weakening class solidarity in the industry.[30] To Corner Brook's manufacturing workers, loggers ordinarily did not appear to be a central part of production. Mill companies passed economic uncertainty onto a large segment of workers who were geographically scattered and disorganized, and that occupational segregation contributed to the higher standard of living for workers at the central production site in Corner Brook.

The 1934 Bradley Report on the state of Newfoundland loggers – an inquiry established by the Commission of Government but later suppressed for its damning critique of the island's paper companies – describes the wide-scale abuse of woods workers. According to F. Gordon Bradley, IPPN's unskilled mill workers made $2.40 during eight hours, while the average logger made less than $1.13 in ten. Loggers' pay and conditions varied among camps, so some woods workers made even less. Bradley concluded that no regulations governed living conditions in the camps. The loggers were almost completely unorganized and were 'reduced to a standard below even tolerable existence.'[31] The Depression had reduced the majority of the population of the logging town of Deer Lake to a 'state bordering on pauperism.'[32]

The detestable conditions that west coast loggers endured and their sporadic but effective mass protests against exploitation are covered amply elsewhere.[33] Unfortunately, those studies do not provide an equally detailed analysis of mill labour. The result is an inaccurate portrayal of mill employees as forming a smug 'aristocracy of labour' that simply ignored the plight of their comrades in the woods. Yet mill workers aided loggers who themselves never expressed industry-wide class consciousness.

Before John Thompson established Newfoundland's largest loggers' union, the Newfoundland Lumbermen's Association, in August 1935,

Newfoundland loggers. (Corner Brook Pulp and Paper Limited Photographic Collection courtesy of the Corner Brook Museum and Archives)

IPPN mill employees backed unorganized loggers in at least two disputes. In the spring of 1932, Deer Lake loggers feared a complete loss of income when IPPN cancelled the annual cut. Pressure from the loggers and Corner Brook mill workers convinced IPPN to make a small cut. Early in 1933 west coast log drivers struck when IPPN slashed their wages by 7.5 cents. Again, pressure from mill workers forced the company to return to the original wage.[34] Mill workers were also affected negatively by the Depression. At times they supported loggers, and at others – particularly once loggers established independent unions in the mid-1930s and Corner Brook mill unions remained unrecognized – they did not. In other disputes between the company and loggers, individual mill workers offered support and others refused to get involved.[35] Mill workers had their own issues with management and engaged in more confrontations with the company during the Depression than at any other time in their history. Before labour and capital compromised on the short time schedule, they shut the mill down for a brief time.[36] Mill workers had never stopped work before.

Few Corner Brook workers were militant. Mill workers preferred to negotiate with the company instead of threatening it. According to long-time mill employee Ches Rendell, workers achieved sporadic and important local victories through cautious dealings with the company.[37] Besieged North American conservative union bureaucracies urged locals constantly to accept extensive wage cuts. IBP President Matthew Burns 'pleaded with the Canadian locals' for years during the Depression 'to take such cuts when they were demanded by the companies.'[38] By the late 1930s IPPN and Bowater viewed the mill unions as an effective check on labour militancy.

Mill workers understood that they were in a better socio-economic position than other Newfoundlanders and hesitated to risk eroding that position by fighting when the company seemed open to compromise. Sutherland's implication that loggers struggled only within a context of a strong company–government alliance that prevented 'relevant' social change applies equally well to mill workers.[39] Loggers, moreover, did not have to contend with hidebound union bureaucracies that were terrified of strikes. It is remarkable that mill workers obtained even meagre gains.

International Paper by 1937 had been battling one labour organization or another since the early 1920s. New president Richard Cullen sought to regain IP's financial equilibrium by recognizing moderate mill unions like the IBP and IBPSPMW. Company officials believed that by aiding and co-opting moderate unions they would forestall further industrial disruptions. In April 1937, IP officials met union leaders in Montreal and signed closed-shop agreements for all International Paper mills in Canada.[40] IPPN recognized unions in Newfoundland the same month. The strategy worked in IPPN's western Newfoundland pulp-and-paper network, but the company sold the operation before it could benefit from the new course.

Mill unionists and their supporters fondly remember April 1937 when IPPN agreed to the first joint mill unions contract. The first agreement was for two years and it raised wages by 2.5 to 3.5 cents.[41] Thereafter, union bargaining committees negotiated contracts periodically with mill management. In their eminently moderate way, Corner Brook's skilled and unskilled mill workers contested and survived a decade of company anti-unionism and economic depression while other IBP and IBPSPMW locals were ruined. When Bowater purchased the mill in the spring of 1938, it maintained union recognition.[42] By then the towns had a population of over twenty thousand people. An 'internal labour market' had developed where mill positions were passed on to the next generation of young men. Around 94 per cent of Bowater employees were Newfoundlanders.[43]

During the Second World War, mill production increased to the point that 'Corner Brook's output was not far short of the entire U.K. consumption.'[44] After the war the company accommodated all of its former employees who chose to serve in the military by counting military service towards job seniority.[45] BNPP fostered the impression that it took great care of its workers on the job and trusted them to take care of each other in the community. The company set up apprenticeship programs and maintained the loyalty of current employees by giving their sons preference in future job openings. BNPP's decision to sell its company town assets after the war enabled Townsite skilled workers to buy quality homes for low prices. The corresponding move toward municipal self-government between 1946 and 1955 eroded claims of company monopoly and provided residents with the belief – usually overstated – that they determined their own fate.

Joseph Smallwood's newly established Canadian provincial government contributed to mill workers' security throughout much of the 1950s as well. Confederation gave all Newfoundlanders a reliable social safety net for the first time. BNPP was one of the province's only industrial success stories, and the inveterate micromanager Smallwood was determined to maintain the smooth, profitable operation of the paper mill and the growth of Corner Brook. There is scarcely a mention of workplace tension during this period. Not even the explosive company–logger conflict at the end of the 1950s shook mill workers' faith in compromise and cooperation.

If mill workers were generally quiescent during the 1940s and 50s, the situation with loggers was one of simmering discontent. In 1940 the Commission of Government created the Woods Labour Board to ease the tensions between paper companies and loggers. The government proclaimed that the board was a multi-party compulsory conciliation committee where disputes could be settled without resort to work stoppages, but it really functioned to foil reforms in the woods. Between 1940 and 1958, the board's most significant accomplishment was ending 'militancy in the woods for almost twenty years' by criminalizing the unions' most effective weapon, the lightning strike.[46] Conditions and pay in the woods remained little better than in the 1920s.

Rank-and-file loggers discovered, as before, that they could not rely on paper companies and the government to give improvements to workers. Historian Ian Radforth argues that 'managers pursued only those kinds of innovations that enhanced their own power and control' but it was not 'a straight managerial conspiracy.' For nearly twenty years under the board, Newfoundland loggers surrendered to management's will. Ontario loggers, in comparison, took part in an ongoing 'process of negotiation' with management from which they were better able to alter corporate plans.[47] By the mid-1950s it was plain to Newfoundland loggers that their once forceful union leaders were tethered to an obstructionist conciliation system. Between January 1957 and New Year's Eve 1958, an overwhelming majority of BNPP and ANDCO loggers voted to join the militant and expanding International Woodworkers of America (IWA). The IWA petitioned the paper companies for a raise of twenty-five cents an hour, better camp conditions, and a reduction in weekly hours from sixty to fifty-four.[48] The companies refused to budge and the loggers struck on 1 January 1959.

Smallwood intervened on the side of Newfoundland's most stable businesses, enforced a harsh union decertification law that was condemned throughout North America, and ordered police to monitor IWA picket lines. On 9 March seventy police attempted to break up a twenty-man picket in Badger, and Constable William Moss was killed in the ensuing melee. Already losing public support among Newfoundlanders who, for the most part, rallied behind Smallwood, loggers ended the strike suddenly on 11 March. The IWA left Newfoundland, the loggers were rounded up into a government-run union, and they signed a collective agreement for a 'five cent an hour increase [that the Grand Falls mill company] had said would cripple it three months earlier.'[49]

Grand Falls mill workers largely rejected the striking loggers. They believed the loggers were asking for too much and that it would cripple the industry they all depended on, whereas Corner Brook's mill workers were slightly more sanguine about the conflict, despite BNPP's 'implacable opposition' to the IWA. According to Harold Horwood, 1,400 BNPP loggers left their camps in protest. Later, some raided the camps when scab loggers replaced them, and the protesting loggers threatened to 'close down Bowater logging operations entirely.' Horwood contends that most of Corner Brook's mill workers 'supported the IWA and gave generously to its strike fund,'[50] but he cites no evidence. Considering the mill workers' history of lending at least minimal support to loggers, it is likely that a number of them did support the strikers morally and financially.

After the 1959 strike, work in the west coast paper industry settled into a groove once more. At times there were fluctuations in production and scattered layoffs because of sagging demand, but over the next two decades minor slumps ended in satisfactory recoveries. BNPP's introduction of modern technology into its woods operations in the 1960s made extraction 'deseasoned' and predictable, and greatly reduced the company's logging workforce.[51] From the pool of thousands of seasonal workers in the 1950s, new owner Kruger employed only 500 full-time professional loggers in 1992.[52] Rationalization in the woods presaged similar trends in the manufacturing arm of the industry.

Bowater allowed the Corner Brook mill to stagnate. Technological upgrades and workforce changes that would have made the local industry more sustainable were sacrificed after 1952 because BNPP's role was as 'cash cow' to finance Bowater's North American operations. BNPP's dwindling income went to maintaining local wages and benefits, and the rest was diverted to mills in places like Calhoun, Tennessee. What that meant was not clear to mill workers until they were faced with the unenviable choice between massive layoffs or plant closure. In 1984, after several years of veiled threats that kept the community on edge, Bowater announced it was selling the mill.

The buyer, Canada's Kruger, arrived with the intention of modernizing the operation and slashing the workforce in order to compete with the low-cost mills in South America, Scandinavia, and Southeast Asia that had been built during the creeping decline of the Corner Brook mill. Unfortunately for the mill workers, no amount of cooperation, compromise, or loyalty could stave off Kruger's decision to achieve 'technical control' of its workforce.[53]

In August 1988, after the first Kruger contract expired, the combined mill unions struck to protest the low wages and job cuts. The strike lasted forty-three days and involved nearly 1,600 workers – the biggest and longest strike in Corner Brook since the 1924 construction strike. Mill workers gained some concessions, but Kruger reserved the right to cut jobs and subcontract the work, with the result that by 1992, there were only 567 permanent hourly workers at the mill – approximately the same number as in the woods and just over one quarter of the number during the 1950s.[54] After nearly seven decades, the largely artificial divisions between Corner Brook's primary extractive and manufacturing workers had disappeared. Both groups were expendable.

In his comprehensive study of unionization among Newfoundland loggers, Dufferin Sutherland calls mill workers and their families a 'well-paid proletariat in prosperous company towns,' and an 'aloof aristocracy of labour.'[55] The labels are misleading. For Sutherland to lump Corner Brook's mill workers into a Marxist category like 'aristocracy of labour' after spending considerable space arguing that *no* Newfoundland workers had knowledge of radical class theory is a logical contradiction that is the equivalent of blaming house cats for not acting like tigers.

Mill workers were not an 'aristocracy.' They were an industrial workforce constrained in their ability to improve their local conditions and effectively support other unions. Inhabitants did not act out of broad identification with the working class. Any sharp sense of class solidarity positing a simple opposition between 'the company' and 'the workers' was diluted by the top-down imposed and bottom-up maintained divisions between workers. Local community issues in Corner Brook tended to take precedence over the politics of capital and labour.

The value of historical comparison is seen when labour relations at Mount Isa are considered. Queensland has a long history of unionism, class politics, and industrial law. It is a jurisdiction where class-based theory is more applicable to the structural economic process of industrial development as well as in the way employers and workers subjectively understood their places in industry and society. However, class in Mount Isa was lived experience, not theory. Tense relations between labour and capital shaped Isa's history in no predetermined way.

Australian mining was undergoing massive changes during the first half of the twentieth century. The realities of the resource required mining companies to focus on new technologies and increased technical training for employees, and pushed owners like Urquhart to plan their industries to an extent never seen in Australian mining. MIM's decision to build mining and processing works on a single site ensured that thousands of extractive and manufacturing, settled and transient workers lived in close proximity to one another. Uncertainty fostered tensions at Mount Isa.

Historians of Mount Isa tend to describe MIM employees as quiescent and tout a record of peaceful employee–company relations. That is a fair assessment when comparing labour history at Mount Isa to a place like Broken Hill – a rare example of a dependent industrial town with a marked degree of worker control – or to a militant occupational group like longshoremen. However, compared to Corner Brook and most other company towns, Mount Isa has a deep history of class conflict.

The basic uncertainty of industry in Australia's isolated outback shaped workers' response to employment. Mobility was the main survival strategy for unskilled Queensland workers and it shaped class development at Mount Isa.[56] That MIM was compelled to continue to build houses four decades into its administration denotes how mobility caused MIM to adapt to pressures from below. The tensions between largely fixed institutions – the mine, the Queensland government, the union, and even skilled workers – and a mass of rough unskilled workers inured to transience entrenched oppositional social relations.

A corporate–government alliance for development shaped local relations. By the early 1920s, the Labor government had settled into conservative habits. It garnered much of its support from the AWU's rural membership while many other Queensland workers were associated with radical unions. After 1917, Queensland's Labor premiers regularly espoused a hatred of anything 'communist.' That term covered any group or idea that the government and its union and business allies believed deviated from orthodox labour, liberal, or conservative politics. The leftist bastion of Broken Hill, New South Wales, with its industrial council, militant working residents, high pay, and high living standards was an example that no capitalist or state politician cared to see repeated.[57]

Conversely, ordinary workers viewed Broken Hill as symbolic of labour's power to fight for its fair share. Workers' belief in 'fair dinkum' relations among all classes did not respect union jurisdiction. In the AWU, for example, local rank-and-file unionists often took matters into their own hands against employers instead of waiting for union officials to speak to company representatives or file a formal arbitration claim in the Industrial Court.

Most labour in Queensland was unionized. The state had a long history of worker organization and labour politics. The prominence of organized labour in the workplace and in the government contributed to the belief in labour's central importance to the economy and society. In large industries like mining, unions were divided into two types: trade and industrial.[58] Industrial unions were massive, often multi-sector organizations that encompassed large numbers of unskilled miners. Trade unions were numerous but smaller organizations that comprised skilled workers like electricians, engineers, and mechanics. Originally a rural, pastoral-based union that had organized sheep shearers in the

1890s, the AWU was an industrial union, the largest in Queensland,[59] its members found in most enterprises in the state.

The state government of Queensland premised its industrial relations laws on keeping the industrial peace and mandating equilibrium between the inimical interests of capital and labour. Conservative labour organizations, private companies like MIM dedicated to avoiding another Broken Hill, and strict industrial relations procedures where state officials bound capital and labour to their decisions comprised the official context of industry in Queensland. Rank-and-file workers and their allies among members of smaller trade unions and town residents were the amorphous countervailing force. After the Labor Party's early nationalization fiascos and resulting credit squeeze, Queensland governments supported trouble-free foreign investment and steady production. The position favoured capital far more than it did labour.

Up to Leslie Urquhart's injection of British capital in 1927, the number of construction workers fluctuated at Mount Isa. The small settlement that hugged the western bank of the Leichhardt comprised itinerant peddlers and an ever-shifting pool of labourers.[60] Constant mobility left the field's industrial relations undeveloped. No significant labour disputes occurred until large-scale construction began. The arrival of Russo-Asiatic signalled greater permanence.

Urquhart was wary of Australian workers and Queensland labour law. He had been warned about the stubborn militancy of workers and knew he would have to contend with formal arbitration. Urquhart believed the solution was to eliminate as many jobs as possible through mechanization, do all secondary processing onsite, and offer skilled workers a range of company housing and welfare provisions to keep them content.[61] Urquhart's distrust of labour and the divisions his comprehensive plan introduced into the nascent industrial settlement proved detrimental for the maintenance of industrial peace.

Between 1928 and 1930 the local labour scene was made up of a jumble of competing unions. When mining and processing began, each union negotiated a contract or 'award' with the company through the state's Industrial Court. Each award set out pay scales, hours of work, and job requirements, and if a breach in the terms of an award occurred, the offended party could apply to the Industrial Court for a formal arbitration hearing. There, an industrial magistrate heard evidence from company and union(s) and made a ruling that bound both parties. Employers wanted their employees to be members of accredited unions so that workers were bound by compulsory arbitration and, theoretically at least, could not easily disrupt production by striking. In 1929, sixteen separate awards covered 700 workers. Considering the labour government's strong interest in Mount Isa, it is not surprising that its main grassroots ally, the AWU, became the official union for Isa miners and the dominant union on the field.[62]

A slew of difficulties confounded Urquhart's vision of industrial order through mechanization and paternalism. ASARCO General Manager Julius Kruttschnitt arrived in December 1930 full of what he described as 'fear and trembling' at the prospect of working out the mine's numerous problems. He had to increase production and cut costs. That dual mandate meant a work speed-up and an overall decrease in pay.[63] Up until that point, labour relations had been peaceful, apart from worker grumbling and threats from union officials. Isa miners and managers alike were more concerned with making the mine viable than demanding higher wages or increased benefits.[64] Pressure from management caused the growing workforce and its unions to apply greater pressure on the company.

Extracting and processing low-grade ore was more demanding and dangerous than mill work. Miners worked in hot, dark, and confined spaces for twelve-hour shifts, six days a week. Back-breaking repetitive work with heavy picks was 'mechanized' by heavy, repetitive, and loud hydraulic picks, while workers still loaded ore-bearing rock onto waiting ore carts by hand. Even experienced miners suffered assorted occupational injuries. Between 1929 and 1932 accidents that ran the gamut from high falls to explosions killed twelve workers. Scores of men suffered crushed and broken bones and lacerations. After 1932, the mine averaged over two fatalities a year.[65]

Employees on the surface in the mineral flotation and smelting plants worked equally long hours and were responsible for difficult maintenance procedures. Along with burning, falling, and electrical hazards, in the 1930s surface workers risked contracting debilitating lead poisoning from the ineffective smelters. The protective gear required to avoid inhaling lead particulate was rarely available to all workers, and some men refused to wear it because of the extreme heat radiated by furnaces of molten metal.

All workers came together in one place. MIM had no unskilled workers on the geographic periphery to exploit in order to reinforce shop-floor stability at the point of production. In Mount Isa primary extractive workers and secondary plant employees experienced similar work conditions. Living and working at the same site engendered a degree of cross-occupational rank-and-file reliance that other industries did not possess. 'Mateship' – an Australian euphemism for homosociability, usually of a tough working-class variety – suffused the mine and plant, the boarding houses and bars. After 1930, the rough group of unskilled workers and a company devoted to controlling every aspect of production combined with the added uncertainty and low pay of the Depression.

To Kruttschnitt, the Depression created an opening for management to increase its control over the workforce. 'There were plenty of men outside the gate at Mount Isa during the Depression. It kept those on the job on their toes because they knew fellows were waiting outside the gate for somebody to be thrown out. [These men waiting for jobs] just camped on the river bank.'[66] Economic collapse eroded workers' confidence in the IR system.

Geoffrey Blainey portrays Depression-era Mount Isa as a place that 'sowed optimism.' To him, MIM was 'radical and courageous' and 'attempt[ed] to create a contented industrial community.'[67] In fact, the mine was in financial trouble and the planned town suffered because the new mine owner prioritized industrial productivity over housing. Itinerant labourers, always abundant in Queensland, soared in numbers during the Depression as the result of mass layoffs in other industries. Thousands 'rode the rattler' to Mount Isa in a desperate search for work. Most men arrived with little more than rough canvas tents and shoulder swags containing a change of clothes and a few personal items. Each morning, hundreds of men queued up at the gates of the mine for the chance that a MIM official would call on them to work for A$2.00 to A$2.50 a day. A day's work was often followed by days without. Later in the 1930s, the company afforded the luckiest workers the luxury of renting a tent from the company. Uncertainty followed uncertainty.

State inquest files are replete with qualitative descriptions of the social consequences of poverty, illuminating the darker corners of mobile workers' lives. In one case, two men spent the day alternating between drinking together and fighting until the man who endured what one witness called a 'terrible hiding' threatened the other with a broken beer bottle and had to be restrained by three prostitutes. Later that night, the bough shack of the man who had been roughed up burned to the ground. In another case, Harry 'Tink' Carter, an itinerant labourer, died in a leaky old tent by the rail junction. The sixty-three-year-old had no valuables and thirteen pounds in savings when he died. After nine or ten days of heavy drinking, William 'Tassy' Burns wandered away from the Cloncurry hotel where he had stayed briefly and died of exposure. The inquest revealed he had four jobs between November 1929 and April 1930 and that he left nothing behind except a tent, a blanket, and some clothes.[68] Life for the itinerant industrial worker was difficult. Some died. Many took refuge in alcohol and violence. Both were easy to obtain.

Mount Isa was male dominated. Men did not bring female companions to the Isa, and it was difficult to meet women there. The rough recreation of binge-drinking sessions around campfires were all-male affairs.[69] Mateship between mobile workers remained the default form of relationship into the late 1960s.

Uncertainty of employment, poverty, loneliness, sexual frustration, and alcohol's depressing effects created tensions in a social environment that prized the goals of masculine independence and toughness. Isa's itinerant workers refused to shy away from confrontations around the campfire or in the workplace. Mateship at camp bled into work relationships. Queensland workers' mobile anonymity and belief in the dignity of labour, their conflict-based industrial milieu, and dangerous occupations fostered 'occupational inter-reliance.'[70] In the mine and smelter, workers directed dissatisfaction at MIM foremen and managers who told labourers how to do their jobs, and then ordered them to do it better and faster.

Employees reacted by staging snap work stoppages during the early 1930s.[71] The brief wildcat stoppages were justified. Ordinary workers complained frequently about verbal abuse and victimization by staff and foremen. Speed-ups resulted in injuries and deaths. From the opening of the smelter in June 1931 up to December 1937, local doctors diagnosed 369 workers with varying levels of lead poisoning caused by defective smelter equipment.[72] Unions applied to the Industrial Court for greater protection, but only MIM and the AWU bureaucracy received satisfaction from the court. In October 1931, at the urging of MIM and AWU, the Industrial Court 'rescinded all [sixteen] existing awards' and replaced them with a single Mount Isa Mines Limited Award, which covered all workers and made the AWU the dominant union on the field.[73] From then onward Mount Isa's smaller militant trade unions tended to act in concert and struggled to get local AWU members onside during their frequent disputes with the company.

MIM's first aggressive attempts to establish strict control over its unruly workforce came in 1933 and 1934. First, Kruttschnitt shut the mine

Argent Hotel, Townside, Mount Isa. (Courtesy Jonathan Richards)

down and locked all workers out from 31 October until late December. The company said 'low metal prices' and 'the enforced stoppages of a section of its employees' made the lockout 'absolutely imperative,' with the result that many workers abandoned the field and went to the coast in search of work. When MIM reopened, management rehired only 350 of its previous 1,200 workers.[74] MIM hired young, inexperienced workers who would work for less pay than veteran miners and whom the company could more easily train in its own work routines. In the ensuing court proceedings, AWU officials alleged widespread victimization, but MIM came out on top. The court ruled in favour of a roster system that gave the company more control over who could work in the mine, and it added penalty clauses to the award for workers who participated in 'illegal' work stoppages. The court allowed a small pay cut as well.[75]

In November 1937 the Industrial Court granted MIM workers a 'lead bonus' of six pence for every one-pound increase in the price of lead up to thirty-one pounds per ton,[76] the second mine in Australia in which such a prosperity bonus was awarded (the first being to Broken Hill workers in 1925). The courts hoped the lead bonus would create 'a buffer against increasingly wide fluctuations in international metal prices' and 'a counter to major industrial disruption.'[77] Mount Isa workers came to view a bonus accurately indexed to MIM profits as their right, but, apart from the rare instances when the Industrial Court awarded substantial increases in the bonus, the bonus declined over the next twenty-five years. By the early 1960s, threats to the lead bonus became an explosive labour relations issue.

MIM never accepted the lead bonus as a perpetual right of workers. In 1936 and 1937 MIM sent staff members overseas to study the newest techniques of scientific management.[78] Managers' fascination with time and motion studies and industrial psychology grew over the following decades. The state government contributed to stable corporate profits by passing the State Transport Act in 1938, which sounded innocuous but actually allowed the Queensland government to declare states of emergency to end labour disputes.[79] The government would apply the act twice in Mount Isa in the 1960s.

Residents who did not work directly for MIM had to court the mobile workforce, and as a consequence the rough transient miners became the customers, tenants, and friends of the settled townspeople. One outcome of the mutual dependency was that many residents adopted class-based positions similar to MIM workers. Owners of small businesses supported rank-and-file miners during labour disputes by reducing rates or granting easy credit. Churches opened charity kitchens. Women in Mount Isa established similar organizations, attended meetings, participated in boycotts, and picketed. The struggle against monopoly was at the base of community politics during this period.[80]

For a short time the lead bonus balanced workers' wage and occupational safety concerns with the company's productivity demands. Historians who emphasize MIM's story of development generally mythologize the years between 1937 and 1960 as the period of labour–capital cooperation, which made MIM one of Australia's most successful companies. Geoffrey Blainey went so far as to call Isa 'the glamour town of the Australian outback, the Mecca for hundreds.'[81] But this depiction is convincing only when labour's clashes with MIM over the following two decades are overlooked. In reality, MIM continued its heavy-handed treatment of its workforce after the Second World War, and workers' collective sense of exploitation in two key areas – lead bonus payments and the accountability of union leaders – festered.

Demands for higher pay were muted for a time after the 1937 bonus award, but they did not disappear. In October 1940, higher pay returned to the agenda when fifty fitters – members of the Amalgamated Engineering Union – struck for a raise of eleven shillings a week. Meanwhile, AWU leaders complained that MIM had lowered contract rates without consulting the union. They asked miners to revert to hourly wages instead of piece rates. MIM accused the AWU of a 'go-slow' strike, arguing that workers on an hourly wage produced less without the incentive of higher earnings. Union leaders fired back, saying the company was victimizing and intimidating its members. In the subsequent arbitration hearings, the Industrial Court ruled MIM's reduction of contract pay unwarranted and suggested the company raise fitters' pay as well. By 25 November all workers were back on the job.[82]

War and industrial recovery threw workplace relations into chaos once more. Many MIM employees joined the military or left the outback to pursue work in coastal war industries, compelling MIM to conscript 'enemy alien' labour in the last years of the war.[83] A captive workforce and strict wartime controls over industrial disputes benefited the company by quelling union activity on the field until the late 1940s. New and returned employees of the ballooning mine workforce pressed the company for higher pay as soon as hostilities ceased.

In November 1946 the combined unions at Mount Isa lodged a claim for rates of pay equal to those at Broken Hill. The impulse to emulate Broken Hill became a general principle for Mount Isa's rank-and-file employees. The court delayed the claim for over a year as a result of the Commonwealth government's extension of national security regulations, saying it would return a decision on 21 January 1948. When it failed to do so, trade unionists in the Mount Isa Trades and Labor Council (TLC) formed a Lead Bonus Dispute Committee and voted overwhelmingly to strike unless MIM increased wages commensurate with the company's 'enormous' profits. MIM's Industrial Officer Stuart Tuck responded, telling strikers that any man failing to show up for work 'would be regarded as having terminated his employment.'[84] The next day, 600 of MIM's 1,500 employees walked off the job.

During the nearly three-week strike that followed, another pattern emerged that – like demands for increased bonus payments, reversion to hourly wages, and the desire to emulate Broken Hill – became a theme in the disputes of the 1960s. Initially, only the trade unionists who ran the surface works struck. AWU miners continued to work. Increasingly out-of-touch and collaborationist AWU bureaucrats refused to commit their workers to the strike, despite strong support for the dispute committee among the local AWU membership. Two weeks into the strike, approximately a third of the AWU's 900 members defied their own union's position and joined the strikers. In sensationalist fashion, a local AWU organizer blamed the defection on the 'communist' dispute committee. In this case the committee's secretary was actually a radical leftist, but the AWU's incendiary rhetoric obscured the fact that the strike was over the mundane issue of higher pay, not a step toward revolution.[85]

On 2 February the local head of police reported 'considerable bitterness' between 'the opposing factions as a result of the efforts of the less militant section to endeavour to call the strike off.' MIM threatened to turn employees out of company barracks and make them pay cash for meals, but strikers refused to return to work until 5 February, when the industrial magistrate agreed to a full investigation and audit of the company's books. In the subsequent hearings, the Industrial Court refused to hear representatives from the dispute committee, even though its members led the strike, and the dispute broke down into employee group infighting.[86] Four months later in June 1948, disgruntled AWU members tried unsuccessfully to form a new union at Mount Isa.[87] These episodes reinforce a sense of pervasive disquiet. For a decade after the failed breakaway bid, outright industrial strife receded. Low attendance at AWU meetings expressed the apathy many workers felt towards stodgy labour politics.[88] Yet the absence of overt protest is deceptive.

The number of non-English-speaking European immigrants grew during the 1950s. Poles, Czechs, Greeks, Australia's largest Finnish community, and people from dozens of other countries flocked to the outback town after the war. The reassuring tone adopted by company organs that there was 'no animosity among the nationalities' was wishful thinking.[89] Oddly enough, company promoter Gordon Sheldon contradicted his own statement about ethnic harmony when he stressed the 'big part' Finnish miners played in 'leading a return to work' in the 1961 strike.[90] Before the mid-1960s, the Finns formed a particularly close community with their own social clubs. Finns preferred to work exclusively with countrymen.[91] The raw nativism of 'white Australians' also makes claims of easy harmony suspect. Aboriginal Australians, for example, are absent from the frequent pronouncements about MIM's multi-ethnic workforce during this period. While I have seen no direct evidence that the company excluded Aboriginals from its workforce, it is safe to assume that prejudices in unwritten hiring practices barred Aboriginals from working alongside white Australians. The influx of New Australians exacerbated tensions as well.

Prosperity masked fundamental contradictions in the workplace and community. MIM officials instituted strict scientific management procedures at the mine after 1945. General Manager Fisher embraced scientific management wholeheartedly.[92] In 1950, MIM employed 'industrial psychologists,' increased its number of supervisors, and trained them in the most up-to-date industrial management practices. The *Queensland Government Mining Journal* printed regular articles promoting the 'close study of the movements of the worker, the work areas, the housekeeping, materials, machines, tools, and clothing,' and how to 'put workers at ease' while explaining their jobs to them. Along these lines, the journal described a film used to train mining supervisors at Mount Isa in which supervisor 'Erasmus' instructed an anonymous worker to 'repeat all his instructions while he checks them against his notes.' In the film Erasmus's strict devotion to efficiency earned him 'the respect and confidence of all his subordinates,' but it is difficult to imagine how the study and rearrangement by educated supervisors of the most miniscule actions of workers would earn any respect from experienced, independent miners.[93] By the late 1950s, workers complained of over-supervision and being 'sweated,' claiming there was anywhere from one supervisor for every two miners to 'one supervisor for every four men.'[94]

The lead bonus came increasingly under siege during the late 1950s too. Workers discovered that even a bonus of eight pounds was barely enough to cover the high cost of living in the isolated outback. Electricity cost twice as much as in Melbourne and new furniture two times more than in Brisbane. Board was 'difficult to obtain' and rents kept pace with increases to the lead bonus.[95] MIM and its critics agreed on two things: distance added 'to the price of almost every commodity bought in Mount Isa and the cost of living' was high.[96]

MIM officials remained bitter about what they considered forced profit-sharing. The collapse of Labor's dominance – including a fatal split between the AWU and the Labor Party – and the 1957 electoral victory of the Frank Nicklin–Kenneth Morris Country–Liberal coalition opened the door to a more effective company alliance with the government. For the first time, ASARCO-MIM dealt with an explicitly pro-business state government.[97]

From 1957, the Nicklin-Morris government's actions to do away with the lead bonus pushed suppressed local grievances to the fore. Between 1959 and 1964, inter- and intra-union tension formed along local lines. On the one side were staid, distant union officials and the indebted mining families who advocated arbitration and industrial peace. On the other side were militant local rank-and-file workers. The latter felt triply exploited: by a rich foreign corporation, by ineffectual union leaders, and by a supposedly 'fair' industrial relations system stacked against the interests of ordinary workers.

The first cracks in the 1950s facade of prosperity appeared in June 1959 when several hundred MIM employees fought a two-month battle for a higher bonus. By that time the bonus had slid from over seventeen pounds a week in 1951 to under four.[98] In early June the trade unionists in the Mount Isa Industrial Council and a number of AWU members imposed a ban on working overtime at the mine in an effort to force the company to raise the lead bonus to ten pounds per week.[99] Kenneth Morgan, secretary of the Industrial Council, formed the Rank and File Committee and asked employees to decline overtime and work set hours.

On 16 June, the AWU's Northern District Secretary Edgar Williams reported the alarming fact that nearly nine hundred of Isa's AWU members had resigned from the AWU and enrolled in a breakaway Mount Isa Mine-Workers Association that held secret meetings at Morgan's Workers' Club on Townside. Morgan and the Rank and File Committee also expressed solidarity with Clyde Cameron, the former top AWU official who broke with the AWU to form the Committee for Membership Control (CMC), which aimed to make AWU bureaucrats accountable to members in local chapters.[100] Aloof union bureaucrats did not comprehend the cross-union alliance of rank-and-file AWU and trades workers in Mount Isa.

Over the next three weeks recriminations flew back and forth between supporters of the Rank and File Committee and supporters of MIM *and* the AWU. On 1 July, MIM fired Kenneth Morgan and two others for allegedly leaving their jobs to taunt 'scab' workers, and 150 workers walked off the job in sympathy. MIM agreed to rehire the other two men, but not Morgan. Two days later, the local AWU branch voted, by a slim margin, to stage a twenty-four-hour sympathy strike protesting the firings. However, between 3 and 5 July AWU officials signed a separate deal with MIM guaranteeing that the lead bonus would never drop below five pounds for its members. The backroom deal was just enough to convince a majority of AWU members to return to the customary overtime system, and it further isolated the AWU from Isa's more radical trade unions, leaving a bad taste in the mouths of militant rank-and-file AWU members. On 6 July the trade unions, robbed of much-needed AWU support, voted to end the overtime ban but condemned MIM for its acts of victimization.[101]

Up to March 1961, union officials tried to break the wage stalemate and increase the lead bonus through formal Industrial Court proceedings, but the recently re-elected Country-Liberal government agreed with mining companies like MIM that the bonus issue had spiralled out of control. Employees at the nearby Mary Kathleen uranium mine staged three strikes over bonuses in 1960.[102] Early in 1961, the court increased Mary Kathleen miners' bonus to the ten pounds they demanded, and AWU officials believed that, with similar claims lodged for Mount Isa workers, it was only a matter of time until the government agreed. The bonus increase at Mary Kathleen, however, was the last of its kind. In March, Liberal leader Kenneth J. Morris introduced an Industrial Arbitration Amendment Act that separated the arbitration and enforcement functions of the state Industrial Relations Commission. The commission had been able to grant and enforce increases to the bonus, but Morris's amendment took that power away and left the commission with only the authority to reduce or cancel the bonus. The Industrial Court was given wide powers to compel unions to accept the new industrial relations laws and, as Morris said, stop labour from threatening investors.[103] The amendment rendered null and void every claim pending for an increased bonus. In response, unions orchestrated a state-wide walkout.

At Mount Isa on 15 March, the AWU and TLC staged a twenty-four-hour strike to protest the new law, and Isa's retail workers and barmaids walked off their jobs in solidarity. Kenneth Morgan arranged visits from coastal trade union representatives who decried the Nicklin-Morris government as 'an executive for the big monopolies.' The next day, an informal delegation of mine unionists visited MIM General Manager Foots and asked him to intercede with the government to increase the bonus. Foots refused to agree to anything in the informal gathering but said he would be happy to deal with proper union representatives in the proper setting. Two weeks later Isa's rank-and-file AWU members sent Morris a petition demanding the act be repealed or the state would face 'violence and bloodshed perhaps never known in the Commonwealth.'[104]

Throughout the next five months, union officials tried unsuccessfully to boost the bonus through formal means. The national organ of the breakaway CMC reported in April that Mount Isa miners had 'heckled' AWU representatives. By late July 1961, the unions were demanding a lead bonus of twenty-five pounds.[105] Positions had hardened all around and the AWU faced a crisis of legitimacy.

The need to placate the rank-and-file led the Isa AWU to join with Morgan's radical trade unionists in supporting an overtime ban on 20 August. It forced the closure of the copper mill and smelter. Then on 20 September, AWU members voted three to one to strike but took no immediate action. Likely seeking to bring matters to a head, trade unionists walked off the job on 25 September, but AWU members kept working. Foots sent a curt memo to the trade unions ordering their members to return to their jobs and demanding that the unions guarantee they would abide by the arbitration laws. Failure to comply, Foots continued, would 'result in the closure of the Mine and the Plant.' When they did not comply, Foots locked the gates of the mine,[106] and the lockout lasted until 21 November – the town's worst labour dispute since the 1933 lockout.

As in disputes past, the community generally supported employees. Local Anglican and Methodist ministers said the workers' position was based on 'principles' and that they should not settle for 'peace at any price.' The Methodist women's auxiliary opened an 'emergency kitchen to assist miners in distress.' Other women formed the Mount Isa Women's Relief Committee to organize food vouchers for workers at Townside markets. Maintaining its distance from the trade unions, the AWU organized a separate fundraising and distress network.[107] Townside business owners supported their customers by discounting goods and collecting payment from union strike funds.

Miners got little sympathy from the wider public. Government and law enforcement agents said communist rabble-rousers disturbed industrial peace, and the government refused MIM workers' unemployment claims. One week after the lockout began, representatives from Townsville's wholesale businesses – through which many Isans leased household goods – began repossessing whiteware and furniture with 'no allowances for payment failures.' On 13 November, the industrial magistrate ordered all unions back to work. Six days later the AWU complied with his ruling.[108] Again, AWU officials convinced most of its members – many of them new Australians who until then had been courted rarely by labour leaders – that gains were possible only through institutionalized arbitration. Militant local trade workers and their allies in other national unions felt once again that the AWU had sold them out.

The trade unions voted two to one to continue the strike. With labour action running out of steam, the government declared a state of emergency at Mount Isa on 20 November – the fourth such act aimed at crushing a Queensland labour dispute since 1946. Recalcitrant trade unionists returned to work the next day. A few months later, workers threatened to strike if Liberal Party leader Morris – the architect of the despised arbitration amendment act – visited Mount Isa.[109]

The dispute resolved nothing. MIM's easy enlistment of the government's coercive power coupled with the general unwillingness to compromise meant that peace had no solid basis. The 1961 dispute shattered MIM workers' traditional but long-assaulted ideas of how employers and government should behave toward the working class. To the field's militant workers the dispute confirmed that the company and government would have given in if the AWU had not capitulated.

In the wake of the dispute, local police began 'strict surveillance' of 'all activities of all unions.' MIM's net profit, meanwhile, grew from £1,034,495 in 1962 to £5,597,769 in 1963, making it Australia's third-richest corporation that year and an ever more inviting target.[110] The Country-Liberal coalition government won a third consecutive term.

Between July and October 1964, the government's bandage solution to Mount Isa's industrial relations haemorrhage was ripped clean: one of Australia's worst labour disputes began, pushing Pat Mackie, a genuine rank-and-file leader, to the fore.

Pat Mackie (born Maurice Patrick Murphy) was born into an itinerant New Zealand logging family. In his late teens, he made a living as an unskilled manual labourer while moonlighting as masked Brazilian wrestler Giorgio Cortez in New Zealand's amateur wrestling circuit. That persona was the first of many – including the name Mackie – he assumed over the next three decades. His ability to effortlessly adapt to new settings jibed with the formative experiences of many of Mount Isa's workers. According to Mackie, to get from place to place with no money you had to be clever.[111]

The ability to blend into specific rough masculine work cultures – to be a good mate – and also to create a larger-than-life persona was important for success as a mobile worker. New arrivals on mining fields often needed other workers' acceptance to get hired. They then had to internalize quickly and observe informal codes of behaviour in order to avoid ostracism and unwanted physical violence. Mount Isa police and court files testify that many workers never mastered that social balancing act, but that identity play was quite common.

Mackie stowed away on a ship to North America and worked in longshoremen's unions in British Columbia, Montreal, and in the northeastern United States from the mid-1930s to the end of the Second World War. He associated with remnants of North America's Industrial Workers of the World – a loose collection of anarcho-syndicalists dedicated to establishing democratic control in industry – and played a leading role organizing unions and leading strikes. During his time on the East Coast Mackie was arrested for possession of marijuana while re-entering Canada from a union trip to the United States. He pleaded guilty. Mackie understood that 'the likelihood of a string of such convictions is a normal occupational hazard, built into the nature of things.'[112] He maintains that Communists who were angry with his success in organizing workers and his anti-Communism set up the arrest. Mackie says he was interested not in middle-class, 'theoretical' politics, but dedicated to immediate rank-and-file worker struggles.

Mackie shared his focus on 'getting by' with mobile Queensland labourers. Itinerant workers' survival strategies shifted constantly and to middle-class observers they were rarely 'pretty' or neat. Perhaps the fundamental inconsistency of those individual approaches cannot be adequately summed up in reasoned historical analysis. Only in moments of collective activity and dialectical conflict – usually accompanied by written records and multiple reminiscences of shared experiences – does anything resembling a broad working-class consciousness or 'movement culture' become apparent. The mundane details of workers' immediate social and domestic lives differ from person to person, but Mackie's ability to navigate serious obstacles and never lose heart later earned him the deep respect of most MIM employees.

Mackie left North America in 1944 and he ended up in Australia, where he became drawn to the prospect of working his own small mine in the Queensland outback. Mackie worked briefly for MIM in the early 1950s, saving enough money to buy a small lead mine at Lawn Hill that he named the Lucky Dollar, where his links to traditional Queensland mining culture are evident. The first Labor governments founded their mining policies on faith in the resourcefulness of independent gougers. By the 1950s networks of citizen-gougers had been supplanted by massive, foreign corporations like MIM, but the labouring idyll of living off your own piece of land still resonated with many Queenslanders. Mackie later said it was the most demanding work he had ever performed, but that it was also the most peaceful and settled time of his life.

The interlude ended abruptly. According to Mackie, MIM squeezed out the Lawn Hill gougers by lowering its refining quota for the field's untreated ore, and Mackie and other gougers – left with no other profitable buyer for their ore – had to surrender their leases to MIM. In a tremendous affront to Mackie's pride, he had to get a rank-and-file mining job with MIM to make a living and repay debts. He began to work for the company again in December 1961 at the end of the lead bonus strike. Respected by native and new Australians and fully versed in union procedures, Mackie was elected to chair local AWU meetings in early July 1964.[113]

This analysis can only describe briefly the events of 1964 and 1965. Several books contain detailed narratives of the dispute.[114] According to state historian Ross Fitzgerald, whose narrative of the dispute comes closest to an objective account, 'In August 1964, [the combined unions'] application for a rise of four pounds a week was rejected by the Industrial Commission on the grounds that such an increase would ... constitute a bonus rise.' Fitzgerald continues, 'The unions argued that there had been no increase in the bonus since 1956, that their bonus was half that paid to Broken Hill miners, and that the value of [miners'] take-home pay ... was less than it was twelve years earlier.' MIM characteristically refused to consider a raise and the commission refused the application.

'In September [the AWU] decided [again] on "go-slow" tactics and urged miners to switch from contract work to time wages only.' Industrial Court Justice Mostyn Hangar went against the Industrial Commission's conclusion that the slowdown was an acceptable protest. Legalistic industrial relations regulations could not cope with such non-traditional labour tactics, so on 30 September Hangar declared it a strike 'and refused to hear further applications.' Isa's unions argued 'that the dispute was not a strike but a lock-out.'

According to Fitzgerald, 'The AWU ... backed away from confrontation with the government and decided to lift the ban on contractual work.' But, in shades of disputes past, Brisbane union officials made the decision unilaterally without consulting local members. At this point – with Mount Isa workers' confidence in orthodox Australian unionism at is lowest ebb – local AWU chair Pat Mackie began to rally rank-and-file miners around his long-held belief in rank-and-file power and autonomous locals, arguing they should ignore the orders of the compromised AWU bureaucracy and maintain the slowdown. Mackie even organized translators to tap into simmering grievances among the field's new Australians. Then the Industrial Court ruled that the slowdown was a strike. Miners responded by howling down AWU officials at a local union meeting and voted overwhelmingly for Mackie to speak for them.

MIM did not look kindly on disruptions to a bargaining process that generally favoured its positions. Management sacked Mackie on 22 October for being absent from work. Mackie argued he was away on union business – a legitimate excuse, according to the Mount Isa award – but the company said he was not a legitimate representative, nor was he speaking for a recognized union. MIM refused to consider Mackie's re-employment and the AWU executive cancelled Mackie's union ticket. Miners could readily imagine a conspiratorial administrative triumvirate trying to deny Isa workers their due. Three days later, miners supported a non-confidence motion in the state AWU executive, and by the end of October 1964, the dispute had escalated. Mackie and his supporters allied themselves with the CMC – the AWU's bitter national rival. The CMC supported Isa's miners while the AWU supported Queensland's revised industrial relations laws and aligned itself with MIM and the Nicklin government.

Throughout the ensuing conflict most Mount Isa residents – MIM employees, small business owners, service workers, and wives – supported the miners once more. Townside businesses paid Mackie's wages throughout the dispute, and workers' wives and local businesses established vital redistribution centres as they did in earlier disputes.

Management lost patience. On 3 November it secured an injunction ordering employees to resume contract work. Mackie's Isa CMC ignored the order and the Nicklin government rushed through state of emergency legislation that allowed MIM to sack men who refused contract work. Two hundred and thirty-one men were fired within five days. Then, Justice Hangar's about-face decision in late December to increase contract pay by three pounds incensed the miners.[115] In a move reminiscent of Kruttschnitt's uncompromising 1933 position, MIM General Manger Foots shut down the entire operation ten days before Christmas. The company evicted recalcitrant workers from company barracks and the government refused to grant unemployment benefits.[116]

During January 1965 negotiations remained at an impasse over rehiring Mackie. Meanwhile, inter-union politics became front-page news as radical unions championed Mount Isa miners, and the AWU organ, the *Worker*, launched a series of provocative attacks against what it called the 'pseudo-Canadian-Yankee' gangster Mackie and his communist CMC allies. In a public address on 19 January, Premier Nicklin ordered miners to give in. MIM announced its decision to reopen the mine a week later, but the miners refused to return to work. The state government 'issued a drastic Order-in-Council to back up MIM. The new legislation, still more draconian than the December state of emergency, gave police virtually unlimited powers of entry or arrest and placed a ban on all forms of free speech and dissent.' Dozens of new police officers searched houses and confiscated a printing press and banned strike materials. Police patrolled state airports and detained without cause a legitimate trade union official en route to Mount Isa. In response, Isans 'painted the town from one end to the other with hundreds of large swastikas.'[117]

Workers staged sympathy protests throughout Australia. A reciprocal radicalization had gripped all parties. While the government and company campaigned across the state on a trumped-up law-and-order theme, the TLC countered with a pitch for the power of ordinary people over that of uncaring bureaucracy: 'We don't need courts, we don't need governments, we don't need commissions to decide this issue ... Let us be fair dinkum and weigh the issues in this dispute ... Do you believe the company cannot afford to pay? Do you believe the mine would close its gates for one man? Do you believe this huge enterprise is repaying Queensland in any shape or form what it should in the exploitation of our resources? Don't be duped by propaganda and smear tactics. Seek the truth.'[118] Workers voted to stay out by a four-to-one majority. The Nicklin government revoked the order-in-council less than a week later. Undeterred by public opinion, the AWU cut off strike pay to Isa miners in February and asked MIM to order workers who refused to return to work to leave town.[119]

In the following two months the dispute devolved into a national smear campaign and unnecessary violence. MIM reopened the mine on 17 February 1965, and from that point on many Australians considered the majority who refused to return to work as being on strike. Queensland media generally painted Mackie, quite formulaically, as a conniving Communist rabble-rouser, but also as a foreign dope-peddling criminal. Premier Nicklin publicly proclaimed Mackie 'unfit to mingle with decent society.' In a compulsory conference in late February, the president of the Queensland TLC and an AWU representative threw punches over which man was the real scab.[120]

For its part, the Industrial Court refused to entertain calls for Mackie's reinstatement, would not deal with Mackie or other 'unofficial' parties in compulsory negotiations, and ultimately decided not to arbitrate, because Isa workers had placed the proceedings under duress. An anonymous 'Mount Isa Miner' summed up the rank-and-file's frustration: 'I've no particular liking for Pat Mackie – he's not my type ... Pat seemed to be able to put into words what we were thinking. To go back without Pat would be to lose our self-respect, and no other gains could balance that loss. Observance of the law and requirements of British justice, and respect for the rights of the individual, have been thrown to the winds in an effort to paint Pat Mackie so black that we'll dump him.' 'Miner' then cleverly turned the court's refusal to arbitrate on its head, saying, 'Such tribunals can act only during periods of duress – no threats of strikes or lock-outs – conciliation commissioners are not necessary.'[121]

When MIM reopened the mine, miners picketed the roads leading to the site. Initially, only a handful of workers crossed the line. By 3 March, however, over 230 of MIM's 2,000 employees had returned to work. 'When the miners' resolve faltered,' writes Fitzgerald, 'incidents of violence broke out between pickets and workers; these were invariably reported in the press.' Essentially, the three-way assault on Mount Isa had slowly manoeuvred workers into what most regarded as a misdirected strike. Constant administrative pressure wore out the strikers. Small disputes took place on the picket line and the media dutifully publicized two shootings – one fatal but unconnected to the strike – in language that fabricated the lawlessness of Mackie and his supporters. The imagery of violence guaranteed further emergency legislation. An anti-picket law 'was rushed through the House' on 17 March. Again, the government flew extra police to Mount Isa, where they arrested several picketers.[122]

'No industrial solution to the situation at Mount Isa was found. Instead, the damaging dispute ... petered out, leaving homes broken as families saw ... life savings wiped out. In late March, Mackie announced his departure ... and urged a general return to work if a guarantee against victimization was given. The company subsequently wooed the AWU and nine craft unions until a massive meeting of unionists on 7 April voted overwhelmingly to return to work.'[123] Mackie and other critics maintained that MIM's parent company ASARCO made massive profits during the dispute, because the sudden loss of supply from the major Australian producer caused a spike in global base metal prices that benefited ASARCO's numerous mines and smelters in other parts of the world.

MIM and the Queensland government's collusion had solidified after the fall of Labor in 1957. The AWU and trade unions had been fighting internal and intra-union battles for decades, and among the majority of MIM workers the AWU's credibility had diminished greatly by 1964. Into this complex local mix of class conflict stepped Pat Mackie. Mackie was neither 'industrial Casanova' nor a fork-tongued Communist who hypnotized gullible workers. He embodied Australian traditions of rough, working-class dignity, independence, and mobility. Furthermore, he expressed clearly rank-and-file workers' legitimate grievances. When all those forces collided, a battle ensued. Ultimately, the combined forces of the company, government, and conservative unions defeated the workers. By accenting law-and-order, mainstream media coverage made the company seem peripheral to the whole affair. MIM and its parent ASARCO gained the most of all the participants, emerging from the dispute with a thoroughly pacified workforce precisely at the moment of soaring base metal prices. Miners limped back to the conservative AWU.

Scapegoating or glorifying Mackie is too easy. The deep contradictory socio-economic and political roots of the dispute have not been analyzed, despite the fact that it was arguably Australia's most bitter labour dispute since the shearers' strike of 1893–4. The opposing positions on the 1964–5 dispute are the two dominant historiographical explanations of company towns in microcosm: the business-centred and structuralist Marxist interpretations. The peculiar centrality of class in Mount Isa's history is downplayed in favour of the 'Casanova thesis' on the one hand or the meta-narrative of global class conflict on the other. Neither conveys complex lived reality in the outback mining town.

The years following 1965 witnessed little overt class conflict. After the industrial battle, town residents and company and state officials redoubled their efforts to nurture a civic consciousness. The rapid growth of small business and modest diversification away from dependence on one industry fostered an impression that Mount Isa was 'growing up' and leaving behind the difficult days of company control and industrial unrest, and three years after the strike, the Queensland government recognized the new Mount Isa by incorporating it as a city. After 1968, Joh Bjelke-Petersen's government established regional branches of state offices and encouraged large coastal retailers to set up shop in the town. Media in the 1970s promoted the city as 'a town in a hurry.' These glosses contrasted with earlier reports that called Mount Isa a 'black prince among mining towns.'[124] In any event, the people of Mount Isa would have understood that the autocratic Petersen government would have permitted no deviation from the contented Queensland it promoted.

Of course, MIM fully supported plans to shift residents' focus from industrial to civic issues. The 1964–5 strike exposed the simmering class tensions in Mount Isa. After the strike, company officials decided to retreat from direct paternalism. MIM encouraged state government's greater visibility in the town and it welcomed the opportunity to discuss with the Mount Isa City Council civic matters like the takeover of its recreational facilities. The incorporation of Mount Isa as a city had a substantial influence on dampening class conflict.

After the strike, MIM's industrial relations team resigned and the company hired new IR officers who it hoped would bring fresh approaches.[125] Queensland's amended industrial relations framework focused on flexible union–management bargaining instead of mechanically registering claims with the Industrial Court. Management and union negotiated less formal industrial agreements every two years, heading off wage, safety, and benefits issues before they could erupt into stubborn legal challenges or costly industrial disputes.[126] MIM never rehired the forty-six men it blacklisted after the strike, and there was little public pressure for them to do so.

Socio-economic diversification and MIM's new 'good corporate citizen' policy ushered in an era of relative industrial and social calm at Mount Isa, but they fail to explain why the changes were acceptable to the town's residents. We must add ordinary Isans' responses to those top-down considerations. The elimination of the field's contingent of militant workers made other employees reticent to revisit the disappointments of the past. The government's naked strike-breaking in the service of the corporate and union status quo convinced moderate Queenslanders of the futility of battling the system.

This comparison highlights different socio-industrial dynamics, pinpointing their origins in local history. In Mount Isa, divisive class issues often took the forefront in local matters. Industrial protest and other forms of militant, bottom-up, working-class culture also played an important role in fostering community identity. The link between class and community was particularly apparent during the conflicts of the 1930s, and again dramatically during the major strikes in the early 1960s. MIM employees did not act like the fatalistic, exploited proletariat described in Rex Lucas's seminal study of company towns. Their world view remained focused on local experiences and improving the immediate lot of rank-and-file workers and their families. The pre-eminence of class contrasts remarkably to the mill town in the Humber Valley. It is only through a comparative approach to history that this situation appears so starkly, but explicably.

The bulk of MIM's workforce was raised in a culture of homo-sociable 'mateship' and mobility. Unskilled workers moved relatively freely from place to place, seeking the best pay. Rough transience promoted intense but often fleeting relationships between males who worked, lived, and travelled the same way. This mobile but oddly cohesive male proletariat was a major part of Queensland politics and industrial relations. Queensland's industrial legislators struggled for a balance between supporting militant workers, and conservative unions like the AWU that supported the status quo, and private industrial developers. Queensland's political economy balanced on the fulcrum of an entrenched distinct working-class culture.

Workers in pre-Confederation Newfoundland, on the other hand, rarely identified themselves as a working class. Armstrong's workforce of Newfoundlanders was raised in a centuries-old outport fishing culture dominated by a tenacious pre-industrial 'merchantocracy.' Family ties and immediate community relations dominated work and society in Newfoundland. In Corner Brook, community-based issues produced a powerful source of collective action.

Newfoundland's traditional economy thrived on dependent relationships where, ideally, paternalist merchants provided for their clients. Deference to authority was a hallmark of the socio-economic system. Where Queenslanders understood their place in an industrial class structure, Newfoundlanders who joined modern industrial workforces came to them as outsiders. The labour histories of Mount Isa and Corner Brook diverged ever further as workers and managers contested specific issues of work and power over years of local history. The events described here speak more to the flexibility of human experience in cases of economic and industrial development than they do to the confirmation of trends.

Chapter Five

'If I had to get a factory job I'd be fired': Civic Life and Resident-Company Negotiation

We turn now to community life: first to the activities of formal community groups and later to the small autonomies that shaped daily life. To understand local order in Corner Brook and Mount Isa, we must look within the extremities of force and consent that mark the endpoints of Antonio Gramsci's theory of hegemony to the messy midpoints of that continuum.[1] Rather than violent conflict or shrugging resignation, negotiation, compromise, and accommodation were the wellsprings of community growth in Mount Isa and Corner Brook. Society in both locales took place on a negotiated middle ground, the same field of contestation where local authorities and workers had their agency constrained. Highlighting the varied and subtle negotiations that comprised social relations and order in company towns reinforces a critical point. Overly structured readings of social order, to paraphrase labour historian Sean Cadigan, deny the ability of ordinary people to cause change.[2] Actions did not always get the results that agents hoped for. Nor must they meet with the approval of later commentators. But ignoring expressions of agency or writing them off as false consciousness hides the human face of economics and, more ironically, society.

Residents of Corner Brook and Mount Isa articulated a range of formal community organizations and civil societies that went beyond the narrow confines of the company town type. In Corner Brook, and to a lesser extent in Mount Isa, small business, municipal politics, and organized recreation played important roles in producing local identities by bringing residents together in community spaces not explicitly owned or overseen by the company. Community groups sometimes acted as agents of resistance to authority as well. Comparison highlights the subtly different historical processes at work in each town.

The contracts for the Corner Brook mill stressed the company's responsibility to administer the adjunct Townsite. The owners of the mill were expected to provide for skilled workers and, to a lesser extent, all town residents. This responsibility hastened Armstrong's collapse, but later owners retained the mantle of town patron.[3] It is hard to imagine a more pervasive top-down local authority than IPPN or BNPP. Yet even in an isolated company town in an isolated land on the edge of North America and the Atlantic world, the effectiveness of the corporate authority was constrained by ever-impinging global trends and by the obligation to look after residents.

The Corner Brook companies assumed responsibilities that were rarely of one-way benefit to them. The interests of business and civil society rarely coincided, but reconciliation was precisely what the Newfoundland government and the working residents who were essential to industrial success expected the companies to accomplish. The web of reciprocal obligations between the company and denizens of Townsite functioned through negotiation and compromise, and that situation carried over into the fringe towns. Until the mid-1940s there was no effective authority outside Townsite, but the company had a vested interest in ensuring that residents accepted life in the fringe towns. The lack of municipal government meant that resident negotiation came from a variety of sources. The mill company often aided organized community groups, which negotiated effectively with the companies to build a local dynamic that gave people a sense of community beyond dependence on the business of making newsprint.

Small businesses were among the first exemplars of an emerging local identity. When IPPN took control of the mill in late 1927, numerous businesses operated in Corner Brook. Newfoundland's small retail and service providers – consisting mainly of general stores, clothing shops, and restaurants – were active at this time. Curling acted as a regional centre for the Bay of Islands and the Labrador fishery. Competing general stores Bartlett's and Baggs operated for years before NP&P began the Corner Brook paper mill. Owners of the *Western Star* had published the regional newspaper out of Curling for a quarter century when the mill began production in 1925. Many businesses also migrated to Corner Brook when the construction boom began.

Industrial development and its accompanying population explosion quickly realigned the relations between settlements in the region. Before the advent of NP&P, Corner Brook depended on Curling for most services. Prior to 1925, outport residents in the Bay of Islands looked

Dunphy's Limited in Curling, 1925. (Corner Brook Pulp and Paper Limited Photographic Collection courtesy of the Corner Brook Museum and Archives)

towards the sea and lived a cycle of fishing in the spring and summer, fish preparation in the fall, and subsistence and upkeep in the long winters. The paper mill meant that most residents of Corner Brook would instead look to the interior forests for their livelihood. Regular wages replaced infrequent cash payments for fish and meant a growing number of regular customers for small businesses. The mill town easily supplanted Curling as regional business centre.

Unlike some company towns, NP&P permitted free enterprise in its town. The company let the Fisher family live and do business in Townsite. The Fishers opened a tarpaper store in November 1923 and a pharmacy on West Street in the mid-1920s. Private interests also operated Goodyear and House, the first department store in Townsite. Company records do not explain NP&P's peculiar openness to free enterprise.

The company kept essential manufacturing and provisioning trades – like the foundry, the company farm, and the stables – in-house but purchased construction materials from the Fisher sawmill. It set regulations prohibiting alcohol within Townsite and tried to limit competition against the businesses that it permitted in the planned settlement, but tenants could visit the numerous fringe businesses to obtain alcohol or other services if they did not want to shop in West Street. Most likely, the company wanted to show, as Stanley Buder said of Pullman, Illinois, that 'social reform and good business practices were complementary.'[4] By 1925 NP&P had established a mixed economy of company-owned and private businesses in Townsite. The company's legitimation of free enterprise established a lasting pattern of negotiations for greater consumer choice and residential services.

The company wisely made room for the three main religious denominations in Townsite. Town plans and board meetings highlight the company's desire to include places of worship. Early religious services took place in the company's Majestic Theatre, and between 1924 and 1927 the worshippers built an Anglican, Roman Catholic, and United Church. Churches engendered feelings of security, permanence, and continuity in the instant town, helping to minimize religious sectarianism by showing residents that the company did not favour one group over the others. Religious leaders' praise for the companies' social benevolence legitimized the company's role as earthly provider and contributed to community order.[5] The space for modest choice built into the company plan was a small opening for agency from below.

The case of the Townsite school is an early and instructive example of how residents of the planned town lobbied the company for additional services. The reason for NP&P's plan for housing its skilled workers was to make the settlement attractive for essential employees who would relocate permanently to Corner Brook with their families. The upwardly mobile and relatively well-educated skilled men and women who moved into NP&P's houses emphasized early the need for their children's education. In late 1924 – half a year before the mill opened – company town residents approached company managers about building a school in Townsite.

A December 1924 report said that settlers wanted the school because of the rapid influx of families.[6] Parents worried that if they did not press the issue, the company would postpone the project to focus on industrial matters. In late 1925 local manager John Stadler informed company directors that school construction was underway. By January

1926 the spacious, well-staffed Townsite public school opened its doors. The school board of six company-appointed and six elected members admitted children from Townsite first, and the company deducted a twelve-dollar monthly tuition from the pay packets of employees. Children from the fringe communities could occupy the remaining spaces if their parents paid the tuition. The company also allowed a Roman Catholic school in Townsite shortly after it finished the public school. According to an early Townsite resident, the company collected a fee for students who attended the Catholic school as well. Until the Second World War, the mill company augmented teachers' government salaries, and officials regarded the public school as the best in the region.[7] NP&P's educational paternalism was the result of ad hoc decisions made by onsite managers. In fact, up to the early 1950s each company's general rule of administration was to compromise with working families in order to keep them content in their domestic lives. Keeping prized residents happy was sometimes as simple as listening to them and doing what they asked.

Local health care developed out of the necessities of the workplace, but company officials had to compromise and make the hospital accessible to all residents, regardless of their relation to the company, because the Newfoundland government did not have the funds to maintain a government hospital.[8] National economic problems and the inescapable fact of a rapidly expanding but poorly serviced population led the company to the role of a regional health-care provider. This episode shows that sometimes unforeseen consequences – not always the result of organized active pressure from resident groups, but directed by the logic of local circumstances – forced companies to be inclusive.

As in most company towns, organized recreations were popular in Corner Brook.[9] Isolated industrial enclaves were instant societies. They began with few longstanding family and community ties, so residents used organized recreations to make new friendships, establish community and workplace cohesion, and keep busy and fit. The mill hired only male workers, so the first large-scale formal activity those men organized was, not surprisingly, a highly physical sport. In January 1924 Canadian and Newfoundland workers played Corner Brook's first game of hockey in an empty company warehouse. Later that year, Townsite residents – some of them NP&P managers – formed a voluntary winter sports and entertainment association to organize events and acquire company sponsorship. One major coup for Townsite recreation enthusiasts came in late 1925 when NP&P donated an empty pa-

Corner Brook Public School, Townsite. (Corner Brook Pulp and Paper Limited Photographic Collection courtesy of the Corner Brook Museum and Archives)

per shed for use as a permanent ice rink. The rink housed recreational skating and the mill hockey league. Hockey organizers initially structured the league around mill departments – Construction, Accounts, and Electrical were three of the teams – and NP&P donated a trophy for the league champions.[10] The Stadler Cup remained the symbol of local hockey achievement decades after John Stadler had resigned in the midst of NP&P's financial debacle. The paper shed / ice rink survived into the 1950s.

The women of Townsite focused primarily on the formal recreations of church and secular social clubs. One early female resident remarked that her 'husband was always into something,' meaning that he spent much of his free time involved in some type of physical extracurricular activity.[11] The company's community department assumed responsibility for performing many masculine-associated domestic chores like painting, house repair, and winter shovelling, so Townsite men had more leisure time than male breadwinners in the fringe towns. Women's ties to the domestic sphere, meanwhile, remained relatively unchanged. Females cooked, cleaned, laundered, sewed, knitted, nurtured and disciplined children, and maintained the family's reputation and status. The company expected the wives and teenage daughters of skilled mill workers to behave with decorum and participate in more socially than physically oriented activities. Mona Collins recalled bridge games, morning coffees, and afternoon 'sherry gatherings.' Others, like Emily Watson, participated in church societies that organized fundraisers and entertainment nights, or gardening, library groups, and school committees.

Company influence pervaded recreation in Townsite. IPPN kept the promise of former manager John Stadler to make 'every effort' 'to provide a good social and sporting atmosphere in the community.'[12] The American company promoted baseball games and, according to Mona Collins, members of its staff even taught select employees popular new American dances like the Charleston at the Glynmill Inn's 'invitation only' 'fancy dress balls.'[13] British Bowater injected its own forms of recreation. Eric Bowater entertained guests at his country house in Strawberry Hill. It contained 'spacious dining halls and drawing rooms, good kitchens and cellars, and a staff of unobtrusively attentive servants.' BNPP promoted children's groups that focused on outdoor activities and forestry skills. It also paid for a large new park and baseball field and aided residents' efforts to raise money for a modern ice rink to replace the old paper shed.[14]

Rapid town growth on the borders of Townsite expanded community-based tensions between the company's desire to control and resident agency. In Townsite, private businesses needed the mill company's permission to set up shop. In Corner Brook East and West, anyone with enough start-up capital to obtain land and secure space could run a business. The mill company had no legal jurisdiction in the fringe towns and the Newfoundland government did not establish an effective regulatory presence there, so the only operational constraints on business owners then were those of space and consumer interest. Nobody constrained residential or business growth, so fringe development was the messy product of myriad informal negotiations among shifting interests.

Business owners in Corner Brook West made the first collective efforts to improve the town, or at least Broadway. Before the mill opened, business owners like retailers Fred Basha and S.D. Cook, electrician Charles Ballam, and representatives of the established merchant Barry and Dunphy families re-established the defunct Bay of Islands Board of Trade to press for improvements. In February 1925, the paper reported that the Board of Trade was hoping to build a road that would link Humbermouth, Townsite, Corner Brook West, and Curling. It is unclear if the board received financial or material support from the Newfoundland government or the company – support from the latter is likely – but its lobbying efforts for a road between the settlements succeeded. Road crews completed a passable corduroy road connecting Curling shortly thereafter. That the board met in the NP&P boardroom in spring 1925 suggests that the mill company aided fringe business owners in their local improvement initiatives.[15]

The following year the board focused on electrifying the fringe towns. NP&P's hydroelectric system provided free electricity to the company town, but the other settlements went without. The board made little progress on this front early on because the retrenched NP&P was interested only in keeping the mill operational. After IPPN purchased the mill in mid-1927, it quickly reached a deal with the board, and by the end of 1928 Ballam and his associates in the Bay of Islands Light and Power Company had signed a contract to purchase electricity from IPPN and had wired all of the buildings in and around Broadway.[16]

Depending as it did on government patronage, west side water and sewer provision arrived slowly and unevenly. According to Horwood, Richard Squires 'arranged a government grant of $20,000' when seeking re-election in 1928, and the grant was supplemented by $10,000 from Broadway businesses. That money 'financed the first water and sewer mains along Broadway and up Caribou Road, but left the outlying regions of the town as badly off as ever.'[17] But Squires's election-day patronage was a futile gesture. When BNPP asked its engineers to survey the fringe communities in the late 1930s, they were concerned primarily with the lack of utilities. The Goldenberg report of 1950 stressed the same point.[18] The Board of Trade tended to lose interest in civic projects when they no longer benefited its members' main goal of enhancing the downtown commercial district.

Business owners on the fringes had to be more aggressive than those in Townsite in order to succeed without the support that Townsite businesses received from the company. The experience of dry goods salesman John Noah exemplified how the fringe was a place where residents whom the company excluded from mill employment and paternalism could prosper. The son of Lebanese immigrants to Cuba, Noah encountered ethnic prejudice and the need for mobility from an early age. Shortly after his arrival in Cuba, the local government 'decided to purge the country of people whose racial background it disliked.' Persecution forced Noah and his parents to move again, this time from Florida to New York. Noah made his penultimate move to St John's in 1909. As a young man he established himself as a peddler of dry goods. Anticipating the population boom in the Humber Valley, he came to Corner Brook in the spring of 1923, bought land from a local speculator for $600, and built a tarpaper shop on what became Broadway. The dry goods store became one of Corner Brook's primary retail outlets. Noah expanded his business into property rental and collaborated with other local merchants to improve the Broadway area. He also helped his nephew set up a jewellery store. Noah's formative years taught him self-reliance, and his early forays into small business made him a quick thinker and a good judge of financial opportunities. The fringes had many such characters.

The mill company discriminated against ethnic minorities. Residents recalled that the company did not hire Lebanese, Jews, or Chinese.[19] Employment restrictions meant those people could not dwell in Townsite. Instead, they opened small shops on Broadway and Humber Road in Corner Brook East. Levitz, Brenner, Freed, Kaplow, Swersky, and Levine had their names above many of Broadway's early storefronts in the 1920s and 1930s. Corner Brook West had a small synagogue at that time as well. Corner Brook families of Lebanese descent like the Noahs, Bashas, Tumas, and Faours ran numerous businesses and furnished a few of the fringe town's earliest community leaders.[20]

Women often ran hospitality services on the fringes. A Mrs Corbage ran a popular west side saloon at the intersection of Broadway and Caribou Road while a Mrs Buckle kept a busy boarding house nearby.[21] In Townsite, where the Pickering brothers ran the boarding house, feminine self-reliance of that type was less acceptable.

Attaining independence as a self-made business owner was a common goal for wage earners in Newfoundland in the early twentieth century. For women and minorities it provided the only realistic option for upward mobility. The lightly regulated fringe communities thrived on entrepreneurial skill and guile. Without formal authority, they could not function any other way. Residents of the fringe coalesced into a community that functioned internally through constant compromise. Small business owners did not achieve success easily, and many aspirants to local middle-class status failed and/or moved on, but some prospered in ways impossible had they worked for the mill and lived in the planned town. As John Noah said, 'If I had to get a job, I'd be fired ... The best thing that ever happened to me was not getting a [mill] job.'[22] Corner Brook's middle class depended on the neighbouring corporate authority and the Newfoundland government to help develop the fringe towns' infrastructure. That they were able to achieve significant early improvements with little support from either body deserves acknowledgment. However, their dedication to community-based initiatives originated primarily from self-interest. Better amenities and an enhanced civic profile convinced more people to shop and do business on Broadway. Localism – the tendency to understand issues in terms of how they related to specific places rather than to the workplace or larger political considerations – transcended class in Corner Brook.[23]

Mill workers' abortive attempt to form a cooperative department store in 1927 is an example of how ordinary Corner Brook residents achieved small changes by playing local business interests against one another. Grand Falls had a worker-run, profit-sharing cooperative store for several years, and in November 1927 a number of Corner Brook's mill workers advocated a co-op to 'fight modern conditions of competition by modern methods of co-operation.'[24] A co-op promised to act as a buffer against high prices by passing business profits back to members as discounts and savings. IPPN rejected any activities that smacked of expanded worker control, but offered a compromise.

IPPN bought the Fisher family store on West Street and opened a company store that sold goods to mill workers at roughly 10 per cent above wholesale cost. Only workers qualified for store coupons. Worker mobilization for community development failed, but the mill owner, aware of the need to maintain the reputation of benevolent paternalist, appeased its working residents by creating a similar business. Workers again pushed for a co-op ten years later.

In consultation with its employee committees, IPPN tried to ensure that the Depression did not devastate mill workers and their families. It raised credit limits at the company store and deferred rent on company houses to stabilize the towns' occupational-residential nucleus. Workforce stability allowed many local businesses to survive. An empty building on Broadway was rare. In fact, ads in the *Western Star* show that new businesses opened during the Depression.[25] Historian Oiva Saarinen found an 'under-represented' middle class in northern Ontario company towns, but even during the Depression, Corner Brook's middle stratum was larger than in most Newfoundland settlements.[26] Corner Brook still depended on the mill, but the towns became important centres in their own right.

IPPN's concessions buoyed workers' renewed attempts to establish a co-op. A group of skilled workers and mill staff approached the new BNPP managers early in 1938. Montgomery Lewin did not 'think [the plan was] solid enough to make a profit,' and he opposed the scheme, refusing to purchase shares, but he did not veto it. Lewin allowed the co-op committee to build its outlet at the edge of Townsite. The Corner Brook Co-operative Society opened 1 August 1938 and made a respectable $15,000 in its first year of operation. Over the next two decades it established a credit union, health, pension, and life insurance plans, opened a second shop in Corner Brook West in 1949, and expanded its original outlet into a supermarket and department store complex in 1960s.[27] Its success demonstrates the perseverance and resourcefulness of Corner Brook residents.

Before community amalgamation, the willingness to compromise for mutual benefit on local matters depended on the good faith of all parties. Mill unions never demanded official recognition and found that shop-floor issues could be solved through other channels. Townsite residents needed only to suggest the need for some improvement before the company acted to placate them. Fringe denizens enlisted company aid when they could. All parties generally played by the same rules. The injection of new municipal and provincial authorities shortly after the Second World War complicated matters.

The confederation referendum of July 1948 exemplifies how the inhabitants of Corner Brook supported change through the ballot box. Residents used the referendum to oppose company wishes and buck the general voting trend in other large Newfoundland towns. BNPP and local manager Montgomery Lewin were 'strongly anti-confederate.' Lewin made the company's position clear in a series of public pronouncements. However, residents ignored the company's ordinarily weighty opinion, voting nearly 69 per cent in favour of joining Canada.[28]

The popular explanation for the Humber district's sizeable pro-confederate vote is that residents of the district were 'Joey's people.' Smallwood had links to the Squires government that brought the mill to the Humber Valley, he had helped organize the mill workers' Local 64, and he spoke fondly of the west coast centre.[29] The received wisdom, however, fails to account for voters' decision to ignore BNPP, the region's main benefactor. The 'Joey factor' argument oversimplifies the practical reasons – greater protection from economic collapse and expanded social services. Humber voters chose to support confederation. Voters rejected responsible government and chose security within a wider federation.

Lewin pushed for self-government and cooperation between the towns and most councillors agreed with him for their own reasons. The settlements had common problems, and it made sense to pool resources and institute common development and infrastructure policies. In early January 1950 representatives of the Corner Brook councils met in the BNPP boardroom as the Humber Municipal Association and set the terms for a study of the prospects for municipal administration by Carl Goldenberg of Montreal. Goldenberg suggested that amalgamation was the 'boldest' way to make improvements.[30] It is not clear if the elected representatives felt they were being railroaded by BNPP and Smallwood into accepting a political solution their constituents would not support, or if they were just unable to agree on terms of unification, but the report accomplished no immediate substantive changes. Instead, it set the terms of local political debate for the next five years. The Humber Municipal Association met regularly to discuss matters of common interest into 1955.

The councillors from the fringes likely waited to see how the post-Confederation development boom would affect the status of each town before rushing to amalgamate. The Smallwood government channelled considerable funds into a provincial modernization program that helped finance a cement mill and a gypsum plant in Corner Brook East.[31] Those industries contributed to modest diversification and a symbolic move away from dependence on the paper mill. They also aided the Corner Brook–based construction giant W.J. Lundrigan Limited.[32] All in all, the late 1940s and early 1950s was a period of great promise in Corner Brook. The towns seemed finally to have an effective state ally in the provincial government, and resident engagement in local politics and community sentiment was at its height.

Five years after the Goldenberg report, the Humber Municipal Association agreed to hold a public referendum on amalgamation. A decisive 75 per cent amalgamation vote settled the issue in spring 1955. The first amalgamated council – with Allison Bugden as mayor – took control of the city on New Year's Day 1956.[33] City councillors quickly encountered serious difficulties in overcoming a history of dependence and geographic division.

Deep urban structural problems persisted. Put simply, residents paid too little in taxes to generate the funds to improve infrastructure, the council's ward-based electoral structure ensured that councillors remained loyal to their specific neighbourhoods and often delayed broader urban development for relatively petty reasons, and the council had to get the approval of the city's higher authorities – BNPP and the provincial government – in order to undertake reforms. A brief discussion of the school tax dispute of the mid-1950s and the removal of the city council over a zoning permit in 1963 highlights the limits of localism at this time.

No one denied that the city had an overburdened education system. Local school statistics told a sad story. In 1955 Corner Brook had fourteen schools with eighty-four classrooms and 3,289 students. That meant 235 students per school and 39 to a room. The school boards reconditioned temporary structures into classrooms for which they could not find the money for regular upkeep. Annually, 300 local children could not secure school enrolment.[34] Local authorities decided to rectify the shortfalls with a universal tax tied to property values and income.

A loose organization calling itself the Vigilante Committee led by Curling resident Ethel Rowsell spoke out against the tax and circulated a petition proposing its annulment. The self-titled vigilantes argued that residents without children would have to pay the school tax commensurate with the value of their property, and that the School Tax Authority had not been elected and could not decide an issue that required popular support. The authorities brushed aside the vigilantes' concerns, even though an island-wide federation of municipalities had recently rejected the institution of similar taxes. Rowsell added that the Vigilante Committee collected 4,300 names on a petition from residents of Corner Brook, constituting the majority necessary to overturn the legislation. Smallwood removed from the petition the names of 1,400 individuals whom he arbitrarily decided were not residents of the city, and the city council adopted the controversial tax in 1956.[35]

Ethel Rowsell later recalled how the imposition of the school tax and amalgamation indicated that Smallwood and his ally Mayor Allison Bugden wanted to direct development in Corner Brook on their terms, despite significant opposition from the city's politically active residents.[36] Resolved as it was by brute political power instead of public debate, the imposition of the school tax exacerbated rivalries and fostered apathy in the local political process.

Throughout the remainder of the decade and into the early 1960s, the council focused on improving urban infrastructure. Corner Brook had 26,000 residents by this time. Many lacked basic services. The council commissioned various planning studies but their conclusions were disheartening. A 1958 report by Newfoundland's Urban and Rural Planning Department estimated that the city needed $397,000 just to pave and widen five main roads. The planners said they were satisfied to learn that the city council had applied for a $2 million bond issue to implement its suggestions. But borrowing only delayed the reckoning. The city was born in debt. In 1955 it assumed a $3.5 million debt for water and sewerage provision. The only way to maintain regular administration and public confidence was to keep borrowing and paying interest on pre-existing loans. According to former councillor William Brown, Corner Brook had a total debt of $9.2 million in 1962, when in the same year the city revenue amounted to $1,471,000 before subtracting interest payments, the cost of new projects, or annual operating expenses. Over 30 per cent of that sum or $475,000 came from grants from the provincial government and BNPP.[37]

Financial morass was aggravated by intractable personality clashes. Strong-willed Mayor Bugden had enemies among councillors, and the city council split into two factions. Bugden and his allies aimed to slash expenditures and raise revenues through increased taxation. Smallwood, according to Bugden's closest ally Arch Lawrence, urged the mayor to 'cut 'til it hurts.' The other group urged greater economic diversification by encouraging industrial expansion in the city.[38]

The situation deteriorated further at the end of 1961 when the city manager sacked the works superintendent. The anti-Bugden councillors rebelled and deadlocked city administration, demanding their associate's reinstatement. According to Bugden and Horwood, nothing got done for the next sixteen months. Early in 1963 the recalcitrant councillors proposed that the council rezone a section of the city's open space for industrial use so an American company, McNamara Construction, could build a cement plant. Bugden rejected the proposal on the advice of Smallwood, BNPP officials, and the local construction firm Lundrigan Limited, none of whom approved of a new company competing with their local interests. But the proposal carried. Smallwood finally had enough. He acted swiftly. The morning after the meeting the provincial government dissolved the Corner Brook council. Astonishingly, Smallwood – former scourge of the appointed Commission of Government – established an appointed three-man commission of government in Corner Brook. It administered the city behind closed doors for nearly five years. He appointed Allison Bugden chairman. BNPP was awarded a seat on the commission as well.[39]

The commission cut expenditures and raised revenues modestly up to 1967, but it also sapped Corner Brook's vibrant local democracy, diminishing residents' interest in local affairs. By early 1967 apathy had set in to such an extent that BNPP's general manager had to remind residents to show civic pride by voting in the upcoming municipal election.[40] Post-commission councils concentrated on making small improvements that ameliorated urban problems. Tamed councillors did not threaten entrenched industrial or provincial interests.

Formal bottom-up negotiation in Corner Brook shifted after 1955 from one comprising small-business organizations and a variety of community organizations to negotiations in which the voices of multiple parties were channelled through the city council. The city council had to walk a tightrope between satisfying the demands of a concerned electorate, or going it alone and maintaining the entrenched interests of BNPP. It was able to identify the city's problems and make minimal progress towards rectifying poor infrastructure and service provision, but not without incurring a large debt. The introduction of a strong provincial government allied to industry unbalanced the local equilibrium of piecemeal resident–company negotiations. BNPP had ended its interest in town administration, and by the early 1960s Smallwood tired of the city. Opinions on local issues hardened and for a time all parties stopped cooperating, with resident participation in local affairs the main casualty. In Corner Brook, localism, more than class, was the locus of negotiation and contestation. In Mount Isa it was the other way around.

Localism tended to respond to and intensify class concerns in Mount Isa between 1923 and 1965. The concentration of the huge workforce on a single site made class issues paramount and residents' concerns about community stability secondary. The interests of Isa's proletariat and its petite bourgeoisie converged in a loose alliance where considerations of class strongly influenced community issues. Workers and petite bourgeoisie fashioned the cross-class pact during the volatile first years of settlement after the state government relocated the first settlers to the east bank of the Leichhardt.

Mount Isa's pioneering residents moved in from dead mining towns like Kuridala and Hampden. A semi-nomadic streak arose from the region's uncertain boom-and-bust resource economy. Toughness and mobility were operative characteristics. The realities of the outback made Isa's pioneers cagey, resourceful, and stubbornly independent. As business owners, they hoped to get in early to supply the services cheaply that workers demanded and get out fast if the local industry collapsed, as it almost always did, and the transience of mine workers grew out of the same experience.

But outback itinerancy was a survival strategy, not a life objective. Migrants hoped to make stable, prosperous lives for themselves, but the uncertainties of life on the resource frontier mitigated that distant goal. Mine and government officials' regular pronouncements about the size and quality of the Mount Isa deposit, however, caused several of the pioneers to plan for a settled future. Shortly after the discovery of the deposit, the small, unplanned settlement on the west bank of the Leichhardt had a number of businesses whose owners established Isa's first formal organization, a progress association, to procure a steady supply of water and establish a rudimentary local authority. Corbould assured stockholders and residents that the deposit would be a 'Broken Hill–sized' bonanza, but company demands regularly dashed the expectations of the struggling middle class.

Urquhart based his plans on having complete control of industry and settlement on the west bank of the Leichhardt. Company officials convinced top government officials to build a rail link to the mine, with the sole terminal on the west bank. Company plans left no room for the pioneer settlement or its nascent middle class. Eager to aid the owners of the industrial mega-project, state authorities surveyed a new townsite on the Leichhardt's east bank. The government surveyor said the east bank had better access to bore water. The progress association voted unanimously to reject the switch because taxes would be higher on the Cloncurry Shire side of the river, but the state government ignored the protest. Residents then hoped that Townside would get financial and material support from the government and gain adequate services and infrastructure, but subsequent developments disabused them of that notion as well.

Residents had difficulty securing water. A steady supply was not located until August 1926. The mining company, not the state government or shire council, drilled the bore and donated it to the town.[41] Residents complained that postal, police, and educational services were below average, that land cost too much, and that rates in the Cloncurry Shire were far higher than across the river. In 1938 Raphael Cilento, Queensland's director of general health and medical services, repeated to the attorney general Townside residents' complaints that Cloncurry council did 'very little' to improve services in Mount Isa. He added, 'Various demands for immediate action have been made upon the Cloncurry Council who have either ignored these, temporized in respect of them, or sought escape from their obligations by various means.'[42] Townside residents felt that they had been sold a bill of goods. Unaddressed grievances exacerbated imposed social divisions.

By the early 1930s, Mount Isa's roughly one hundred small-business owners lived exclusively on Townside. Small mobile shops like convenience stores, cafes, tailors, and cobblers dominated the retail trade. Recreational services included a 'picture show,' hotel bars, two billiards rooms, and vendors of meat pies, cordials, and ice cream.[43] West Street, a central access that ran north-south, was the main commercial area of Townside. A variety of rough stores were interspersed with rougher houses. From there the settlement spread out to the east, north, and south, becoming progressively more derelict and poorly serviced on the margins. Townside got the bulk of miners who did not plan to stay and who cared more about their pay packet than building a stable community.

In 1929 Mineside workers decided to build a cooperative store. Russo-Asiatic convinced its employees to accept a compromise company-run 'community' store where miners could buy goods for less than in Townside shops. Mineside residents generally approved of the community store until it closed in the late 1950s, but families in the planned town could not get everything they wanted there, so Minesiders shopped at Townside. Relatively high incomes enabled Mineside residents to exploit the duplication of services by shopping strategically.[44]

MIM organized a variety of formal recreations. The company sponsored recreation in Mount Isa the same way it built homes, in waves. MIM managers organized cricket and golf matches, and sponsored a brass band that performed regularly at the company rotunda in the Mineside town centre. Urquhart installed a clubhouse in Mineside and equipped it with a small library, a reading room, and tennis courts. After the Second World War, ASARCO-MIM beefed up its paternalism: it built a swimming pool and contributed to a leading manly Australian pastime by sponsoring the local rugby union.

Formal female activities highlight the differences between community organizations in the different halves of the town. Company organizations afforded wives and daughters 'feminine' pursuits similar to those found in other planned towns at the time: reading groups, charity and

MIM Bowling green. (Courtesy Jonathan Richards)

public health drives, dances, lawn bowling associations, and all manner of school- and church-based social clubs. Julius Kruttschnitt's first wife, Marie, played an instrumental early role in establishing many of Mineside's respectable female activities.[45] Townside women, who were fewer, did not have access to these company-led social groups. More significantly, the women of Townside had less spare time to participate in organized social events. Some joined church and school groups, but formal recreation was not as prevalent in Townside. Fringe residents' preference for hotel bars and informal recreations remained separate from Mineside's well-funded and supported activities.

Townsiders' sense of deprivation relative to Mineside and even to other industrial sites in Australia contributed to the oppositional social dynamic in Mount Isa. The ability of the middle class to influence local events lay in its ability to adapt to changing circumstances. MIM had enormous influence, but the shops, movie theatres, hotel bars, and shacks of ill repute in Townside appealed to many inhabitants, and as a result Townside became a tattered symbol of independence from company control. Pride in going it alone infused Isans' activities in Townside with the satisfaction of subverting the local order, while contradictorily the personal character of most of those actions ensured that inhabitants' subordination within the corporate order went unchallenged.

If adaptation failed, business owners could move on to the next boom town. Sturdy building foundations represented faith in the future of a larger community. As expressed in the airy, hand-me-down vernacular architecture of the outback's petite bourgeoisie, experience proved that a naive belief in industrial bounty was illusory and dangerous for individual well-being. Industries came and went with little regard for the fates of the communities they founded. Governments courted those same firms by offering them generous concessions to development while trying to instil in ordinary Queenslanders a 'grin and bear it' self-sufficiency. External markets were beyond individual control too. Structured underdevelopment in Mount Isa provided the nascent outback middle class with numerous reasons to hesitate in laying foundations.

Local business growth paralleled the fortunes of the fluctuating industrial workforce, and decades of statistics compiled by the Queensland state government confirm this fact. The government had official eyes and ears among the police, mining officers, officials in the industrial court, and unofficial agents inside the AWU. It even had its agents file detailed annual reports on the activities of small business in towns across the state. A local business tax register charted the peaks and valleys of business growth in Isa over five decades and reveals fascinating corollaries to the development of the mine.

Between 1924 and 1927 several shops opened, but business struggled because the state of the mine and town relocation was uncertain. Urquhart's comprehensive construction program and the completion of the railway connection initiated a flurry of activity after 1927. Twenty-nine new businesses opened from 1929 to 1930, most being retail shops, small service firms like Smith's electrical company, or hospitality firms like boarding houses or hotels. After 1930, industrial setbacks, labour unrest, and the Depression caused the local economy to decline, and the establishment of new businesses did not match the level of 1929–30 for nearly two decades. Before MIM's post–Second World War construction bonanza, Mount Isa's small businesses concentrated in the retail sector, because setting up a small convenience store or restaurant was not as risky as building a hotel or establishing an electric power utility.

After the war, the number of local businesses expanded alongside the ballooning industrial workforce. Between 1949 and 1951 fifty-seven new businesses opened in the town, nearly half of which were in the retail sector, but the service and hospitality sectors expanded significantly as well. Then, after the inauguration of Fisher's house-building schemes in the mid-1950s, business growth truly exploded. Between 1953 and 1955, ninety-seven small firms opened. This time, along with the predictable rise in retail and service providers, entrepreneurs opened eleven contract building firms. Eighteen gougers started independent mining ventures, Pat Mackie's Lucky Dollar mine being one of them.

Between 1956 and 1959, MIM retreated from overt paternalism by demolishing its old planned townsite on the far side of the hills and closing the company store. Small business boomed again. Between 1956 and 1960, 222 new businesses opened in Mount Isa. By 1960, the town had 517 small businesses, nearly 400 of which began after the 1949 boom. Local economic dependence on the prosperity of the mine is clear.

Townside's reliance on the mine was pronounced during industrial unrest. Local economic growth crashed in 1933 and 1961. Those years witnessed the two biggest and longest-running labour disputes in the years covered by the tax registers. The onset of the Depression did not affect the local economy to as great an extent as disruptions to the immediate workforce – the consumer base that was the lifeblood of Townside business. After the settlement of the 1961 dispute, there was an unparalleled rise in businesses openings.[46] Tax records are not available after 1963, but later statistics would likely confirm the dependent relationships and show a precipitous drop in business activity during the 1964–5 dispute, followed by sharp growth in the years of industrial stability and civic government that followed.

MIM did not buy from the Townside businesses, but its workers did. The high turnover of the mine workforce did not trouble small business owners as long as the total number of workers remained high. Strikes and industrial-economic downturns shrank the workforce and its buying power. Business owners had to attune their behaviour to that of their unstable consumer base. When strikes stalled the local economy, Mount Isa's constrained business owners threw in their lots with the workers, believing that stance would serve them better than being associated with the monopoly corporation. There was a range of local community issues, but most highlighted the class divisions at the heart of daily life.

A beer strike in 1929 indicated the confluence of middle- and working-class interests early in Mount Isa's development. The two hotels on Townside were the only places in Mount Isa where residents could purchase alcohol legally. Miners and publicans butted heads over the price of alcohol. In October 1929, miners organized a Beer Strike Committee and scheduled a revolving paid picket outside the hotels and urged miners to boycott them. The first strike in the town was a protest in favour of workers' right to an affordable drink, and it lasted one year. The beer strikers declared that anyone who drank at the Townside hotels during the strike earned the label 'defaulter' or 'black' and was to be shunned. By January 1930, the committee ruled sixty-four Isans – some who operated small businesses – in default of the strike. The momentary convergence of interests created by the beer strike saw company managers and police officers heartily supporting the strikers because the grassroots prohibition increased worker productivity and reduced arrests for drunk and disorderly conduct.[47]

Most business owners courted the beer strikers by letting the committee put donation boxes in their shops or by discounting services for striking families. Retailers who aided the workers fared well. Isa's police inspector reported in that most of Townside's older businesses did 'better trade ... than prior to the beer strike.'[48] The strike petered out, but it forced publicans to lower the price of most beverages by 20 per cent. The working-class consumer boycott highlighted the divisions among members of the middle class in Mount Isa and demonstrated to individual business owners the wisdom of at least tacitly supporting the goals of the organized industrial workforce, as opposed to relying on an indifferent company and government for help.

A hospital dispute during the 1930s illustrates the confluence of middle- and working-class interests as well.[49] MIM and Townside residents vied for the new Mount Isa hospital. Jurisdictional and funding disagreements ensued so that hospitals operated on both sides of the Leichhardt from 1930. One hospital was company funded and the other financed by local subscription. Townside residents believed the company concerned itself only with the health of managers and miners – not all residents like a proper community hospital. Class issues soon intervened, further polarizing the company–community standoff.

Throughout the lead poisoning crisis between 1931 and 1933, miners and other Townside residents vigorously defended the redundancy of two hospitals on the grounds that doctors at the Mineside hospital failed to diagnose lead poisoning for fear of company censure.[50] The dangers that workers encountered in ASARCO's speed-up and the deepening Depression invested the local dispute with anti-monopoly and anti-capitalist sentiments. Middle- and working-class residents of Townside were incensed that the state government supported the demands of a foreign company over those of Australian citizens. Events came to a head in 1933, first through the government lead-poisoning report that attributed the lead-poisoning crisis to workers, blaming them for breathing too much polluted air in the workplace, and MIM's year-end lockout further complicated the struggle over the hospital. With the mine closed, residents could no longer pay for the Townside hospital, so the state assumed control of it. What appeared on the surface as a compromise solution to the hospital dispute benefited MIM the most, because the company hospital no longer had to compete against a neighbouring medical board that opposed its very existence.[51] Government intervention first and foremost stabilized the company.

A variety of local issues cropped up between the late 1930s and early 1960s, but residential efforts to develop Townside into an attractive community ran into the hard rock of government neglect, the mobility of workers, and oppositional class politics. Most workers had little stake in Mount Isa and were loath to invest time or money in improving a place they planned to leave. In separate reports in 1955 and 1960, outside commentators specified the lack of paved roads and the near-total lack of landscaping or gardening in the fringe town. Both writers complained that educational facilities were below average, that recreation rarely took place without the consumption of alcohol, and that there were no strong public bodies to mobilize and direct community sentiment.[52] Mount Isa's population ballooned with MIM's profits, but Townside grew without any commensurate improvements to infrastructure or amenities. Advocates for an enlarged civic identity in Mount Isa could not surmount political neglect and could not enlist residents because most were there to make money and leave. It took a resurgence in industrial and class unrest to open the door for more explicitly localist forms of community identity to find an effective role in the local order.

Working residents grew discontented in the late 1950s. The 'community' store and Olympic-sized swimming pool in Mineside did little to bridge the three-decade gap between company paternalism and structured underdevelopment. MIM tried to manage its rough Australian workforce scientifically with characteristic heavy-handedness, and the mine turnover rate soared. Many workers found themselves outside of the paternalist network. Led by militant labour leader Kenneth Morgan, the smaller trade unions decided to expand their influence into the community. Members raised £4,000 in donations and, in late 1956, began building a Workers' Club in Townside. By October 1959 the club claimed roughly four hundred paid members.[53]

Workers complained throughout this period that the town had too few drinking establishments. Two and later three hotels for a workforce of several thousand thirsty miners could not handle demand.[54] MIM consistently discouraged alcohol consumption, and the established Townside publicans had a vested economic interest in funnelling access to the bottle through their establishments. Morgan and the militant trade workers, however, built a place of their own. They failed to secure a liquor licence, but that did not stop a Queensland alcohol wholesaler from supplying the club with alcohol, which the club then sold onsite illegally. Morgan and his associates corresponded frequently with the Queensland Licensing Commission about obtaining a licence while local law enforcement looked the other way.

During the industrial standoffs of 1959 and 1961, police and company officials fingered the Workers' Club as the epicentre of radicalism. Police increased surveillance of the club, and early in 1962 they raided it, charged four men with illegally dealing liquor, charged six more with drinking on an unlicensed premises, and confiscated thirty-four kegs

Star Pictures, Townside, Mount Isa. (Courtesy Jonathan Richards)

Boyd's Hotel, Townside, Mount Isa. (Courtesy Jonathan Richards)

of beer. All ten men were convicted. The licensing commission inquired among town residents into the club's dealings. Anonymous complaints in 1961 and 1962 cited overall increases in drunkenness, 'Sunday drinking,' operating after hours, club owners allowing patrons to take alcohol home, gambling, and an accusation that Morgan was skimming the club's profits. The commission patently refused to grant the Workers' Club a licence. Morgan complained bitterly about the decision and wondered 'why other clubs in the past were able to obtain licenses so readily with so little to offer their members.'[55] That the commission kept the club in regulatory limbo for five years and then pounced only after a difficult industrial dispute suggests ulterior motives.

Three decades after the 1929 beer strike, residents, workers, and local authorities fought similar battles for the right to have a reasonably priced beer with workmates. The episode highlights the continuing but shifting entanglement of class and community politics in Mount Isa. Restricting access to alcohol dominated the discussion, but it also challenged the legitimacy of company authority, the appropriateness of class politics in public space, and whether the Isa would remain a mine with an adjunct settlement or become a community that housed a mine. The failure of the Workers' Club represented a diminution of class influence in local affairs. The long industrial dispute in 1964–5 eroded workers' power substantially.

Before the 1960s, community groups in Mount Isa often described the prevailing hegemony as a grasping monopoly versus legitimate inhabitants whose demands deserved priority over those of the foreign corporation. Scholars have located a similar form of egalitarianism in the 'producer ideology' of nineteenth-century American workers. Historian T.J. Jackson Lears sums up those studies: the producer ideology 'animated mass movements from the Knights of Labor to the People's Party,' but those working-class movements 'never became hegemonic' because their world view 'blurred class distinctions and propelled workers into the arms of middle-class radicals who focused on financiers rather than employers and worked through existing political institutions.'[56] Mount Isa's worker–middle-class alliance was an Australian variation on this theme. Working- and middle-class interests intersected in Mount Isa, painting many local issues with a class brush. When labour disputes occurred, Townsiders generally supported the workers. Local business owners and other groups fostered a small degree of community sentiment, but they did so under specific constraints and with a particular tone and effect.

The socio-economic dislocations caused by the labour disputes of the 1960s realigned the local middle class toward reliance on company aid. MIM had been trying since the late 1950s to stabilize its workforce by convincing workers to buy its houses, but the local middle class had no reason to count on the success of a new scheme to create permanence in the entire town. The wide-scale social unrest in the early 1960s made the company and state government refocus their attention on solving the problems of instability and gave the middle class a new ally. The economic boom MIM experienced during and after the 1964–5 strike established the company's financial security and the basis for civic stability.

In July 1963 Mount Isa overcame a longstanding political constraint when the state government made it the seat of its own shire council. After four decades of neglect from Cloncurry, the Mount Isa middle class selected its own political body that could negotiate directly with MIM and the state government for aid. Residents' control over the direction of town development grew as coastal retailers moved to Townside, and the council directed its energies towards enhancing infrastructure by paving streets and supplying all homes with water and electricity. The 1964–5 dispute eroded the tacit cross-class alliance and stigmatized class issues.

The company and town's middle class finally found themselves on the same side. Their latent shared interests in stability, permanence, and investment in a civic identity now became manifest. Blainey says that after the Queensland government classified Mount Isa as a city in 1968, state and company assistance 'fell in one paternal shower.' MIM and the government provided direct assistance to residents who wanted to build houses in Townside, the council introduced a previously unheard of level of zoning and town planning to Townside, and dozens of new buildings – most housing coastal chain stores – replaced Townside's ramshackle structures. In 1972 the city's population exceeded twenty-seven thousand, with most residents living in affordable, well-serviced suburban homes. MIM's turnover rate decreased steadily as well. In a matter of years Mount Isa became a shire, a city, a regional hub, and, most important to MIM and the local middle class, a community that housed a mine.[57]

Dependence persisted, despite the grant of self-government. The company and state government heavily subsidized urban development because city revenues did not finance the growth. MIM owned the electrical and water supply, and the nearly six-thousand-strong mine workforce still comprised the largest occupational and consumer group in the city. The first city councils were a lightning rod that directed resident concerns away from MIM while the company maintained its influence behind the scenes. Local histories by Geoffrey Blainey and Noreen Kirkman implicitly recognize these facts: they laud the switch to self-government but describe the era not by what successive councils accomplished but how they were showered with largesse from above. The descriptions of the era of local government in both books are curiously abbreviated.[58] Recognizing dependence and constrained agency is not a suitable ending for popular histories.

Civic agents operating in a web of complex historical relations helped shape contrasting local orders in company towns to a degree that most writers never grant. This point expands our understanding of dependent industrial towns. That these residents did not always achieve the intended outcome of their actions does not demonstrate a lack of agency, only the myriad potentialities of social interaction. Chance constrained local authorities, too.

Upon closer examination, broad similarities of corporate order in Corner Brook and Mount Isa dissolve into a number of place-specific contrasts. The relations among workers, company, and the middle classes began and remained fairly peaceful in Corner Brook, compared to the oppositional relations so prominent throughout the history of the Isa. Corner Brook was already a regional centre in 1925 and, collectively, the communities comprised the island's second biggest 'city' by the end of the Second World War. Queensland governments selectively neglected Mount Isa's development and fostered deep grievances among permanent residents. In Corner Brook the rapid achievement of regional prominence resulted in localism that tended towards compromise. In Mount Isa neglect reinforced a localism that mimicked oppositional behaviour at the mine.

In post-Confederation Corner Brook, as the provincial government sought to centralize power in its hands, good relations between local boosters and the company grew strained, while recurring industrial unrest in Mount Isa in the 1960s caused the interests of MIM and the local middle class to dovetail to a greater degree than they ever had before. Both local orders stayed between the poles of force and consent but on different sides of the centre. Smallwood's dictatorial decision to end local democracy in Corner Brook was roughly equivalent to Nicklin's state of emergency in the 1964–5 Mount Isa dispute, but the former action was prompted by community problems, not industrial unrest. The difference is quite telling.

We can take this reappraisal deeper, though. Residents' daily navigation, internalization, and constant refashioning of their place in the local order formed the basis of bottom-up agency. Everyday experience connected work to the public and private spheres. An evaluation of the small autonomies chosen by the residents of Corner Brook and Mount Isa and the local structures of feeling that grew out those autonomies completes this comparison.

Chapter Six

'Personal Relationships and Private Worlds'? Structures of Feeling in Company Towns

Industrial relations established the framework for company towns, but the collective daily experiences of thousands of residents created dynamic communities. The corporations that founded Corner Brook and Mount Isa avoided conflicts that could have overturned the advantageous power relations they had initiated. There were serious disputes, of course, but the companies held on to their local balance of authority. Corporations retained hegemony, partially by persuading and coercing residents to accept their role as authorities. Like other layers of history in the two communities, the tones of daily life in the communities differed from one another. Social relations in Corner Brook tended toward accommodation and in Mount Isa toward opposition.

Partial consent to corporate order occurred at its most basic level in the perceptions and actions of ordinary people. Every day in each locale, individuals' imperfect comprehension of self and of the wider structural limits to their lives combined with complex external familial, social, and occupational relations to foster 'contradictory consciousness.' Local orders preserved degrees of open-endedness that persuaded people to trade immediate inequality for personally acceptable measures of autonomy and security, and to hold onto the possibility of upward social mobility in the future. Choices and opportunities, even small ones as measured against major historical events, represented spaces for negotiation and independence. They made life in company towns bearable and sometimes even attractive to residents. The prosaic but critical contradiction at work here, however, was that inhabitants' resort to innumerable small autonomies protected the corporations' right to rule.[1]

The sum of residents' internalizations of the legitimacy of corporate order in Corner Brook and Mount Isa were 'structures of feeling.'[2] In Corner Brook the rapid achievement of demographic stability and residents' ability to recast traditions to mitigate feelings of exploitation established a tendency toward uncritically accepting a 'natural' order. Residents of Corner Brook also compared their local experience favourably to life in Newfoundland's poor rural outports. In comparison, Isans developed a far more oppositional tone. Residents gauged life in Mount Isa against the bustling cities on the coast and the bastions of labour power like Broken Hill, with the result that the outback mine town did not come off well in these comparisons. In addition, antagonism sprang from the binaries of daily life like the town's large sexual imbalance and the enmity between settled families and itinerant males. Within Mount Isa's oppositional structure of feeling, the company earned legitimacy most often by exercising power rather than by compromising with subordinate groups. Put simply, MIM used the stick, Bowater the carrot.

Daily life in the western Newfoundland mill town had several characteristics that set it apart from other dependent resource towns. The rapid growth of a sizeable urban settlement presented men and women with numerous opportunities that they could not find elsewhere on the island. Mill workers got steady, well-paid wage work in place of an unreliable living through seasonal fishing, subsistence provisioning, and credit. Women found employment in domestic service and retail outlets or, for smaller numbers of trained females, teaching or secretarial positions. Rural Newfoundland offered little independence and few paid jobs for women.

Life in the urban industrial setting opened up individual choices. Thousands of children in Corner Brook grew up in neighbourhoods larger than most outports. Children went to school and socialized in wider networks than they did in fishing villages. Dozens of shops, movie theatres, dancehalls, and bars gave Corner Brook's wage workers things to do in their spare time. In fact, the availability of these facilities for popular culture expanded the very idea of unstructured leisure time. A large population enlarged the pool of potential mates for both sexes, and unsupervised leisure time gave young adults a sense of expanded personal control over friendship and courtship.

The choices residents encountered in the city, however, could cause individual social dislocation as well. The erosion of traditional family and communal ties, the pressure to meet the unattainable standards of peer groups, the deprivations of under- or unemployment, and the expanded opportunities for antisocial behaviour accompanied the benefits of greater choice. Yet many people chose the possibility of creating prosperous lives for themselves in the mill town over the probability of communal poverty in the outports. Newfoundlanders' recognition of Corner Brook's regional centre status confirmed its appeal.

Gaining the benefits of urban life did not cause new arrivals to abandon traditional domestic and social practices completely. Amalgams of traditional and modern practices shaped a number of daily behaviours. Historical geographer Glen Norcliffe points out how today residents of Corner Brook use time in the woods – be it snowmobiling, hunting, fishing, or trips to 'the camp' – to affirm a shared sense of place in the face of the homogenizing pressures of globalization.[3] Residents had practised similar strategies from the mill's inception. Corner Brook's new proletarians adapted traditional survival tactics to the new industrial setting and affirmed sentimental ties to their rural upbringings.[4] Inhabitants took comfort from and achieved personal validation in self-provisioning and wilderness recreations. Hunting, fishing, and wilderness sojourns enabled a temporary escape from the depersonalizing routine of industrial wage labour. Other historians have demonstrated similar hybridizations of past customs.[5] Among residents of Corner Brook, recasting traditional activities proved effective enough to offset the alienation of conforming to industrial discipline in the town's first decades and resilient enough to subtly subvert trends toward global standardization today.

The emotional importance of hybridized customs tells only part of the story. Crucial material benefits accrued from these practices. In a locality where mill labour was the main occupation, catching fish, hunting, gathering berries, and raising modest vegetable gardens became ways to not only subsist but to save money. Families established informal trading relationships with networks of relatives and friends by giving surplus goods to neighbours. The recipients' obligation to respond in kind at some future date went unspoken, but the reciprocity exerted a powerful push toward cohesion and conformity. The ability of residents to use traditional subsistence practices to complement wages meant that the economic viability of the average Corner Brook family was steadier and its income greater than that of outport families.

Corner Brook settlers practised ways of living that existed outside the company's efforts to define work and social life in corporate terms. What social control theorists regard as workers' retreat to pre-modern modes of existence when faced with corporate dominance actually comprised a practical accommodation to industrial work rhythms by borrowing from pre-existing customs and practices, in a conscious strategy rather than through instinct.

The attraction of the instant city pulled scores of Newfoundlanders to the area. Women and men settled in Corner Brook in roughly equal numbers. The 1935 census listed one third of the Humber District's population as married – an uncommonly high proportion of married couples for a company town. The census estimated that the district also had more single women than men. Females comprised a sizeable portion of the local population. Ten years later, most areas of Corner Brook had achieved sexual parity. Townsite had more female inhabitants than males, and with two males for every female, Corner Brook West – the still-expanding fringe town – was the only area with a considerable sex imbalance.[6] The town based on the male-only exploitation of forest resources achieved rapid sexual equilibrium.

The statistical parity of sexes did not mean gender equality. The company barred women from shop-floor employment, making Corner Brook's best-paid occupations off-limits. One woman recalled that Bowater did not employ married women in any capacity. Women worked mainly in the retail sector or as domestics and usually only until they got pregnant or married. Women of all ages and skill levels received considerably less annual income than males.[7] After marriage, accepted gender roles assigned workers' wives to the domestic realm of child-rearing, family upkeep, and small, private get-togethers with neighbourhood wives. Women consented to the scaled authority of corporate father and male breadwinner because of improvements to their lot relative to life in the outports or in volatile resource settlements like the nearby logging town of Deer Lake. The frequent refrain among women that they 'didn't want for anything' signifies real material and social improvement, not consent and resignation.

The uncharacteristic prevalence of women in Corner Brook reined in extreme homo-sociable male behaviour such as transience, displays of public violence, drunkenness, and petty crime. Set hours of work, the general certainty that one had a steady job, and life among other Anglo 'whites' who shared similar cultural and personal traits contributed to stable routines. Sexual parity also increased chances for both sexes to find partners. By 1945, Corner Brook had more than seventy-six hundred married residents.[8] That, in turn, reduced forms of self-harm like high alcohol consumption and acts of casual and habitual violence brought on by loneliness and sexual frustration.

Demographic characteristics intersected with the vicissitudes of built environment and cultural beliefs to reinforce the disposition toward accommodation in Corner Brook's structure of feeling. The Humber region is cold and snowy for half the year. Settlers could not reside in tents or breezy shacks. The company offered skilled workers sturdy, well-sealed, and warm houses for modest prices. That made settling into domestic relationships easier for essential workers. Less-skilled migrants sought similar permanence on their own terms. Before industrial Corner Brook was a decade old, sturdy owner-built dwellings comprised most of the structures outside Townsite.[9] The time, money, and assistance fringe-dwellers required to build their own houses constituted a major investment in the future that would be jeopardized by industrial or social unrest.

Most settlers placed a premium on respect for and loyalty to family and friends and on deference to authority. Respect, loyalty, and deference were not trivial sentiments. Emotional attachment overlaid the crucial strategies of material reciprocity and mutual assistance among kin, neighbours, and merchants that enabled generations of Newfoundlanders to snatch hope from scarcity. Such relations stressed compromise – sometimes 'grinning and bearing it' – over confrontation.

Those attitudes jibed nicely with the eager paternalism and outward interest successive mill managers advanced in their dealings with residents. Corner Brook union leaders reminisced how they 'took what they could get' from the company without misgivings, while a housewife from Townsite stated quite matter-of-factly that she stayed with her husband through several rough periods because she felt a responsibility to raise her children as best she could.[10] These are not expressions of defeatism. They are the sensible acknowledgments of concrete limitations with which participants felt they had successfully dealt. Satisfaction in industrial relations and in domestic life came through patience and compromise. Self-restraint and amelioration tended to get the best results fastest.

Corner Brook's settled couples conceived many children. The average Corner Brook household had 5.3 inhabitants in the mid-1940s.[11] Parents perceived many relative advantages for children in urban Corner Brook over child-rearing in rural areas. The city had better schools than most other Newfoundland settlements, and not only was the quality of instruction superior than in the one-room, all-grade outport schoolhouses, but children had cause to stay in school longer and socialize in wider peer groups. Extended social networks meant that city

Palace Theatre on Broadway, Corner Brook West, 1950s. (Corner Brook Pulp and Paper Limited Photographic Collection courtesy of the Corner Brook Museum and Archives)

kids had greater opportunities to select their own partners and obtain steady work later in life.

Not all children in Corner Brook could access these opportunities in equal measure. Children in the fringe towns faced poverty and a suite of problems associated with it. Few childhoods escaped hardship. The lessons of growing up in Corner Brook, however, instilled in many young adults desires to establish and maintain close family relations and lasting friendships. Continuity, moderation, and the importance of individual and small group autonomy prevailed. Formative experiences shaped inhabitants' later accommodation to industrial and civic issues and fostered a steadily reproducing industrial workforce. Large families meant also that mill workers were continually alert to the need for a steady and reliable income flow.

The idea that fringe towns acted as a safety valve for the tensions created by a company-imposed social hierarchy is a prominent description of company town experience but the concept is underdeveloped. In Corner Brook, the separation between Townsite and the fringe settlements, and the social inequalities that stemmed from spatial and social segregation did not evoke sustained vocal criticism of the company. Patterns of deference and the lack of identification with wider class issues comprised two significant reasons for the lack of complaint, but the daily experiences of most residents with the bustling fringe settlements downplayed resentment as well. Broadway on Corner Brook's west side emerged as the main commercial centre in the city, where all inhabitants shopped and bartered for goods. Fringe residents' experiences in dealing with scarcity and the absence of a reliable central government taught them to make their own luck and not to protest against things they could not change. Settlers on Corner Brook's fringes assumed when they arrived that they would go it alone.

Newfoundlanders expected to squat on or lease a plot of land and to build and own their own dwellings without the help of authorities. A number of skilled mill workers rejected company rentals in favour of owning a house on the freer fringes. The expectation of self-reliance downplayed in fringe-dwellers' minds the frequent criticisms of the poverty of Corner Brook's fringes, where residents viewed spatial and social inequalities as badges of independence and hard work, not as character flaws. They believed tenants in the planned town valued company-defined status above substance. Outside Townsite, 'English snobbery' did not sit well with people, but insults and fights over such issues were confined mainly to the young.[12] Fringe-dwellers inverted the corporate order by elevating self-reliance over close relations with managers and company handouts. Like so many aspects of daily life in Corner Brook, residents internalized hierarchy in personal terms, not as social structures that could be changed through collective action.

That this relatively compliant attitude benefited the mill company is without question, but authorities had not imposed it and could not govern it. The corporation cultivated residents' good favour by adopting its own accommodationist posture. The company's frequent compromises with and aid to various segments of the community proved to residents its genuine goodwill. For all of these linked reasons, most residents internalized the local order smoothly. Even inhabitants' daily encounters with unsavoury or antisocial behaviour like alcohol consumption and crime affirm a context of local accommodationism.

In the 1920s and 1930s Newfoundland law proscribed and the rapidly expanding population outpaced the supply of alcohol. The company initially forbade the sale of alcohol in Townsite to abide by the Newfoundland government's monopoly on the sale of spirits (excluding beer, which private vendors could obtain a licence to sell). Mill management also sought to instil Victorian notions of sobriety and industry in its essential workers. One manager's summation of the construction period revolved around the lack of alcohol. In a book of poems commemorating the construction period, H.A. Ogden voiced the men's repeated complaints that the planned town was 'dry.' In over-indulgent verse, Ogden intoned,

> Drink to me only with thine eyes,
> For we cannot get champagne;
> And being overruled by 'Drys'
> We call for drinks in vain.
> But soon we hope this Act will cease,
> Which spurns the use of wine,
> And Glynmill profits will increase
> At your expense and mine![13]

Other skilled workers were less verbose in their resistance to company prohibition. They purchased either a weekly supply from St John's or, more likely, crossed into one of the fringe towns to buy illegal alcohol.

Early settlers reminisced humorously about bootlegged liquor and illicit beer vendors in Corner Brook. Smugglers brought spirits from the French-controlled islands of St Pierre and Miquelon and distributed it around the island's bays and coves. Rum-runners sailed under cover of darkness into Cook's Brook cove in the Humber Arm and unloaded their contraband. From there, local agents distributed it throughout the Bay of Islands. Parson's sawmill in Curling functioned as a 'hideout' for spirits bound for Corner Brook. Long-time residents Ethel Rowsell and George Basha recalled that by the late 1920s 'every second place' in Corner Brook 'was a blind pig' or an illicit alcohol vendor.[14] Residents obtained alcohol easily in prohibition Corner Brook.

The local police force had few officers in the early years. They operated out of a multi-purpose company-built government building and patrolled the town on company horses. Officer Walter Mugford recollected that 'every three or four' houses in the 1930s had a home brew still. Police officers nicknamed Corner Brook West the 'Western Front' for its ramshackle appearance and number of blind pigs. Police had to obtain sufficient evidence – the testimony of neighbours – to search suspected premises. Then the law required them to 'take a sample and seal it in front of the suspect, so that no one could be accused of tampering before it was sent to St John's for testing.'[15] If the sample had alcohol content the suspect would be arraigned. Sentences tended to be fines of varying severity. For local officials, the enforcement of prohibition took a lot of time and had little effect. Police constables' inability and disinclination to stem the illicit alcohol trade confirmed locals' perception of the fringe communities as free spaces, beyond the influence of authorities.

Police invested in the neighbourhoods too, for they had to maintain good relations with the majority of inhabitants. Ethel Rowsell and George Basha recalled that some police officers turned blind eyes to what most people considered the minor infraction of an unenforceable law. Rowsell called them 'very good policemen,' adding that one officer 'never got anybody into trouble unless he really had to.'[16] In certain cases, horizontal personal ties to the community overrode the top-down duty to administer order impartially.

Over the following years, legal access to alcohol increased and authorities placed few limits on the size of the trade. Local merchant John Bartlett opened the first liquor store in the mid-1930s, and by the early 1940s Corner Brook had several small taverns. According to George Basha, women ran many of the bars. Women avoided patronizing the rough watering holes, however, preferring to imbibe at private gatherings – known locally as 'times' – or at licensed dances. Florence Ledrew said that bars like Mrs Corbage's on Broadway 'were always packed, especially on paydays.'[17] The buildings were small. Few could accommodate more than a couple dozen patrons. Fights occurred, but the dispersal of bars around town militated against brawls or roaming gangs of inebriates.

Other deviant and criminal activities seldom appear in the historical record. Harold Horwood says in his local history that 'there was little serious violence' and 'the cases were simple ones' involving 'liquor … and fighting.'[18] Such a description, however, could describe any small or mid-sized town anywhere in the Western world at any time. Court records reveal a clearer picture of crime in Corner Brook: drunk and disorderly behaviour dominated, but judges heard cases of domestic violence and abandonment frequently as well. One resident remembered 'three or four' prostitutes working Broadway in the early years, but available bench books mention no trials for prostitution. Most of the remaining cases dealt with vagrancy, unpaid debts, petty thefts, minor frauds, and, from the mid-1940s on, motor vehicle violations. Murder, sex crime, and grand theft rarely occurred, and newspapers publicized only the most spectacular court cases.[19]

Peering briefly into the dark recesses of everyday life in Corner Brook reveals hidden frustrations and anger. Communities like Corner Brook did not produce just emotional contentment and 'good' relations. Many residents consented to authority only partially, but undeveloped or misdirected grumbling about personal dissatisfaction did not provide the basis for well-organized resistance to corporate authority. In keeping with Corner Brook's inward-looking local culture, authorities investigated and prosecuted offences with discretion, and the media behaved similarly. Most inhabitants viewed crime as the exception to the rule and believed Corner Brook's social order reasonably good and fair.

Corner Brook inhabitants negotiated their immediate social and occupational lives and daily surroundings by tying traditional ideas and activities to industrial life. Social and industrial stability took root early and accommodationist attitudes followed. The generally conciliatory bottom-up approach to authority suited the corporate hegemon but was not imposed by it. The mill companies had little influence over the daily lives of the majority of residents of Corner Brook and acted in response to this grassroots dynamic. Ordinary people's ability to pursue numerous small autonomies convinced them that 'the line between dominant and subordinate cultures [was] a permeable membrane, not an impenetrable barrier.'[20] Unsurprisingly, the residents of Corner Brook had little appetite for critical social theory or collective resistance. Social cohesion and locally defined good fortune pointed residents toward negotiated consent to corporate authority. The daily autonomies that the inhabitants of Mount Isa developed within the mine town's starker social limits fostered a divergent confrontational structure of feeling.

The constant struggle to control the temperamental outback environment and deal with what later writers called 'Isa-lation' made toughness and creativity important personal attributes for the residents of Mount Isa. Few single women migrated to the rough mining town. The resulting sexual imbalance made homo-sociability the default relationship and promoted rough demeanours. The spatial and social inequalities between settled residents and the anonymous mass of transient inhabitants added to the tensions of daily life in the Isa. Attitudes that developed out of thousands of daily relationships scaled up to local authorities in the form of an oppositional stance. Standoffish inhabitants conditioned decidedly anti-labour companies to confront the bluster from below with a 'my way or else' attitude, leading to a cycle of dissatisfaction and conflict.

Settling Mount Isa with married couples proved difficult. Di Perkins, an analyst of life in northwest Queensland says, 'The heat, the dust, the flies, and the unrelenting superiority of nature over man are irrefutable aspects of this area.' She contends that the stark environment created a 'special type of community.'[21] Workers and residents toiled in manic conditions without the technological safety net of air-conditioners or cars, and often without four solid walls and a roof. Long-time MIM boss Julius Kruttschnitt recalled that 'there was plenty to struggle against.'[22]

Still, some early settlers arrived with wives and children in tow. In a few short years, the company recruited a seed population of skilled workers and their families to live in the new company houses. Leslie Urquhart's first houses had a good water supply, individual septic systems, and considerable living space, but housing construction did not continue along those lines. High labour turnover made the demand for company houses and the quality of dwellings inversely proportional. During the Depression, families who arrived intending to settle had to live in humpies thrown together on the fly until the company 'could wangle [*sic*] a house or some sort of shelter for them so they could live together.'[23] The volatility of natural and built environments shot deeply into the daily experiences of highly prized married workers.

The married men who moved their families from coastal cities and established inland towns and who secured a company 'house' often got a tent or a tin hut. The company repaid the risk that families took to resettle with a dwelling that could only be considered temporary. One early couple remembered cooking and eating on potato and onion boxes in their company dwelling. Families in the dozens of post-Urquhart houses shared outhouses. Bathroom facilities remained communal affairs until the massive planning initiatives of the 1950s. Keeping cool at home was another struggle. Men and women slept on screened-in verandas outside and on particularly hot nights slept between wet towels. According to an unnamed wife of a Mineside worker, 'cheap rent' that 'was more than fair' convinced working-class families to tough it out

The mine from Townside. (Courtesy Jonathan Richards)

in the Isa instead of chancing the dodgy Depression-era Queensland labour market.[24] Working families found the Isa relatively appealing in the worst years of the Depression, but comparisons to 'better' coastal or industrial settlements lingered. Settlers found little cause for boosterism in early Mount Isa.

The hardships of the outback also qualify later boosters' refrain that Mount Isa was 'a good place to raise children.'[25] Developing constitutions surely had trouble adapting to the region's oppressive climate. School officials complained throughout the late 1920s and 1930s about crowded classrooms and the lack of basic institutional implements like chairs, tables, proper buildings, and playgrounds. Di Perkins's *Outback Insights* contains a memorable photo of a class of children swatting in unison at a swarm of mosquitoes. One can imagine the pleasures of sitting through an arithmetic lesson in such conditions. On top of material hardship, children attended school irregularly. When mine walkouts or lockouts occurred, the schools emptied like the rest of the town.[26]

Improvements in childcare arrived piecemeal. A 1948 report for the state co-ordinator general entitled 'Northern Australia Nutritional Survey' suggests major differences between the formative experiences of Mineside and Townside children. The company settlement had two schools, a kindergarten and baby clinic under construction, a dental clinic, and a sports oval. A community swimming pool followed. The brief description of facilities for Townside children is telling. Surveyors mention private dwellings made of galvanized iron, and a 'hospital' with only one doctor. According to them, 'coloured' – a word designating Aboriginals or mixed race – children and kids from 'broken homes' comprised 70 per cent of the 150 pupils at the Townside state school. The survey also noted that children seldom stayed in school past early adolescence because fourteen-year-old boys could get high wages at the mine.[27] The comprehensive civic planning projects of the 1960s greatly enhanced learning and leisure opportunities for all children in Mount Isa, but the records contradict the less-than-critical appraisals of local promoters.

Few single women migrated to the mining town. Limited employment opportunities comprised one reason. A few dozen young women worked as secretaries, waitresses, or laundresses for the company, but such jobs promised no upward mobility. Few jobs existed outside company employment. Before the mine opened, some of the region's pioneer women opened boarding houses. After the government relocated the township to the east side of the river, however, men purchased most of the lots and supplanted women as business owners.[28] After 1930, women either moved to the Isa with their husbands or were born there.

In an outback town built by rough male hands, single females encountered a range of gender constraints. According to one historian, 'In an environment where a woman was rare, it was her "femaleness" that was the dominant characteristic rather than her personality as a whole.'[29] Three decades after its founding, men continued to outnumber women seven to one in Mount Isa.[30] A report in the *Australian* in 1973 described how married men in the Isa preferred to spend free time 'redoing their eight hours' work' in the company of other males, instead of spending time with their wives. The report also claimed a greater amount of male homo-sociability – mateship – in Mount Isa than anywhere else in Australia.[31] The large sexual imbalance meant that transient male labourers socialized only with other males. Romantic and sexual frustration mingled with a host of other daily difficulties and made the floating population domineering, unpredictable, and difficult for authorities to deal with.

Single men who relocated to the Isa believing rumours of easy work and money became quickly disillusioned. They cultivated standoffish and bogus personas as a result of their working-class upbringing and personal experiences riding the rattler from job to job. Anonymity in life and labour generated actions geared toward securing immediate gains, not establishing stability and permanence.

If a newly arrived worker found a vacant room at one of the Townside hotels, he lived in uncomfortably close proximity to others. Rooms were cramped and dusty. If the water supply to the hotels stopped unpredictably, as it often did, frustrated tenants lived conveniently above the only establishments in town licensed to serve alcohol. Boarding houses offered worse accommodations. In a 1935 letter to the Department of Education, local teacher C.H. Christiansen described sixty men living at a boarding house comprising several ramshackle structures. The men ate 'in a dining room of bush and sawn timber' and washed 'under a bucket shower suspended from a tree' with no privacy.[32]

The public character of transient workers' lives was an important fact. Mount Isa workers 'lived a more public life in every sense.'[33] They used tents and humpies only for sleeping and the odd sexual encounter, spending the rest of their time among masses of men in the mine or in the hotels, and in smaller gatherings around campfires in the spaces between tents or out in the bush. They experienced the gamut of human emotions in the public eye. Transient inhabitants blocked the public gaze by adopting false identities, by fudging the truth to keep their pasts private, or by verbally or physically attacking those who got too close. If circumstances came to a head, men simply packed their meagre belongings and left.

Inquest files describe how in 1930 the twenty-one-year-old daughter of a prominent local business owner died after a self-administered abortion turned septic. Police found that the deceased woman was 'keeping company' with a young man who lived at the boarding house where she worked. The woman's father told police the man had left town around the time his daughter's pregnancy began to show. When pressed by investigators, local physician Dr Pincus suggested that similar circumstances in the past had prompted abortions.[34]

This episode illustrates how the local sexual imbalance, gender inequality, and the unpredictability of male workers played out, pointing to the deep opposition between invested stability and anonymous mobility in Mount Isa. The unpredictability of flow-through workers made people wary of establishing personal relationships. Those tendencies were writ large during labour disputes. Most people fled to the coast. In 1960 a commentator made the telling statement that local home-owners 'invested only in such [household] articles as are easily moved.'[35] In this tense social setting, investing in the future was not easy. Residents did not consent readily to anything, let alone a foreign company's pretensions to local authority.

The peculiar bottom-up social milieu of Mount Isa led permanent and transient residents to develop different kinds of small autonomies, ranging from personal hobbies like gardening to casual visits and parties to binge drinking and casual violence. Residents gained degrees of relative autonomy and a fleeting sense of escape from company rule from those activities, but the contradictory implications of small autonomies also reinforced MIM's hegemony.

Many of Mineside's settled residents took advantage of MIM's offer to supply its tenants with gardening and construction material. Beginning with Leslie Urquhart, the company promoted planting and maintaining tidy household lots. Company organs like *MIMag* publicized families that maintained well-kept grounds and compared diligent gardeners to the anonymous 'Mr and Mrs Don't Cares' who took no pride in the appearance of their homes. Company officials said 'a good garden [was] generally the sign of a good man – a contented man with a sense of pride.'[36] Time spent gardening or building an addition to a tent house meant the people in question had invested in the future of the town. Convincing more residents to take pride in 'their homes' was a primary way the company tried to implant its corporate vision for Mount Isa.

But this explanation is one-sided. Gardening and all forms of domestic 'puttering' satisfied residents' personal needs too. The men and women who spent time making their domestic spaces more attractive did not do it to please company officials or to raise the building's resale value. They worked to make a more liveable atmosphere for themselves, their children, and their friends.[37] Gardening and carpentry enlarged social networks by introducing people with similar interests to one another. For them, manual labour was not simply a menial chore. Labour could be a recreation, an escape, a parenting strategy, or a half-conscious compulsion – the perennially unfinished project or work for work's sake – as well as wage work. Working around the house preoccupied miners, solidified ties with family members and friends, and gave tenants a sense of personal accomplishment that they could not achieve in the crush of managed bodies at the company mine and smelter.

Other pastimes were more clearly recreational. Noreen Kirkman mentions settlers' informal 'community singing,' and Julius Kruttschnitt recalled that people took part regularly in picnics and dances. Cinemas and dancehalls drew large crowds as well.[38] Residents engaged in leisure activities to experience comfort and satisfaction and to engender control over their own lives in the face of subordination and dependence. The company could not dictate how people spent their free time, but MIM benefited indirectly from residents' decisions to 'blow off some steam' and lose themselves in ephemeral distractions.

Absent from the company town narratives are comparisons and contrasts between places that give a sense of wider connections or local peculiarities. Neither Geoffrey Blainey nor Noreen Kirkman compares Mount Isa to other industrial centres. What a comparison shows is that an accepting, conciliatory tone is not nearly as prominent in Mount Isa's historical record as it is in Corner Brook's. Difference emerges most strikingly in the behaviour of the Isa's amorphous but, in many respects, defining population group.

The large transient population developed small autonomies formed from elements of rough and mobile working-class existence. Workers' reactions to 'Isa-lation' arose out of their immediate experiences with the availability of alcohol and the lack of personal privacy. The local climate made thirsts heavy. Townside's 'hard' bore water was not particularly palatable or abundant, and workers considered sharing beers with mates after a shift a mark of proper comradeship. Flow-through workers in the first four decades of Isa's existence experienced little privacy. Thousands of men lived in the open. The shortage of females highlighted other stark material contrasts between life in Mineside and in Townside. After work, settled workers in Mineside returned to wives, children, and domestic privacy, but transient inhabitants had none of the basic amenities that fostered sobriety, stability, and fear of the company. Approximately half of the miners had little else to do with their money and free time than to drink with their mates, so the mixture of individual frustrations and inescapable spatial and social inequalities proved an explosive cocktail.

The structure of the local alcohol trade fostered tensions as well. Up to the mid-1940s, the thousands of parched miners had only two licensed establishments at which to drink. Mineside residents had to walk to the east bank of the Leichhardt for a glass of beer, so the effort required to get a drink did not promote moderate consumption. Locating the two hotels a few paces apart in the heart of downtown Townside confined scores of drinkers to a small area, and shift work at the mine ensured a steady supply of drinkers. The cavernous insides of the hotels functioned not as places to relax and enjoy a drink, but palaces of dingo piss. On paydays, men 'four or five deep' crowded the bars passing dripping glasses over the heads of the waiting throng to their friends in the back. The beer itself 'came from Townsville [on the coast] and traveled out to the Isa in wooden kegs in an open truck, merely covered by a canvas tarp. The beer must have been well-heated during the trip and was then chilled at the Isa. The resultant brew was fighting beer.'[39]

Persistent complaints from residents during the employment boom following the Second World War convinced authorities to allow local publicans to open a third hotel downtown, but that did not reduce crowding or binge drinking. Meanwhile, other residents complained about the inability to procure fresh bread.[40] Throughout this period, police, court, and military records suggest scores of arrests every month on charges of profanity, assault, and public mischief stemming from intoxication. Between June and September 1929, for instance, police arrested 216 people on one or more of these common 'trifecta' charges.[41]

The limitations of drinking at the hotels prompted a number of spin-off activities. Sly-grog shops peddled bootlegged or home-brewed spirits that residents could take home or to the camp. Prior to the Second World War, Boyd's Hotel had attached to the enclosed drinking area what residents called a 'bullring.' According to publican Harry Smith, 'Any man who felt like a fight, and there were quite a few in the early days, could go and punch it out in peace.' The town doctor got into the act as the bullring's unofficial referee and medic. The sheer number and variety of these anecdotes implies a pervasive sense of social dislocation and unease. Alarmed permanent residents described the prevalence of drunkenness as a macho reaction to loneliness and the scarcity of female companionship.[42]

Most drank to quench thirst and to socialize in a rough fraternity that remained virtually the same, no matter faces or place. By shouting rounds, hotel patrons showed workmates and neighbours that they were ordinary blokes and not company snobs. The more incisive workers viewed alcohol consumption and its informal customs as ingredients of class solidarity and a mild subversion of management's attempts to instil in them middle-class values of sobriety, hard work, thrift, and respect for the company. Police complained that workers of the 'nomadic type' had 'little or no respect for law and order' and usually found the men unresponsive when police asked them for statements about unsolved crimes.[43] Workers' distrust of authorities stemmed from their daily experiences. MIM compelled workers to accept policies that invaded their bodily space such as mandatory medical exams, recurring speed-ups, and lectures by managers on how to perform their jobs more efficiently. The company even tried to regulate employees' sleep patterns, their alcohol and cigarette intake, and the regularity of their bowel movements.[44]

Workers, especially those who did not plan to settle in the Isa, scoffed at MIM's attempts to control their bodies and what they regarded as police nosing about in their private business. Veteran industrial labourers understood that the police were 'most anxious to prevent any industrial unrest' and desired to, as one local police officer put it, 'assist the Mines management to carry on the peaceful and satisfactory working of their great Industry.'[45] The shared consumption of alcohol represented to workers a small rebellion against propriety and authority, affirming their fundamental control over their own bodies and tying mobile labourers to a working-class culture with its own unwritten rules and codes of behaviour. A former Isa miner recalled that when passed a bottle he never wiped the top. 'It was a sign of bad faith.'[46] Boozing also served as a temporary escape from social pressures. Ingrained resignation does not appear to have been the motivator.

Despite the ritual equality and reciprocity of shouting rounds at the bar, despite the comradeship of mates collectively hoisting a cold one, Mount Isa's culture of drink entrenched inequality – a fact that the record bears out time and again. High alcohol consumption among workers helped MIM legitimize its local authority by intensifying disagreements between workers and personal posturing, and altercations distracted men from fundamental issues of worker subordination to capital. Magistrates' bench books and inquest files show that drunkenness resulted in petty crime and frequent outbursts of physical violence between workers and residents. Alcoholism ravaged bodies and minds and, if unchecked, could lead to creeping decline and death.[47]

In drinking, workers reacted against subordination by inflicting physical and psychological injuries on themselves and those in their immediate circle, not on the corporate authority. Drunken or hung-over workers may have threatened productivity to a miniscule degree but the company had men eager to replace them. Craving another pot of beer did not prompt rational collective action but the disintegration of interpersonal relationships, class solidarity, and community. It divided workers – particularly the settled employees from the flow-through workers – instead of uniting them. Intoxication in Isa's intensely macho culture resulted in drinkers' heightened sensitivity to character slurs and melodramatic displays of chest-beating. In rank-and-file industrial politics, extreme behaviours and lack of patience among workers contributed to the tendency for snap work stoppages and disorganized attempts at forcing MIM managers to heel instead of calmly negotiating compromises or planning systematically to overturn the local order.

The regularity of other unsavoury activities confirms the tone of opposition in the town. The local print media as well as regional and state news organs published articles about drunken rowdiness and the sordid details of assaults and murders. The leaning of the Queensland press toward Tory sensationalism and issues of law and order is evident throughout the record. In Mount Isa before the end of the Second World War, local magistrates' bench books filled quickly with cases of verbal (swearing was punishable by fining) and physical violence, petty frauds and thefts, and all types of public mischief. Perusal of court records of each town suggests that the number of prosecuted crimes in Corner Brook – by no means small – pales in comparison to the number of cases heard at Mount Isa.[48]

Descriptions of the town from the 1960s onward used the roughness of the early decades in Mount Isa to link the town's past to national ideals of indomitable masculinity and stubbornly independent bloke-ism popular among Australians of all political stripes. Later commentators always compared the roughness of the early years to Isa's current settled character. By the late 1950s, just a few short years before the town's two most explosive labour disputes, *MIMag* gushed about the settlement's new-found 'dignity' and its 'miraculous' progress. Geoffrey Blainey's company-sponsored local history described post-war progress in glowing terms. By the early 1970s, state and national media described how Aussie pluck and persistence turned Mount Isa into the suburban 'hub' for a vast, valuable hinterland.[49] Noreen Kirkman's 1998 assessment portrayed the Isa as a paradisiacal *Oasis of the Outback*. But using the history of Mount Isa as a tale of national vigour and progress obscures the conflicts at the heart of the town's history, whitewashing the conflicts that created a settled society between the 1950s and 1970s.

The company struggled mightily to acclimatize its workforce to its conflicted corporate temperament by which MIM demanded strict control on the shop floor but wanted to be seen as the caring father beyond the gates. In neither capacity did it willingly negotiate, compromise, or concede. Subsequently, few workers or residents saw MIM in the same light as its directors and mangers did. For most of Mount Isa's history all inhabitants of Townside balked at what they perceived to be corporate arrogance. Grievances against local authority took hold quickly among the egalitarian, independent-minded population. But the oppositional tone did not arise just out of direct relations with the company. It grew out of multiple personal experiences of place and relations with other subordinate people over whom the company had little or no influence. The gradual shifting of thousands of individual mindsets as well as top-down coercion from the company and Queensland government generated stability in the town.

Australians emerged from the economic collapse and unparalleled global bloodletting of the first half of the twentieth century into an era of domestic plenty. By the early 1950s general economic prosperity and governments' commitment to social spending made it possible for well-paid workers to buy houses, appliances, and cars. MIM had attempted home-purchase schemes in the early 1930s but employees smartly refused to be tied down. The first post-war company housing initiatives continued to be based on tenancy, not ownership. Change occurred as a process, not in a moment.

Between the mid-1950s and mid-1960s the majority of Isa's former tenants and flow-through workers decided to buy houses and settle down. MIM officials caught on to Australians' growing desire for ownership. Private ownership drives began in the mid-1950s. Settled residents bought houses first. Mortgaged houses and leased appliances and cars cultivated the desire for local stability and opened up the small freedoms of holiday vacations and family pride in private property. But this burst of materialism closed off the willingness of some to stand up to the company. The crackdown by MIM and the state government's on labour militants – personified by rough mobile workers like Pat Mackie – confirmed the tendency toward settled relations by the end of 1964–5 dispute.

But top-down directives could not manufacture stability. Regardless of company coercions, residents had to choose ownership and permanence over tenancy and mobility for true stability to grow. Individuals accepted the responsibilities of permanence largely on their own schedules and for their own reasons. Alex Pavusa, the president of the Isa TLC, in the early 1970s summed up the miners' internalization of corporate authority. After the 1964–5 dispute 'the bachelors left the town' he said, 'but the married people hung on. They always have to hang on.' As a result, the town was more peaceful and workers and management did not 'snarl at each other anymore.'[50]

Home-ownership and the trappings of permanence never fully transformed the tone of local society though. Transient workers continued to comprise approximately one fifth of the workforce. Some residents' enduring fondness for 'the turps and the piss' remained high, though increasingly spread among air-conditioned clubs or drunk at home. Overall a confluence of reciprocal local and global – bottom-up and top-down – circumstances in the 1950s and 1960s shifted the structure of feeling at Mount Isa from one in which the company had to struggle for legitimacy with an antagonistic population to one where residents' desires for social stability jibed with directors' wishes for stable production and profits.

For six decades, underlying demographic and social tensions had made Mount Isa's structure of feeling oppositional. Yet the ability of inhabitants to leave at a moment's notice, the legacies of tense domestic and social interactions, and the allure of high pay also confirmed a measure of open-endedness and personal autonomy. Workers and residents ridiculed the company and tried to resist or circumvent its most objectionable practices in a variety of formal and informal ways. Few tried to overturn MIM's authority, and none did so systematically. During the 1960s and 1970s, as they internalized notions of homeownership and permanence, Isans developed better relations with the company. Change occurred at the level of thousands of real lives and was only partial.

Closer examination reveals exceptions to observations made from afar. According to Rex Lucas, inhabitants of company towns reacted to corporate control by withdrawing from the public and industrial spheres into 'private worlds' and 'personal relationships.'[51] But his influential fatalism thesis, much like the overarching structuralist definition of company towns it seeks to confirm, obscures more than it illuminates.

Residents of Mount Isa and Corner Brook used small autonomies for a variety of reasons. Fatalism was only one sentiment in the constellation of emotions arising out of the richness of daily life. In contrast to the accommodationist disposition in Corner Brook, the contradictions at the heart of daily life in Mount Isa fostered antagonism. People in Corner Brook preferred conciliation and the avoidance of serious conflict. Many Isans, meanwhile, lived involuntarily in the public eye and presented tough personas that made social cohesion difficult. Divergent local structures of feeling like these forced corporations to adapt to local peculiarities in order to gain consent for their authority. More crucially still for a study of company towns, the unique structures of feeling that rose out of residents' daily navigation of immediate relationships and structural limitations stamped the societies of Mount Isa and Corner Brook with peculiar dynamics that confirms deep variety in the broader structures of industry and economy.

Conclusion

The people of Corner Brook who 'didn't want for anything' did not mean that they experienced no conflict, sorrow, or unfulfilled dreams in the western Newfoundland mill town. In a similar way, residents who fought for 'fair dinkum' relations between townspeople, the mining company, and the government in Mount Isa certainly did not harbour the illusion that they would achieve perfect equality in the Queensland outback. These impressions capture diverging social attitudes in two company towns but they do not tell the whole story. To uncover the subtle but crucial differences between company towns like Mount Isa and Corner Brook and to explain the reasons for those differences, it is necessary to look more broadly and probe more deeply into the living histories that intersected to make them.

Those histories do not follow the paths laid out in structuralist accounts of wilderness transformed instantly by courageous capitalists into productive land, or of company control and resident resignation. Women like Corner Brook housewife Marian Oxford, whose breadwinner husband asked her to guide the family's finances through the Great Depression, participated actively in local history. So did the men of Mount Isa when they engaged in rough mine work and Queensland labour politics and spent their free time perfecting home gardens. Neither case conveys predictability or fatalism. Local characters like Pat Mackie and John Noah each in his own way epitomized the dynamism and agency of ordinary people as well as the tones of social life in the two towns. Then, a couple rungs up the social ladder, company managers like John Stadler and Julius Kruttschnitt had the difficult job of navigating local and global obstacle courses. Stadler failed in his task where Kruttschnitt succeeded. The sheer diversity of personal experience – from bottom to top, from the home outward into the broader socio-economic arena – reveals a range of agency and constraint, negotiation, struggle, and accommodation that turns the simple company town type into distinct communities with historical value far beyond the clumsy banalities of structure.

The current trajectories of Corner Brook and Mount Isa confound the accepted model of company town demise as well. After more than eight decades, the Corner Brook paper mill is now the only operating paper plant in Newfoundland and one of a dwindling number of mills in eastern Canada, many of which began operations after Corner Brook. Industrial restructuring has slashed the mill and woods workforces to fractions of their 1950s levels while, on a more positive note, the mill has diversified into making paper from recycled material. Like its industrial patron, the town of Corner Brook has for several decades been in a state of slow decline. It is highly likely that the mill will close in the coming decade and that Corner Brook will shrink as a result, but its status as a regional service centre will help it remain a viable town.

Mount Isa, on the other hand, experienced resurgence in the past decade. The collapsing American Smelting and Refining Company sold MIM to global metals giant Xstrata PLC in 2003 for more than $2 billion. The Swiss conglomerate expanded mineral exploitation in the region to benefit from Queensland's close market ties to the surging economies of Asia. The population of the town is now over thirty thousand and growing. In August 2008, Mount Isa Mayor John Molony raised the ire of Australians and sensible people everywhere when he placed ads with Australian media outlets asking 'ugly duckling' and 'beauty-disadvantaged' women to move to the mining town, where he said men outnumbered women five to one.[1] Census figures from 2006 reported the sexual imbalance to be much smaller than Molony claimed, but the point remains that more than eighty years since its founding, Mount Isa is still a rough mining town.

From similar beginnings, the histories of Mount Isa and Corner Brook are still diverging from one another and from the course company towns are supposed to follow. The same distinct, living histories doubtlessly exist in other human settlements too often considered overly structured by external forces.

Corporate Order and Community shows that company towns differ from one another not just in eras of origination and local timelines but also substantively in the processes that fuelled industrial and town construction, and workforce and community development. It takes the analysis several levels deeper than do the conventional accounts and by doing so shows the sorely neglected but central roles human agency, unintended consequences, and adaptation play in making company towns distinct from one another. Corporations and governments did not conspire in a void to bring Corner Brook or Mount Isa into existence. Critical comparison shows that the companies navigated – sometimes cleverly, sometimes foolhardily – external constraints while struggling to secure the consent of workers and residents whom they defined as subordinates. When people settled each place, however, only the barest physical and administrative outlines of society existed. Residents' myriad negotiations, accommodations, and resistances played a vital unquantifiable role in creating the distinct character of each place. In this way, the study speaks more generally to the relationships between people and place, power and subordination in history, and to how global capital assumes different forms at the local level.

The expansion of capital into the Newfoundland forest and Australian outback in the 1920s followed highly dissimilar paths. In terms of capital risk, a Newfoundland paper mill was a known quantity, but an outback silver-lead mine was a serious gamble. The companies' front offices and financial situations differed. Armstrong came out of the First World War with tremendously expanded capacity but with no market for its weapons, while Bolshevik expropriations erased Leslie Urquhart's Russian mining empire overnight. Here individual personalities came into play. Glyn West, chairman of Armstrong, approached the Humber project with unshakeable confidence in his company's ability to succeed in whatever industry it undertook. Desperation fuelled Urquhart. His single-minded determination to regain stolen industrial glory made him attempt to micromanage the outback industrial scheme.

Managerial will ran into economic, political, geographical, and local human constraints on corporate action. The base-metal market in Queensland had been declining since the turn of the century. The isolation of the deposit on the sparsely settled western edge of the Cloncurry field forced Urquhart to build the highly mechanized mine, processing plants, and employee settlement on one site instantly, but his decision lowered even further the chances of suitable short-term returns on his investment. North American newsprint markets, by contrast, had been booming since the end of the First World War. Armstrong, however, entered the market at the bursting of the bubble. It spent lavishly on construction and on establishing market links from western Newfoundland to the mainland, and the island's crisis-prone political administration could not cushion Armstrong's fall when the financial crunch came. Added to these structural constraints were the demands of thousands of working residents that both companies had to deal with. Both foreign developers failed, but for different reasons, at different times, and with different local outcomes.

Corporate-sponsored town planning and the growth of fringe communities delineated the unique built environment of each town and its social inequalities. Armstrong built the 'one-off' Garden City–style Townsite at Corner Brook between 1924 and 1930. Newcomers to the region who were not part of the company's core of skilled specialists created sprawling but vibrant fringe communities. Industrial stability and the generally cordial relations between residents and managers enabled the separate communities of Corner Brook to grow together gradually from the 1930s on. Russo-Asiatic's planned town was but the first in a pulsating sequence of mass house-building projects at Mount Isa. The Mount Isa companies' wildly fluctuating industrial fortunes contributed to chronically high employee attrition. MIM felt compelled to build, retrofit, demolish, and build anew thousands of dwellings. Meanwhile, many Isans viewed Townside as the legitimate settlement of Mount Isa. State and regional governments neglected their charge, however, and Townside became the fringe to Mineside's planned town. For much of its history Townside comprised rough local businesses, the tents and 'humpies' of transient labourers, and the only saloons in the area. The Corner Brook fringe towns acted like safety valves for the local corporate order. Mount Isa's Townside acted more like a geyser. Despite the superficial similarities of planned and fringe towns, the spatial orders of Mount Isa and Corner Brook were unique and they generated distinctive social dynamics.

The towns' labour histories contrast strikingly. At Corner Brook, skilled and unskilled mill workers had far greater financial and social security than their 'contracted' forestry counterparts. Newfoundlanders also had little knowledge of class politics, and the international unions they chose as representatives shied away from challenging capital. Labour relations in Corner Brook evinced little outright class conflict. Urquhart's fateful decision to mine and process ore at Mount Isa made all employees live and work together on a single field. The prominent position of labour in Australian society made workers intensely territorial when management encroached on areas of traditional worker control. In the culture of labour independence and radicalism in Queensland,

MIM pre-empted labour militancy with mechanization, speed-ups, and scientific management. Tension multiplied in the mine and the town. Periodic wildcat strikes, lockouts, and government-enforced states of emergency troubled the mine for decades until company, state government, union bureaucrats, and mass media combined forces to neuter and discredit labour in the mid-1960s. Local expressions of class conflict were central to community character and the maintenance of social order at Mount Isa.

Until the early 1960s, Mount Isa's small business owners depended on unpredictable mine workers for their survival. Formal civic life at Mount Isa was infused with anti-company sentiment that did not cease until MIM gradually ceded local control to residents. Self-government cemented boosters' new ties to its number one corporate citizen, Mount Isa Mines. The history of Corner Brook differed in this respect too. Residents of Corner Brook never rallied to class issues the way that Isans did. Denizens of the quickly settled mill town considered themselves residents first. Small businesses crowded the hillsides bordering Townsite as soon as mill construction began, establishing a local small business sector larger than that in most other Newfoundland settlements. Residents accepted company aid in establishing utilities and creating community organizations. After 1955 supporters of municipal unity tried to assuage long-running parochial gripes to no avail. The substitution of amiable, aloof paterfamilias Bowater by the 'fearless' political leader Joseph Smallwood compounded local civic divisions. Class had no direct bearing on the divisive and dramatic protest over the school tax or Smallwood's end to local self-government.

Finally, differences in ordinary Isans' and Corner Brookers' experience of daily life produced different structures of feeling in each town. The company had almost no power over the ways residents felt or acted in their personal lives. Feeling shaped residents' perceptions of and approaches to corporate order and created community identities.

Corner Brook settled quickly and achieved rapid sexual parity. Newfoundlanders viewed the area as relatively attractive compared to the insecurity of the outports, whereas Mount Isa's geographic isolation and extreme climate reinforced migrants' rough working-class attitudes, fostering the persistent and well-founded belief that the Isa was a place for tough male miners. Few women settled there and tense homo-sociable relationships dominated. Isans tended towards antagonism and opposition while residents of Corner Brook favoured conciliation, accommodation, and minimizing conflicts.

The intersections of all of these histories formed webs of power relations always in process. The company town was not a uniform or mechanistic social system. My demonstration of top-down and bottom-up interactions on multiple levels of company-town society directs the study of company towns away from clichéd structural determinism to a critical historical perspective that portrays company officials and residents alike as constrained agents in an ongoing fashioning, contesting, and refashioning of local hegemonies.

We can understand company towns fully only by understanding the wider histories of industrial and economic development in concert with the people who inhabited them. The same point is true for the industrial enclaves in today's globalized world. The reluctance to deepen the understanding of borderland industrial sites like company towns prevails in contemporary studies of export-processing zones. Many works on such zones downplay the struggles of working residents in favour of broad structural analyses and the belief that corporations have such control over workers that ordinary people have no agency worth writing about. But just like John Noah, Pat Mackie, and the cast of thousands in Corner Brook and Mount Isa fashioned distinct ways of dealing with corporate power, zone residents, too, exhibit a broad range of negotiation and struggle in their daily lives. From the Southeast Asian assembly lines shut down over workers' claims of 'spirit possession' to the community improvement and education centres of northern Mexico and the burgeoning global micro-credit movement, ordinary people are active participants in the shaping of their societies. Company towns are object lessons in the value of historicizing and humanizing dependent industrial enclaves.

The study of surviving and vanished company towns can be expanded into emerging fields of historical inquiry as well. Environmental and public health historians may find research gold mines in the towns based on the extraction of primary resources. Mount Isa's problems with lead poisoning in the 1930s have again become front page news following new evidence of high ambient lead levels in the community. The Corner Brook mill has its own murky history of industrial pollution. The growing realization that the waste from industry may have had as big an impact on the world as the products of industry could be better contextualized by studying how people dealt with – or more likely ignored – environmental protection in the places where the staples of consumer capitalism came from.

The contrasts that emerge from this study are not attributable to a single factor like capitalism, industry type, or national identity. Instead, the tense interactions among the organizing powers of abstract structures like market forces, governments, and labour mixed with the active reinterpretation of structure by people in specific moments and places to cause divergence at the local level. Difference matters. It matters not just to inhabitants or to local historians but to anyone trying to understand the countless ways power, agency, and subordination are expressed in society.

A goal of history is to explain change over time by analysing past human motivations and events. It is these details that make company towns historical subjects in their own right and not the standardized product of global capitalism. Only capitalists and their political allies benefit from overly structured readings of the past. Corporations in company towns appear as a priori authorities instead of what they truly were: fallible, socially constructed groups struggling to secure the consent of ordinary people. Human agents with all their imperfections and constraints prompted change. Nothing was preordained. The considerable and substantive differences between the local orders at Mount Isa and Corner Brook affirm the inestimable potential of human agency, even in places that developed out of tremendous structural asymmetries.

Notes

Introduction

1 Marx and Engels, *Communist Manifesto*.
2 The seminal studies tend to describe company towns in structuralist terms. See Blainey, *Rush That Never Ended*; Bradbury, 'Towards an Alternative Theory of Resource-Based Town Development in Canada'; Bulmer, 'Sociological Models of the Mining Community'; Institute of Local Government, *Single-Enterprise Communities in Canada*; Lucas, *Minetown, Milltown, Railtown*; McCann, 'Changing Internal Structure of Canadian Resource Towns'; Saarinen, 'Single-Sector Communities in Northern Ontario'; and Stelter and Artibise, 'Canadian Resource Towns in Historical Perspective.'
3 http://en.wikipedia.org/wiki/Ghost_town#Australia; Australian Government, Australian Mines Atlas; Carlson, *Company Towns of the Pacific Northwest*, 3, 6.
4 Lucas, *Minetown, Milltown, Railtown*, 15, 17; Canadian Encyclopedia, *s.v.*, 'Resource Towns,' http://www.thecanadianencyclopedia.com/index.cfm?PgNm=TCE&Params=A1ARTA0006789.
5 Eklund, '"Intelligently Directed Welfare Work"?,' 126, 129; Eklund, 'Managers, Workers, and Industrial Welfarism,' 138, 146–7, 153; Mouat, *Roaring Days*; Silverstein, 'Shopping for Sweat,' 42–4; White, 'Global Industrial Enclaves,' 118–19.
6 Lucas, *Minetown, Milltown, Railtown*, xii.
7 Comparison has been employed in industrial and labour histories of industrial towns, but less so in questioning the assumptions about company towns. See Eklund, 'Managers, Workers, and Industrial Welfarism'; Faue, 'Community, Class, and Comparison in Labour History and Local History'; Mouat, 'Industry and Community'; Parr, *Gender of Breadwinners*;

Patmore, 'Working Lives in Regional Australia,' 1, 3, 6; Rollwagen, 'When Ghosts Hovered.'

8 Inglis, *Clifford Geertz*, 3, 19; Geertz, *After the Fact*, 19–20; Geertz, *Interpretation of Cultures*, 17–20.

Chapter 1

1 Scott, *Vickers*, 126.
2 Braverman, *Labor and Monopoly Capital*; Chandler, *Visible Hand*, 24, 285–489, 491–500; John, 'Elaborations, Revisions, Dissents,' 155–6, 158, 187–94, 199–200.
3 Dougan, *Great Gun-Maker*, 62–3, 90–2, 167–8.
4 Scott, *Vickers*, 129; Dougan, *Great Gun-Maker*, 143–7, 152, 177–8.
5 Scott, *Vickers*, 137.
6 Ibid., 143–4; Reader, *Bowater*, 33.
7 Irving, 'New Industries for Old?,' 15; Scott, *Vickers*, 137, 152.
8 Hiller, 'Politics of Newsprint,' 13.
9 Irving, 'New Industries for Old?,' 163.
10 Ibid., 163; Scott, *Vickers*, 91, 153.
11 Hiller, 'Origins of the Pulp and Paper Industry in Newfoundland,' 46–68.
12 W.H. Greenwood to Douglas Spencer, July 1920, file 22, box 1, MG17, The Rooms Provincial Archives (hereafter Rooms), St John's; Harry Reid to Douglas Spencer, 1920, file 22, box 1, MG17, Rooms; Reid to Spencer, 27 April 1921, file 22, box 1, MG17, Rooms; Hiller, 'Politics of Newsprint,' 12–13.
13 Alexander, 'Newfoundland's Traditional Economy and Development to 1934,' 69–70.
14 Ibid., 64; Noel, *Politics in Newfoundland*, 28–31.
15 'Fisher Agreement,' 1902, file 27, box 2, MG17, Rooms; Norcliffe, *Global Game, Local Arena*, 54–5.
16 Hiller, 'Politics of Newsprint,' 4–6; Noel, *Politics in Newfoundland*, 29, 62.
17 Hiller, 'Politics of Newsprint,' 6; Noel, *Politics in Newfoundland*, 153–5, 157–8.
18 Elliott, 'Newfoundland Politics in the 1920s,' 183, 185.
19 Noel, *Politics in Newfoundland*, 151–2; *Times* (London), 12 April 1916, 7; 27 March 1918, 8; 14 May 1919, 8; 25 October 1919, 9; and 28 April 1922, 11.
20 House of Assembly, *Journal of the House of Assembly of Newfoundland*, 526.
21 Hiller, 'Politics of Newsprint,' 7–12.
22 Douglas Spencer to W.H. Greenwood, July 1920.
23 Douglas Spencer to Harry Reid, spring 1920, file 22, box 1, MG17, Rooms;

Douglas Spencer to Harry Reid, 23 and 27 April 1921, file 22, box 1, MG17, Rooms; Arthur Whiteley to Glyn West, 26 May 1924, box 56 (Corner Brook Material box 1), MG17, Rooms; Hiller, 'Politics of Newsprint,' 12–13.

24 Hiller, 'Politics of Newsprint,' 12–13; J.A. MacDonald to Harry Reid, 15 July 1921, file 22, box 1, MG17, Rooms.

25 Walter Preston to Harry Reid, 8 July 1921, file 22, box 1, MG17, Rooms; Harry Reid to Douglas Spencer, 13 July 1921, file 22, box 1, MG17, Rooms.

26 Hiller, 'Politics of Newsprint,' 14–15.

27 Ibid., 15.

28 Sir W.G. Armstrong, Whitworth and Company, Ltd, Agreement, 5 July 1922; Hiller, 'Politics of Newsprint,' 16.

29 Hiller, 'Politics of Newsprint,' 16.

30 *Western Star* (Corner Brook), 8 November 1922, 2; 16 May 1922, 1.

31 Provisional Board of Directors Meeting, 31 October 1922, box 56 (Corner Brook Material box 1), MG17, Rooms; Secretary London Committee, Minutes 1922–3, box 56 (Corner Brook Material box 1), MG17, Rooms; Arthur Whiteley to Glyn West, 26 May 1924, box 56 (Corner Brook Material box 1), MG17, Rooms; Douglas Spencer to Harry Reid, 23 and 27 April 1921, file 22, box 1, MG17, Rooms; Provisional Board of Directors Meeting, 17 November 1922, box 56 (Corner Brook Material box 1), MG17, Rooms.

32 Ankli, 'Canadian Newsprint Industry, 1900–1940,' 8.

33 Hiller, 'Politics of Newsprint,' 17–18.

34 Reader, *Bowater*, 34–6.

35 Newfoundland Power and Paper Company, *Corner Brook Development for Messrs Sir W.G. Armstrong, Whitworth and Company Ltd.*

36 George Carpenter to Charles Conroy, 11 March 1924; Charles Conroy to George Carpenter, 28 March 1924, box 56 (Corner Brook Material box 1), MG17, Rooms.

37 Scott, *Vickers*, 154.

38 *Times* (London), 17 May 1923, 11.

39 Arthur Whiteley to Glyn West, 26 May 1924, box 56 (Corner Brook Material box 1), MG17, Rooms; NP&P Board of Directors Meeting, 18 June 1924, file 306, box 15, MG17, Rooms; *Western Star* (Corner Brook), 2 July 1924, 3.

40 *Western Star* (Corner Brook), 1 October 1924, 1; R. Burns to William Monroe, 4 December 1924, file 226, box 22, GN8, Rooms; Scott, *Vickers*, 153.

41 *Times* (London), 22 May 1924, 24.

42 Hiller, 'Politics of Newsprint,' 22; Scott, *Vickers*, 161; *Times* (London), 29 November 1927, 25.

43 Hiller, 'Politics of Newsprint,' 22; Scott, *Vickers*, 154–5; Arthur Whiteley to

Glyn West, 26 May 1924, box 56 (Corner Brook Material box 1), 6, MG17, Rooms.

44 *Times* (London), 9 June 1926, 22 and 24.

45 Scott, *Vickers*, 163 and 166; *Times* (London), 23 December 1926, 16.

46 *Times* (London), 9 June 1926, 25; Hiller, 'Politics of Newsprint,' 23.

47 H.B. Clyde Lake to William Monroe, 27 March 1926, file 226, box 22, GN8, Rooms; Harry Reid to W.H. Leese, 6 November 1926, box 57 (Corner Brook Material box 2), MG17, Rooms.

48 Hiller, 'Politics of Newsprint,' 24, 29.

49 *Times* (London), 9 June 1926, 24.

50 Ankli, 'Canadian Newsprint Industry,' 8; Hiller, 'Politics of Newsprint,' 24; *Western Star* (Corner Brook), 21 December 1927, 2.

51 Ankli, 'Canadian Newsprint Industry,' 7–9; Nelles, *Politics of Development*, 346, 348, 344.

52 Boothman, 'High Finance / Low Strategy,' 654, 656.

53 Ankli, 'Canadian Newsprint Industry,' 8.

54 *Times* (London), 4 and 10 June 1927, 16 and 20.

55 Heinrich, 'Product Diversification in the U.S. Pulp and Paper Industry,' 474–6, 480.

56 Ibid., 478, 480.

57 Harry J. Crowe to Patrick T. McGrath, 2 April 1926, file 182, MG8, Rooms.

58 Hiller, 'Politics of Newsprint,' 26–30; Horwood, *Corner Brook*, 38; International Paper Company, 'Survey of Expansion of International Paper Company during 1927.'

59 Hiller, 'Politics of Newsprint,' 10–11; Horwood, *Corner Brook*, 39; *Western Star* (Corner Brook), 24 June 1931, 9.

60 Ankli, 'Canadian Newsprint Industry,' 8; Hiller, 'Politics of Newsprint,' 31.

61 Department of Public Health and Welfare, *Tenth Census of Newfoundland and Labrador*, 1:595; Government of Newfoundland, *Eleventh Census of Newfoundland and Labrador*, 1:12.

62 Alexander, 'Newfoundland's Traditional Economy and Development to 1934,' 73, 76; Peter Neary, *Newfoundland in the North Atlantic World*, 12–13.

63 Ankli, 'Canadian Newsprint Industry,' 8, 15; Hiller, 'Politics of Newsprint,' 31–3.

64 *Western Star* (Corner Brook), 6 July 1932, 2; Bowater Oral History Project (hereafter BOHP), tape B-5, side A; Newfoundland Royal Commission, *Report*, 150.

65 Neary, 'Bradley Report on Logging Operations in Newfoundland, 1934,' 208–9, 212.

66 Ankli, 'Canadian Newsprint Industry,' 15–16.
67 Heinrich, 'Product Diversification,' 488, 492–4.
68 Noel, *Politics in Newfoundland*; Neary, *Newfoundland in the North Atlantic World*.
69 Hiller, 'Politics of Newsprint,' 33.
70 Reader, *Bowater*, 134, 139–41, 145–6.
71 *Globe and Mail*, 3 June 1938, 20; Hiller, 'Politics of Newsprint,' 36.
72 Hiller, 'Politics of Newsprint,' 31; Horwood, *Corner Brook*, 71–4, 82; Reader, *Bowater*, 178–9.
73 Horwood, *Corner Brook*, 86–8; Norcliffe, *Global Game, Local Arena*, 71–2.
74 Norcliffe, *Global Game, Local Arena*, 72–3.
75 Reader, *Bowater*, 172, 223, 231.
76 *Western Star* (Corner Brook), 28 May 1948, 1.

Chapter 2

1 Blackmur, 'Arbitration, Legislation and Industrial Peace,' 133.
2 Fitzgerald, *History of Queensland*, 6–7; Sherlock, '"Good-bye the State's Progress,"' 63.
3 K.H. Kennedy, 'Mining,' 282–3; Sherlock, '"Good-bye the State's Progress,"' 61–2, 65.
4 K.H. Kennedy, 'Mining,' 291; Blainey, *Mines in the Spinifex*, 106; Fitzgerald, *History of Queensland*, 8–11, 54; MacIntyre, *Concise History of Australia*, 162–3.
5 Peter Bell, 'International Investment in Early Mount Isa,' 2:293–4; Blainey, *Mines in the Spinifex*, 77.
6 K.H. Kennedy, 'Mining,' 283; McGowan, 'Class, Hegemony and Localism'; Mouat, 'Industry and Community,' 268, 274
7 Mouat, 'Industry and Community,' 268.
8 Blainey, *Mines in the Spinifex*, 9–10.
9 Armstrong, *Kalkadoons*, 150.
10 Gibson and Horvath, 'Global Capital and the Restructuring Crisis,' 183.
11 Blainey, *Mines in the Spinifex*, 34, 43, 48.
12 Blainey, *Mines in the Spinifex*, 54; Eklund, *Steel Town*; K.H. Kennedy, 'Mining,' 284; MacIntyre, *Concise History of Australia*, 152; Sheldon, *Industrial Siege*, 3.
13 Blainey, *Mines in the Spinifex*, 68–9; Kirkman, *Mount Isa*, 4–5; Sheldon, *Industrial Siege*, 1–2.
14 Blainey, *Mines in the Spinifex*, 78; Kirkman, *Mount Isa*, 5.
15 Steinkamp, 'Mining Town in the Social Environment,' 2.

16 Blainey, *Mines in the Spinifex*, 83–5; Ian Hore-Lacy, ed., *Broken Hill to Mount Isa*; K.H. Kennedy, 'Mount Isa Mines,' 54; Kirkman, *Mount Isa*, 5–6.

17 Kirkman, *Mount Isa*, 7–9; *Queensland Government Mining Journal* 25 (December 1924): 488.

18 'Correspondences regarding Squatters and Town Planning, 1948,' Mines Department II, A/8430, Queensland State Archives (hereafter QSA); Drynan, 'The History of Mount Isa'; Kirkman, *Mount Isa*, 9–10.

19 K.H. Kennedy, 'Mining,' 288–89; Kirkman, *Mount Isa*, 14; Steinkamp, 'Mining Town in the Social Environment,' 2.

20 Blainey, *Mines in the Spinifex*, 98–100.

21 K.H. Kennedy, 'Mount Isa Mines,' 54; *Queensland Government Mining Journal* 28 (June 1927): 245.

22 *Queensland Government Mining Journal* 28 (January 1927): 2; Blainey, *Mines in the Spinex*, 118; Hore-Lacy, *Broken Hill to Mount Isa*, 193–9; Kirkman, *Mount Isa*, 16–17; *Times* (London), 24 June 1927, 24.

23 Blainey, *Mines in the Spinifex*, 118; Hore-Lacy, *Broken Hill to Mount Isa*, 199.

24 Blainey, *Mines in the Spinifex*, 121–2; K.H. Kennedy, 'Mount Isa's Russian Connection,' 195–6.

25 K.H. Kennedy, 'Mount Isa Mines,' 55.

26 Ibid.

27 *Times* (London), 25 April 1928, 25; Blainey, *Mines in the Spinifex*, 125.

28 Blainey, *Mines in the Spinifex*, 125; Chaput and Kennedy, *Man from ASARCO*.

29 *Times* (London), 1 July 1927, 24; K.H. Kennedy, 'Mount Isa Mines,' 55.

30 *Queensland Government Mining Journal* 29 (February 1928): 55.

31 Bell, 'International Investment in Early Mount Isa,' 291; Gibson and Horvath, 'Global Capital and the Restructuring Crisis in Australian Manufacturing,' 187; K.H. Kennedy, 'Mount Isa's Russian Connection,' 196; *Times* (London), 25 April 1928, 25. Urquhart's reliance on mechanization and scientific management to stem labour militancy presaged developments in Mount Isa and in the national Australian industrial economy after the Second World War.

32 K.H. Kennedy, 'Mount Isa Mines,' 56.

33 *Times* (London), 1 July 1927, 24; Blainey, *Mines in the Spinifex*, 138.

34 Blainey, *Mines in the Spinifex*, 135.

35 *Times* (London), 5 June 1929, 22; Blainey, *Mines in the Spinifex*, 137–8.

36 *Times* (London), 5 June 1929, 22; and 13 November 1929, 23; *Queensland Government Mining Journal* 31 (April 1930): 176.

37 *Times* (London), 13 November 1929, 23; 16 May 1930, 26.

38 *Queensland Government Mining Journal* 31 (May 1930): 189.

39 K.H. Kennedy, 'Mining,' 291; Moore's Address to Parliament, 17 July 1930, *Queensland Parliamentary Debates*, 63.
40 K.H. Kennedy, 'Mount Isa Mines,' 56.
41 Blainey, *Mines in the Spinifex*, 139–44; Chaput and Kennedy, *Man from ASARCO*, 134.
42 K.H. Kennedy, 'Mount Isa Mines,' 56–57; Chaput and Kennedy, *Man from ASARCO*, 142; *Times* (London), 18 December 1931, 18.
43 Marcosson, *Metal Magic*, 87–9, 158–9, and 163.
44 Interview with Julius Kruttschnitt, 1972, box 7, Mount Isa Mines (hereafter MIM) Collection, Mount Isa City Council Library (hereafter MICCL).
45 K.H. Kennedy, 'Mount Isa Mines,' 57–8; J. Mullan to J. Webster, 1 November 1933, A/7309/33/8274, QSA.
46 Interview with Julius Kruttschnitt, 7.
47 Ibid., 5; Mouat, 'Industry and Community,' 273, 277.
48 Interview with Julius Kruttschnitt, 2; Marcosson, *Metal Magic*, 101–102; Penrose, 'Occupational Lead Poisoning,' 125.
49 Interview with Julius Kruttschnitt, 3; Blainey, *Mines in the Spinifex*, 161.
50 *Queensland Government Mining Journal* 34 (August 1933): 241.
51 Interview with Julius Kruttschnitt, 1–2.
52 Ibid., 9.
53 Ibid., 5; Marcosson, *Metal Magic*, 119.
54 Blainey, *Mines in the Spinifex*, 174; *Queensland Government Mining Journal* 34 (November 1933): 369.
55 Blainey, *Mines in the Spinifex*, 179–80.
56 Fitzgerald, *History of Queensland*, 102–8; MacIntyre, *Concise History of Australia*, 188–95.
57 Kirkman, *Mount Isa*, 73; Tanner, *Long Road North*, 37, 39.
58 *Queensland Government Mining Journal* 42 (March 1941): 61.
59 Ibid., May 1941, 94; Blainey, *Mines in the Spinifex*, 183; *Queensland Government Mining Journal* 42 (October 1941): 209.
60 Interview with Julius Kruttschnitt, 4.
61 *Queensland State Mining Journal* 43 (January 1941): 18; 44 (August 1943): 20.
62 Blainey, *Mines in the Spinifex*, 190–3; K.H. Kennedy, 'Mount Isa Mines,' 58; *Times* (London), 13 February 1947.
63 *Queensland State Mining Journal* 46 (December 1945): 346; Kirkman, *Mount Isa*, 76; Thomas, *Buried Treasure*, 27.
64 Cummings, 'Neighbourhood for Mount Isa,' 10; Kleinschmidt, 'Socio-Educational Study,' 5.
65 *Mount Isa Mines Magazine*, March 1949, 7.
66 *Times* (London), 31 December, 1952, 10; 4 January 1955, 10; 12 December

1957, 18; 21 October 1960, 22; Blainey, *Mines in the Spinifex*, 200; Kirkman, *Mount Isa*, 93.

67 K.H. Kennedy, 'Mining,' 302; Thomas, *Buried Treasure*, 27.

68 Blainey, *Mines in the Spinifex*, 219–21.

69 Kirkman, *Mount Isa*, 102–3; *Queensland Government Mining Journal* 55 (March 1954): 206; *Mount Isa Mines Magazine*, July 1960, 19.

70 Blainey, *Mines in the Spinifex*, 225; Drynan, *History of Mount Isa*; Kirkman, *Mount Isa*, 102

71 Kirkman, *Mount Isa*, 102–3; *North-West Star* (Mount Isa), 21 June 1973, 6.

72 *Mount Isa Mines Magazine*, August 1959, 10; *Report of the First Executive Working Party: A Review of Australian Industry*, 1954, box 7; MIM Collection, MICCL; *Queensland Government Mining Journal* 54 (October 1953): 737.

73 Fitzgerald, *History of Queensland*, 223; Pat Mackie with Elizabeth Vassilieff, *Mount Isa: The Story of a Dispute*. Hawthorn, AU: Hudson Publishing, 1989, 19.

74 Fitzgerald, *History of Queensland*, 224; *Times* (London), 18 October 1961, 15.

75 Fitzgerald, *History of Queensland*, 235; K.H. Kennedy, 'Mining,' 302, 304; Mackie and Vassilieff, *Mount Isa*, 174.

76 Evans, *History of Queensland*, 220–2.

77 Ibid., 227, 229.

78 Foots, 'Businessmen's Seminar Speech.'

79 *MIM Today* quoted in Kirkman, *Mount Isa*, 109.

Chapter 3

1 Fishman, *Urban Utopias*, 46–7; Griffiths, '"Give My Regards to Uncle Billy,"' 25–7; Harrison, *Bourneville*, 14, 46, 87.

2 Simpson, *Thomas Adams*.

3 Buder, *Visionaries and Planners*, 98; Ravetz, *Government of Space*, 126; *Times* (London), 10 December 1904, 6; Crawford, *Building the Workingman's Paradise*, 72.

4 Fairfield, 'Scientific Management of Urban Space,' 181; Stelter, 'City-Building Process in Canada,' 27.

5 MacKinnon, 'Company Housing in Wabana,' 67; Neary, '"Traditional" and "Modern" Elements."'

6 Botting, 'Getting a Grand Falls Job,' 76–80.

7 'Trust Deed for Securing $10,000,000 5½ Per Cent "B" Mortgage Debenture Stock.'

8 Colonial Secretary's Office, *Census of Newfoundland and Labrador, 1921*, 1:290, 294–7.

9 Armstrong, Whitworth and Company, Ltd, 'Property Map of Corner Brook, c. 1922.'
10 'Abe Gushue Residence,' *Corner Brook Architectural Inventory*, uncatalogued accession at CBMA as of August 2005; BOHP, tape B-22, side A; Elton, 'Christopher Fisher,' 129.
11 Buder, *Visionaries and Planners*, 81; Simpson, 'Thomas Adams in Canada,' 5; Simpson, *Thomas Adams and the Modern Planning Movement*, 75–7; Saarinen, 'Influence of Thomas Adams,' 269, 288.
12 Provisional Board of Directors Meeting, 17 November 1922 and 19 April 1923, box 56 (Corner Brook Material box 1), MG17, Rooms; BOHP, tape J-8, sides A and B; Transcript of Oral Interview, file 24 (1-B-24), TR117(b), A000-013, CBMA; *Times* (London), 17 May 1923, 11; Provisional Board of Directors Meeting, 27 February 1923, box 56 (Corner Book Material box 1), MG17, Rooms; 'Humber Strike, 1924,' file 202, box 20, GN8, Rooms; *Western Star* (Corner Brook), 31 August 1922, 2; 20 December 1922, 1; and 21 March 1923, 2; BOHP, tape B-1, side A.
13 Adams, *Design of Residential Areas*, 258.
14 Adams and Thompson, 'Preliminary Sketch'; Symonds, *Architecture and Planning*, 5–6.
15 Symonds, *Architecture and Planning*, 7.
16 Institute of Local Government, *Single-Enterprise Communities in Canada*, 211.
17 Weir, *Rich in Interest and Charm*.
18 White, 'Creating Community,' 49.
19 Symonds, *Architecture and Planning*, 8.
20 Reid, *Townsite Heritage Conservation*; Symonds, *Architecture and Planning*, 9.
21 Crawford, 'World in a Shopping Mall,' 9; Ogden, *Ballads of Corner Brook*; Symonds, *Architecture and Planning*, 9.
22 BOHP, cassette B-46, sides A and B; Symonds, *Architecture and Planning*, 9; White, 'Creating Community,' 50.
23 Minutes of NP&P Board of Directors Meeting, 29 September 1925, file 306, box 15, MG17, Rooms; Board of Directors Meeting, 27 November 1925, box 57 (Corner Brook Material box 2), Rooms.
24 Charles Conroy to George Carpenter, 28 March 1924, box 56 (Corner Brook Material box 1), MG17, Rooms; 'Reid vs. NP&P, NP&P Utilities Corporation, and Armstrong, Whitworth, 1926'; *Times* (London), 9 June 1926, 24; Scott, *Vickers*, 154.
25 *Bowater World* (New York) 6 (Autumn 1962), 5, file 27, box 2C, A001-027, CBMA.
26 BOHP, tape B-5, side A, and tape B-46, side A; Ogden, *Ballads of Corner Brook*.

27 *Times* (London), 9 June 1926, 24.
28 Adams, *Outline of Town and City Planning*, 283; Adams, *Recent Advances*, 163; Simpson, *Thomas Adams*, 114–15.
29 *Times* (London), 3 May 1928, 21; International Power and Paper Company of Newfoundland (hereafter IPPN), 'Regulations.'
30 *Western Star* (Corner Brook), 23 November 1927, 5; Furnace Man, Staff House, Cobb's Quads, Masonic Lodge, *Corner Brook Architectural Inventory*, uncatalogued accession, CBMA; Reid, *Townsite Heritage Conservation*.
31 *Western Star* (Corner Brook), 19 October 1927, 1–2.
32 Government of Newfoundland, *Eleventh Census of Newfoundland and Labrador*, 1:12.
33 BOHP, tape B-46, sides A and B, and tape J-3, side A; Carlson, *Company Towns*, 24–5, 32; Institute of Local Government, *Single-Enterprise Communities in Canada*, 95–7; *Mill Basket*; Reid, *Townsite Heritage Conservation*, 10.
34 Heinrich, 'Product Diversification,' 488, 492.
35 *Western Star* (Corner Brook), 8 February 1939, 5.
36 Bowater Contract; *Western Star* (Corner Brook), 17 August 1927, 2.
37 Reader, *Bowater*, 154.
38 *Bowater World* (New York) 6 (Autumn 1962): 5, file 27, box 2C, A001-027, CBMA; Reader, *Bowater*, 136, 154–5, 183; Wonders, 'Parasite Communities,' 29.
39 Reid, *Townsite Heritage Conservation*.
40 BOHP, cassette S-19, side A; Goldenberg, *Report on Municipal Administration and Services*, 3; BOHP, tape S-19, side A, and cassette B-46, side A.
41 BOHP, cassette B-16, side A.
42 *Western Star* (Corner Brook), 28 May 1948, 1; Horwood, *Corner Brook*, 87.
43 Goldenberg, *Report on Municipal Administration and Services*, 5; Horwood, *Corner Brook*, 85.
44 BOHP, tape S-40, side A, and tape B-11, side A; Horwood, *Corner Brook*, 134.
45 BOHP, tape B-16, side A, and tape S-8-C, sides A and B; Horwood, *Corner Brook*, 92, 162–3; Government of Newfoundland and Labrador, 'Population.'
46 Armstrong, Whitworth and Company, Ltd, 'Property Map of Corner Brook'; Government of Newfoundland, *Census of Newfoundland and Labrador, 1921, Table 1: Population, Sex, Condition, Denomination, etc.* ... St John's: Government of Newfoundland, 1923, 290.
47 BOHP, tape B-22, side A; tape B-27, side A, tape S-25, side A; Government of Newfoundland, *1921 Nominal Census*, 3–13.
48 NP&P Board of Directors Meeting, 27 November 1925, box 57 (Corner

Brook Material box 2), MG 17, Rooms; Horwood, *Corner Brook*, 37; BOHP, cassette B-5, side A; cassette B-46, side A.
49 BOHP, tape S-11, side B.
50 BOHP, tape B-46, side A; Ogden, *Ballads of Corner Brook*, 47.
51 Bowater Newfoundland Pulp and Paper Mills Limited, *Report on Existing Conditions*; BOHP, tape J-6, side A; Goldenberg, *Report on Municipal Administration and Services*, 9.
52 *Western Star* (Corner Brook), 3 September 1924, 1; 29 October 1924, 1; 4 March 1925, 2; Goldenberg, *Report on Municipal Administration and Services*, 3, 6–7, 11; Government of Newfoundland, *Eleventh Census*, 1:12.
53 Bowater Newfoundland Pulp and Paper Company, *Report on Existing Conditions*, 7–8; *Western Star* (Corner Brook), 16 September 1925, 2; 27 January 1926, 2; 5 October 1927, 2; and 9 November 1932, 5.
54 BOHP, tape S-8-C, side B; tape S-14, side A; tape S-20, side A; *Western Star* (Corner Brook), 9 November 1932, 5.
55 *Times* (London), 6 March 1935, 13.
56 *Western Star* (Corner Brook), 23 November, 1927, 5.
57 *Western Star* (Corner Brook), 10 November 1926, 3; 24 August 1927, 4; 27 May 1931, 7; and 2 September 1931, 2.
58 *Western Star* (Corner Brook), 8 February 1939, 3.
59 Bowater Newfoundland Pulp and Paper Company, *Report on Existing Conditions*, 1–3, 5, 9.
60 Department of Justice, Justice Files, Re: Municipal Government for Corner Brook West, 1935–36, file 94, box 167, GN13/1/B, Rooms.
61 *Civic Administration*, March 1952. Quoted in Institute of Local Government, *Single-Enterprise Communities*, 88.
62 *Globe and Mail*, 6 April 1953, 12; BOHP, tape J-5, side A; and tape S-11, side B.
63 Goldenberg, *Report on Municipal Administration and Services*, 3, 6–8, 11–12; Wonders, 'Parasite Communities,' 27–8.
64 Goldenberg, *Report on Municipal Administration and Services*, 1, 5, 22.
65 Bland and Spence-Sales, *Urban Development of Greater Corner Brook*, 13; BOHP, tape T-20, side A; Corner Brook Housing Corporation, *Report of Operations – 1967*, 3–4; Newfoundland Design Associates Limited, *Corner Brook Housing Area Study*; Peat, Marwick, Mitchell, *Local Government in Corner Brook*; Pickett and Allston, 'Planning for Corner Brook,' 180.
66 BOHP, tape B-6, side A; tape S-22, side A; tape S-26, side A; tape S-34, side B.
67 BOHP, tape J-6, side B.
68 *Mount Isa Mines Magazine*, April 1956, 24.

69 Bell, 'Essay on North Queensland Mining Settlement,' 41; Bell, 'Houses in North Queensland Mining Towns,' 302.
70 K.H. Kennedy, 'Mining,' 282–3, 291; Bell, 'International Investment in Early Mount Isa,' 293–4; MacIntyre, *Concise History of Australia*, 162–3; Fitzgerald, *History of Queensland*, 8–11, 54; Blainey, *Mines in the Spinifex*, 77, 106.
71 *Queensland Government Mining Journal* 29 (February 1928): 55; *Queensland Government Mining Journal* 30 (August 1929): 331.
72 Kirkman, *Mount Isa*, 6–9.
73 *Queensland Government Mining Journal* 25 (May 1924): 167; 25 (October 1924): 383; 27 (September 1926): 330; and 27 (November 1926): 408; Kirkman, *Mount Isa*, 8.
74 Forster, *Australian Cities*, 12; Frost and Dingle, 'Sustaining Suburbia,' 25, 27; Kirkman, *Mount Isa*, 9–10.
75 Kirkman, *Mount Isa*, 11–12.
76 'Correspondences regarding Squatters and Towns Planning,' Mines Department 1948, A/8430, QSA.
77 Bell, 'Essay on North Queensland,' 16, 19; Bell, 'Houses in North Queensland,' 302.
78 Berkman, *Making the Mount Isa Mine*, 127; Kirkman, *Mount Isa*, 14–15.
79 K.H. Kennedy, 'Mount Isa's Russian Connection,' 188–90; Kennedy and Kirkman, 'Evolution of Company Welfare,' 1157.
80 Chaput and Kennedy, *Man from ASARCO*, 146; *Queensland Government Mining Journal* 29 (February 1928): 55; 28 (July 1928): 322.
81 Bell, 'Essay on North Queensland Mining Settlement,' 27; Bolton, *Spoils and Spoilers*, 126; Chaput and Kennedy, *Man from ASARCO*, 147, 149; Kirkman, *Mount Isa*, 26; Berkman, *Making the Mount Isa Mine*, 129.
82 Chaput and Kennedy, *Man from ASARCO*, 147; MIM Community Department, 'Description of Mount Isa, 1935'; Mining Trust, 'Plant Inventory.'
83 Kirkman, *Mount Isa*, 25–37.
84 Chaput and Kennedy, *Man from ASARCO*, 148; Drynan, *History of Mount Isa*; Kennedy and Kirkman, 'Evolution of Company Welfare,' 1162; Kirkman, *Mount Isa*, 30; MIM Ltd, 'Plant Inventory'; *Queensland Government Mining Journal* 29 (February 1928): 55; 29 (June 1928): 267; 29 (July 1928) 321; 30 (August 1929): 359; 30 (September 1929): 401; 30 (August 1929): 332; *Times* (London), 25 April 1928, 25;
85 *Times* (London), 25 April 1928, 25; 5 June 1929, 22; 13 November 1929, 23; Hore-Lacy, *Broken Hill to Mount Isa*, 200; *Queensland Government Mining Journal* 29 (February 1928): 55; 30 (September 1929): 401.
86 *Financial Times* 18 December 1931, 6.
87 Interview with Julius Kruttschnitt, 4, 9.

88 Kennedy and Kirkman, 'Evolution of Company Welfare,' 1161–2.
89 *Queensland Government Mining Journal* 32 (May 1931): 198; 32 (July 1931): 287.
90 Mouat, 'Industry and Community,' 275.
91 Kirkman, *Mount Isa*, 62.
92 Marcosson, *Metal Magic*, 278.
93 Kirkman, *Mount Isa*, 65–6.
94 Ibid., 64.
95 *Queensland Government Mining Journal* 46 (December 1945): 346; Blainey, *Mines in the Spinifex*, 188.
96 Tanner, *Long Road North*, 37–40; Blainey, *Mines in the Spinifex*, 187–8; Kirkman, *Mount Isa*, 73–4.
97 Kirkman, *Mount Isa*, 76–7.
98 *Mount Isa Mines Magazine*, March 1949, 7, 14–15; July 1950, 3; September 1951, 2; *Mount Isa Standard*, 3 December 1948, 1; 29 January 1949, 1; 19 February 1949, 1; Cummings, 'Town of Mount Isa Map'; Kirkman, *Mount Isa*, 77–81, 93.
99 *Mount Isa Mines Magazine*, April 1948, 14, January 1949, 2; June 1952, 10.
100 *Mount Isa Mines Magazine*, February 1948, 12; July 1950, 4; November 1951, 7; Kennedy and Kirkman, 'Evolution of Company Welfare,' 1163; Blainey, *Mines in the* Spinifex, 230.
101 Chaput and Kennedy, *Man from ASARCO*, 214.
102 *Mount Isa Mines Magazine*, February 1957, 10; July 1957, 3; *Queensland Government Mining Journal* 60 (April 1959): 234; Chaput and Kennedy, *Man from ASARCO*, 214; Kirkman, *Mount Isa*, 94–7.
103 Blainey, *Mines in the Spinifex*, 226.
104 Karl Langer, 'Plans for Mount Isa Mines'; *Mount Isa Mines Magazine*, January 1956, 8; April 1956, 24; June 1956, 16; 'May 1957, 14–15; July 1957, 3; January 1959, 2 and 24; *Mount Isa Mail*, 12 January 1955; 12 May 1955, 1; Cummings, 'Neighbourhood for Mount Isa,' 31–2.
105 Kirkman, *Mount Isa*, 107–8; Mount Isa Shire Council, 'Explanation of Proposals.'
106 Mount Isa Mines Ltd, *Annual Report*, 1968, 4; 1972, 9; Queensland State Government, *1971 Census*, 576, 578–9.
107 L. Landy to police commissioner, Brisbane, 1925, A/67562, QSA; S. Wilson to J. Stopford, 8 and 23 August 1930, A/8645, QSA; Kirkman, *Mount Isa*, 19.
108 L. Landy to police commissioner, Brisbane, 18 August 1930, A/64261, QSA; G. Gray to L. Landy, 8 January 1930, A/64261, QSA; H.J. Reinke to L. Landy, 7 January 1930, A/64261, QSA.

109 S. Wilson to under-secretary of mines, 27 October 1930, A/8645, QSA; *Smith's Weekly* (Sydney), 24 December 1932, 11; *Cloncurry Advocate*, 8 April 1933; Kirkman, *Mount Isa*, 39.
110 S. Wilson to J. Stopford, 12 June 1931; S. Wilson to J. Stopford, 17 January 1933; Hector MacDonald to J. Wilson, 11 December 1933; Hector MacDonald to J. Stopford, 11 March 1934; S. Wilson to J. Stopford, 16 June 1934; S. Wilson to J. Stopford, 1 August 1934, A/8465, QSA.
111 *Smith's Weekly* (Sydney), 24 December 1932, 11; Kirkman, *Mount Isa*, 38–47; Penrose, 'Occupational Lead Poisoning,' 128.
112 Kirkman, *Mount Isa*, 44.
113 O'Callaghan to under-secretary for mines, August and September 1935, A/8465, QSA.
114 Fitzgerald, *History of Queensland*, 321; Kirkman, *Mount Isa*, 63–6.
115 Justice Department, 'American Military Misconduct.'
116 F.H. Kennedy, 'General Report,' 6; *Mount Isa Mines Magazine*, January 1958, 3.
117 Curtis, 'Civilization in the Spinifex,' 14.
118 *Mount Isa Standard*, 25 March 1948, 1; 24 December 1948, 2; and 25 February, 1949, 1; Our Neighbour, recurring section in *Mount Isa Mines Magazine*, 1951–3.
119 Kleinschmidt, 'Socio-Educational Study,' 5–6, 8, 13–15.
120 Curtis, 'Neighbourhood for Mount Isa,' 9, 29.
121 *Mount Isa Standard*, 26 November 1948, 1; Kirkman, *Mount Isa*, 91–2.
122 Curtis, 'Neighbourhood for Mount Isa,' 32.
123 Ibid., 30.
124 D.J. Dwyer and Associates, *Proposal for Development*; Dryan, *History of Mount Isa*; Kirkman, *Mount Isa*, 102–3, 107–8; Mill, *Report upon Population Growth*, 2; Mount Isa Shire Council, 'Explanation of the Proposals,' 3–4.
125 *Courier-Mail* (Brisbane), 5 September 1972, 4; *North-West Star* (Mount Isa), 21 June 1973, 6; 'Hub of Queensland's North-West,' special supplement, *Australian* (Sydney), 3 July 1978; Blainey, *Mines In the Spinifex*, 233, 235.
126 *Mount Isa Mines Magazine*, April 1963, 3.
127 Mount Isa Mines Ltd, *Annual Report*, 1968, 4; 1972, 9.
128 Faue, 'Community, Class, and Comparison,' 160.

Chapter 4

1 Greening, *Paper Makers in Canada*, 92; Machlis and Force, 'Community Stability,' 221, 229.
2 Gillespie, *Class Act*, 38; Greening, *Paper Makers in Canada*, 71; Sutherland,

'Newfoundland Loggers,' 99; Zeiger, *Rebuilding the Pulp and Paper Workers' Union*, 47.

3 Sutherland, 'We Are Only Loggers,' 37.

4 Botting, 'Getting a Grand Falls Job,' 100; Gillespie, *Class Act*, 57; Zeiger, *Rebuilding the Pulp and Paper Workers' Union*, 46–8.

5 William Scott to William Warren, 3 April 1924, GN8/20/202, Rooms.

6 *Western Star* (Corner Brook), 21 November 1923, 2; 18 June 1924, 2; 20 August 1924, 3; and 17 June 1925.

7 Patrick Hayward's Deposition; Major Betram Butler's Deposition; Dr W. Weekes' Deposition; Magistrate William Scott's Report, 26 March 1924; Government Report on the Humber Strike, 4 April 1924; 'Humber Strike, 1924,' GN8/20/202, Rooms; Macleod, 'Death at Deer Lake, 179–91.

8 Government Report on the Humber Strike, 4 April 1924, 2–3; J.M. Alexander to William Warren, 3 and 4 April 1924, GN8/20/202, Rooms.

9 Corner Brook Strike 1924, 2, GN8/24/237, Rooms.

10 William Coaker to J.M. Alexander, 31 July 1924; J.M. Alexander to William Coaker, 31 July 1924; William Coaker to J.M. Alexander, 31 July 1924; J.M. Alexander to William Coaker, 1 August 1924, GN8/24/237, Rooms.

11 William Scott to William Monroe, 2 August 1924; Corner Brook Strike 1924, 2–4; William Coaker to J.M. Alexander, 2 August 1924, GN8/24/237, Rooms.

12 J.M. Alexander to William Monroe, 5 August 1924; Glyn West to J.M Alexander, 4 August 1924, GN8/24/237, Rooms.

13 Corner Brook Strike, GN8/24/237, Rooms; *Times* (London), 4 August 1924, 7.

14 'Job Applications, Humber Project,' MG17/10/217, Rooms.

15 BOHP, tape S-25, side A.

16 Gillespie, *Class Act*, 57; Horwood, *Corner Brook*, 43–4; Sutherland, 'We Are Only Loggers,' 187–9.

17 BOHP, tape B-7-A, side A.

18 BOHP, tape B-22, side B; tape S-25, side A.

19 Zeiger, *Rebuilding the Pulp and Paper Workers' Union*, 50–2; Greening, *Paper Makers in Canada*, 22.

20 BOHP, tape S-25, side B.

21 IPPN, 'Rules 1928,' 12 and 14–15.

22 Corner Brook Co-operative Society Limited, 'Golden Anniversary,' 1.

23 BOHP, tape T-13, side A; tape B-46, side A; tape B-7-A, side A; tape S-25, side B; Horwood, *Corner Brook*, 44; *Western Star* (Corner Brook), 29 June 1932, 7.

24 BOHP, tape B-5, side A.

25 BOHP, tape J-3, side A.
26 BOHP, tape B-46, side A; tape J-3, side A.
27 BOHP, tape S-29, side B; tape B-1, side A; tape B-5, side A.
28 Relief Division's Comparative Expenditures, 1932–1935, GN38/S6-6-1/1, Rooms.
29 Sutherland, 'We Are Only Loggers,' iii, 335.
30 Sutherland, 'Newfoundland Loggers Respond,' 100.
31 Gillespie, *Class Act*, 58; Neary, 'Bradley Report,' 209, 211.
32 Newfoundland Royal Commission, *Report 1933*, 151.
33 Gillespie, *Class Act*; Neary, 'Bradley Report'; Sutherland, 'Newfoundland Loggers Respond'; Sutherland, 'We Are Only Loggers.'
34 Sutherland, 'Newfoundland Loggers Respond,' 87–8, 100; Sutherland, 'We Are Only Loggers,' 164–5, 189.
35 Commissioner for Natural Resources to the Commission of Government, 18 February 1938, GN38/S6-1-6/7, Rooms; 'Corner Brook Labour Situation, March–April 1938,' GN38/S5-6-1/4, Rooms; Norcliffe, *Global Game, Local Arena*, 68–9; J.C. Puddester, *Report on the Loggers' Dispute at Robert's Arm, 1 November 1937*, GN8/S2-3-2/7, Rooms; Sutherland, 'Newfoundland Loggers Respond,' 108; Sutherland, 'We Are Only Loggers,' 238–9.
36 Sutherland, 'We Are Only Loggers,' 97–8.
37 BOHP, tape B-7-A, side B.
38 Greening, *Paper Makers in Canada*, 29.
39 Sutherland, 'We Are Only Loggers,' 12, 162.
40 Heinrich, 'Product Diversification,' 495; Zeiger, *Rebuilding the Pulp and Paper Workers' Union*, 144–8, and 181.
41 'The Labour Movement,' in *Corner Brook's 50th Anniversary Souvenir Booklet*; BOHP, tape B-7, side A.
42 *Newfoundland Register of Trade Unions, 1938*, GN22/1/1, Rooms.
43 Norcliffe, *Global Game, Local Arena*, 81; 'Population of Incorporated Cities, Towns, and Villages,' Centre for Newfoundland Studies (hereafter CNS), QEII Library, Memorial University of Newfoundland (hereafter MUN); Sutherland, 'We Are Only Loggers,' 95.
44 *Bowater World* (New York) 6 (Autumn 1962): 9.
45 'Labour Agreement between Bowater's Newfoundland Pulp and Paper Mills Ltd and the International Brotherhood of Papermakers, June 1946,' 14, CNS, QEII Library, MUN; BOHP, tape B-46, side A.
46 Sutherland, 'We Are Only Loggers,' 209, 311–12.
47 Radforth, *Bushworkers and Bosses*, 202, 243.
48 Gillespie, *Class Act*, 110.
49 Ibid., 115–16; Neufeld and Parnaby, *IWA in Canada*, 159–62.

50 Horwood, *Corner Brook*, 127–9.
51 Radforth, *Bushworkers and Bosses*, 180, 190, 218–19.
52 Norcliffe, *Global Game, Local Arena*, 103.
53 Ibid., 90; Radforth, *Bushworkers and Bosses*, 208–9.
54 Norcliffe, *Global Game, Local Arena*, 103, 120.
55 Sutherland, 'We Are Only Loggers,' 41, 48–9.
56 Bell, 'Essay on North Queensland Mining Settlement,' 41; Mouat, 'Industry and Community,' 275.
57 Aungles, 'Structural Conflicts,' 26–7; Blackmur, *Strikes*, 23; Ellem and Shields, 'Making a "Union Town,"' 116; Fitzgerald, *History of Queensland*; Mouat, 'Industry and Community,' 275; *Brisbane Courier*, 24 April 1927, 13.
58 McCrystal, 'Metal Mining Industry,' 23.
59 Hearn and Knowles, *One Big Union*.
60 Blainey, *Mines in the Spinifex*, 149–53; Kirkman, *Mount Isa*, 6–8.
61 *Brisbane Courier*, 23 August 1929, 20.
62 Blackmur, 'Arbitration, Legislation and Industrial Peace,' 133; McCrystal, 'Metal Mining Industry,' 2; Penrose, 'Occupational Lead Poisoning,' 124; *Brisbane Courier*, 23 August 1929, 19.
63 Interview with Julius Kruttschnitt, 1; Penrose, 'Occupational Lead Poisoning,' 125, 129.
64 *Cloncurry Advocate*, 4 November 1929, A/64261, QSA; interview with Julius Kruttschnitt, 1.
65 *Queensland Government Mining Journal*, 1929–44; Queensland Inquest Files into Deaths, Industrial Accidents, and Fires, JUS/N series.
66 Interview with Julius Kruttschnitt, 9.
67 Blainey, *Mines in the Spinifex*, 158–9.
68 Queensland Inquest Files, JUS/N923/31/112, JUS/N910/30/439, JUS/N911/30/465, QSA.
69 *Cloncurry Advocate*, 11 April 1931, 5; Perkins, *Outback Insights*, 81.
70 Perkins, *Outback Insights*, 83.
71 E. Dore to L. Cahalane, 10 August 1932 and 3 February 1933; L. Cahalane to W.H. Ryan, 7 February 1933, A/64268, QSA; *Worker* (Sydney), 9 August 1933, 11.
72 Penrose, 'Occupational Lead Poisoning,' 123.
73 McCrystal, 'Metal Mining Industry,' 2.
74 *Courier-Mail* (Brisbane), 3 November 1933, file 538, A/64269, QSA; *Queensland State Mining Journal* 34 (November 1933): 347; Blainey, *Mines in the Spinifex*, 170–1; *Queensland State Mining Journal* 35 (February 1934): 35.
75 *Worker* (Sydney), 6 December 1933, 8; 13 December 1933, 12; 31 January 1934, 4; Penrose, 'Occupational Lead Poisoning,' 129, 134.

76 *Queensland Government Mining Journal* 38 (November 1937): 387.
77 John Shields, 'Lead Bonus Happy: Profit-Sharing, Productivity and Industrial Relations in the Broken Hill Mining Industry, 1925–1983,' *Australian Economic History Review* 37, no. 3 (November 1997): 222–3.
78 *Queensland Government Mining Journal* 37 (May 1936): 155; Fisher, 'Staff Reports on Overseas Trips, 1937.'
79 Fitzgerald, *History of Queensland*, 96.
80 S. Wilson to J. Stopford, 27 October 1930, A/8465, QSA; Community Department, 1935, 4, box 19, MIM Collection, MICCL; *Worker* (Sydney), 9 August 1933, 11.
81 Blainey, *Mines in the Spinifex*, 195–200; Fitzgerald, *History of Queensland*, 318–19; Kirkman, *Mount Isa*, 86, chapters 6 and 7; Sheldon, *Industrial Siege*, 9–10, 12; H.B. Waldegrave, *'Ya Gotta Be Jokin'!'* 64–9, 164.
82 Sergeant, Mount Isa, to sub-inspector, Cloncurry, 11 and 26 November 1940; *Courier-Mail* (Brisbane), 3, 7, 11, 12, and 15 October 1940, RSI13214, A/64282, QSA.
83 M. McAulley to J. O'Keefe, 22 December 1941, A/8362 (RSI1356), QSA.
84 Denning to H.W. Scott, 22 January 1948; Lead Bonus Dispute Committee, 'Lead Bonus Information,' 2 February 1948, file 735, A/64292, QSA.
85 Denning to H.W. Scott, 2 February 1948; *Courier-Mail* (Brisbane), 2 February 1948, file 735, A/64292, QSA.
86 Denning to H.W. Scott, 2 and 6 February 1948; *Courier-Mail* (Brisbane), 5 February 1948, file 735, A/64292, QSA.
87 J. Mullins to H.W. Scott, 28 June and 13 October 1948, file 742, A64298, QSA.
88 McCrystal, *Metal Mining Industry*, 23–4.
89 *Mount Isa Mines Magazine*, June 1952, 10; and July 1960, 19; Sheldon, *Industrial Siege*, 11.
90 Sheldon, *Industrial Siege*, 11.
91 Klemola, 'Mount Isa Finnish Community,' 1–3; Mackie, *Mount Isa*, 32.
92 *Queensland Government Mining Journal* 47 (June 1946): 167–8.
93 *Queensland Government Mining Journal* 47 (September 1946): 257; 51 (August 1950): 697; 54 (October 1953): 737.
94 Mackie, *Mount Isa*, 5; Carthey and Potter, *Mount Isa*, 6.
95 Carthey and Potter, *Mount Isa*, 6; Cummings, 'Neighbourhood for Mount Isa,' 21; regional director of education to minister of education, 1966, EDU/AB843, QSA; *Mount Isa Standard*, 3 December 1948, 1.
96 Sheldon, *Industrial Siege*, 11; *Mount Isa Mines Magazine*, August 1959, 15; Thomas, *Storm in the Tropics*, 17.
97 Fitzgerald, *History of Queensland*, 143–7, 221–3.

98 Hearn and Knowles, *One Big Union*, 269.
99 F. McNamara to Quinn, 3 July 1959, A/64307, QSA.
100 Edgar Williams to J.J. Bukowski, 16 June 1959, A/64307, QSA; Hearn and Knowles, *One Big Union*, 262–3.
101 Quinn to Cooke, 30 June, 1 July, 2 July 1959; F. McNamara to Quinn, 3 and 7 July 1959, A/64307, QSA; Carthey and Potter, *Mount Isa*, 7; Hearn and Knowles, *One Big Union*, 269.
102 File 850, A/64307, QSA; files 861 and 870, A/64308, QSA.
103 Fitzgerald, *History of Queensland*, 223; Queensland Trades and Labor Congress, 'Hands Off the Trade Unions,' 2–3.
104 F. McNamara to T.H. Codd, 14 March 1961; F. Palethorpe to T.H. Codd, 29 March 1961; T.H. Codd to Bischoff, 30 March 1961, file 878, A/64308, QSA.
105 *Voice of the Rank and File* (Sydney), April 1961, 1; Blackmur, 'Arbitration, Legislation and Industrial Peace,' 116, 133; McCrystal, 'Metal Mining Industry,' 25–6.
106 Mumford to Bischoff, 26 September 1961, file 889, A/64309, QSA.
107 *Truth* (Melbourne), 1 October 1961; Roberts to Michael, 12 October 1961, file 889, A/64309, QSA.
108 Mumford to Bischoff, 26 September 1961; *Truth* (Melbourne), 1 October 1961; Roberts to Michael, 17 October 1961; *Courier-Mail* (Brisbane), 20 November 1961, file 889, A/64309, QSA.
109 Mumford to Michael, 22 November 1961, file 889, A/64309, QSA; Fitzgerald, *History of Queensland*, 224.
110 Walker to Michael, 12 March 1962, file 889, A/64309, QSA; Licensing Commission, Re: Application for Liquor License, TR1873/1, QSA; *Times* (London), 9 September 1963, 15; Fitzgerald, *History of Queensland*, 319.
111 Mackie, *Many Ships to Mount Isa*, 5, 11, 38.
112 Ibid., 94–5, 112–13, 127, 136–7; Mackie and Vassilieff, *Mount Isa*, 12–13; Burgmann, *Revolutionary Industrial Unionism*, 3. According to Burgmann, Pat Mackie was still the 'accredited Delegate for the IWW in Australia' in the mid-1990s.
113 Fitzgerald, *History of Queensland*, 230; Mackie, *Many Ships to Mount Isa*, xxiii, 275, 318, 365–7, 370–1; Mackie and Vassilieff, *Mount Isa*, 16.
114 Blainey, *Mines in the Spinifex*, 236–41; Carthey and Potter, *Mount Isa*; Collins, *Copper Crucible*; DeLacey, *Blood Stains the Wattle*; Fitzgerald, *History of Queensland*, 229–36; Kirkman, *Mount Isa*, 106–107; Sheldon, *Industrial Siege*; Thomas, *Storm in the Tropics*; Williams, *Yellow, Green, and Red*. Several Australian newspapers carried extensive, if skewed, coverage of the dispute. Many of those articles were collected by the Department of Labor (file 45, TR1735/1, QSA).

115 Fitzgerald, *History of Queensland*, 229–36. Most of the information in this section comes from Fitzgerald's section entitled 'The Mount Isa Dispute.'
116 Mackie, *Mount Isa*, 85–6, 89, 91.
117 Carthey and Potter, *Mount Isa*, 14; Fitzgerald, *History of Queensland*, 233.
118 Mount Isa Trades and Labor Council, 'The Truth Will Out,' reprinted in Carthey and Potter, *Mount Isa*, 11–12.
119 *Times* (London), 19 February 1965, 10; 27 February 1965, 1; 15 March 1965, 11.
120 *Telegraph* (London), 20 February, and 4 March 1965; *Courier-Mail* (Brisbane), 18 February, and 5 March 1965, file 45, TR1735/1, QSA; Fitzgerald, *History of Queensland*, 234.
121 *Australian* (Sydney), 19 February 1965, file 45, TR1735/1, QSA.
122 Fitzgerald, *History of Queensland*, 234; *Telegraph* (London), 23 February 1965, file 43, TR1735/1, QSA.
123 Fitzgerald, *History of Queensland*, 235.
124 *Courier-Mail* (Brisbane), 5 September 1972, 4; *North-West Star* (Mount Isa), 19 June 1973, 6, and 21 June 1973, 6; *Australian* (Sydney), 3 July 1978, 9 and 13; Mackie, *Mount Isa*, vi.
125 McCrystal, 'Metal Mining Industry,' 29–30.
126 Ibid., 7.

Chapter 5

1 Adamson, *Hegemony and Revolution*, 170–1, 243–4; Anderson, 'Antinomies of Antonio Gramsci,' 21, 26, 49.
2 Cadigan, 'Power and Agency,' 242.
3 Bowater Contract, file 5, box S2-3-2, GN38, Rooms.
4 Buder, *Pullman*, xii.
5 BOHP, tape S-1, side A; tape S-26, side A; and tape T-13, side A; Minutes of NP&P Board of Directors Meeting, 18 June 1924, file 306, box 15, MG17, Rooms.
6 *Western Star* (Corner Brook), 17 December 1924, 2; Government of Newfoundland, *Report of the Commission of Enquiry*, 12.
7 Board of Directors Meeting, 27 November 1925, box 57 (Corner Brook Material box 2), Rooms; BOHP, tape S-8-C, side A; and tape B-5, side A; Doris Cross Interview, August 1997, TR117(b), 1-B-24, file 24, A000-013, CBMA; Government of Newfoundland, *Report of the Commission of Enquiry*, 12; Institute of Local Government, *Single-Enterprise Communities*, 185; Minutes of NP&P Board of Directors Meeting, 18 June 1924, file 306, box 15, MG17, Rooms; *Western Star* (Corner Brook), 27 January 1926, 3.

8 BOHP, tape S-14, side A; and tape S-20, side A; Collins and Caines, 'Development of Hospital Services'; Newfoundland Royal Commission, *Report, 1933*, 150; *Western Star* (Corner Brook), 9 November 1932, 5.

9 Carlson, *Company Towns*, 80; Lucas, *Minetown, Milltown, Railtown*. Institute of Local Government, *Single-Enterprise Communities in Canada*, 243.

10 *Western Star* (Corner Brook), 9 January 1924, 2; 26 November 1924, 2; and 11 February 1925, 2; NP&P Board of Directors Meeting, 27 November 1925, (Corner Brook Material box 2), box 57, Rooms.

11 BOHP, tape B-1, side A.

12 *Western Star* (Corner Brook), 1 October 1924, 1.

13 BOHP, tape S-41, sides A and B; tape S-46, side B.

14 Horwood, *Corner Brook*, 64–5, 143; BOHP, tape S-41, side A.

15 Horwood, *Corner Brook*, 53; *Western Star* (Corner Brook), 29 October 1924; 25 February 1925, 2; 8 April 1925, 2.

16 Baker, 'Interplay of Private and Public Enterprise,' 278; BOHP, tape S-25, side A; Horwood, *Corner Brook*, 53–4; NP&P Board of Directors Meeting, 27 October 1926, file 302, box 15, MG17, Rooms; *Western Star* (Corner Brook), 10 November 1926, 3.

17 *Western Star* (Corner Brook), 3 February 1926, 2; and 24 August 1927, 4; Horwood, *Corner Brook*, 54, 138.

18 Bowater Newfoundland Pulp and Paper Mills Ltd, *Report on Existing Conditions*, 2; Goldenberg, *Report on Municipal Administration and Services*, 7, 11–12.

19 BOHP, tape J-6, side B; tape B-6, side A.

20 BOHP, tape B-5, side A; tape B-6, side A; tape B-42, side A; tape J-6, side A; and tape S-46, side A; Corner Brook Downtown Business Association, 'Historical Survey of Broadway Businesses.'

21 BOHP, tape S-46, side A; tape B-42-A, side A; and tape B-22, side A.

22 BOHP, tape J-6, side B.

23 Eklund, '"Place" of Politics,' 105; Eklund, *Steel Town*, 191.

24 *Western Star* (Corner Brook), 16 November 1927, 2; and 4 April 1950.

25 Department of Public Health and Welfare, *Tenth Census of Newfoundland and Labrador, 1935*, 2:114–15.

26 Saarinen, 'Single-Sector Communities,' 230.

27 BOHP, tape B-7, side B; Corner Brook Co-operative Society Limited, 'Golden Anniversary,' 2–3; Corner Brook Co-operative Society Limited, *Silver Anniversary*, 4, 12–13.

28 'Voting Percentages: Second Referendum,' Heritage, http://www.heritage.nf.ca/confederation/stats.html.

29 Horwood, *Corner Brook*, 91–2.

30 Ibid., 133–4; Goldenberg, *Report on Municipal Administration and Services*, 22.
31 Horwood, *Corner Brook*, 89, 94–5.
32 Letto, *Chocolate Bars and Rubber Boots*; Bassler, *Alfred Valdmanis.*
33 Horwood, *Corner Brook*, 134, 137.
34 Government of Newfoundland, *Report of the Commission of Enquiry*, 27, 64.
35 BOHP, tape B-11, side A; Horwood, *Corner Brook*, 134–6.
36 BOHP, tape B-11, side A.
37 BOHP, tape T-20, side A; Horwood, *Corner Brook*, 138–9; Peat, Marwick, Mitchell, *Local Government in Corner Brook*, appendix entitled 'City of Corner Brook: Summary of Revenues 1962 to 1965'; Pickett and Allston, 'Planning for Corner Brook,' 25.
38 BOHP, tape S-8-A, side B; tape S-40, side B.
39 BOHP, tape B-11, side A; tape S-8-B, sides A and B; tape S-29, sides A and B; tape S-40, side B; tape S-44, side A; Horwood, *Corner Brook*, 139–41.
40 Bowater Newfoundland Limited, 'Bowater's News and Views'; Greenland, Redden, and Snow, *Survey of Recreation*, appendix entitled 'Summary of Cash Collections and Comparative Figures for 1967.'
41 Annual education statistics, Mount Isa, EDU/AB1067, QSA; 'Correspondences regarding Squatters and Town Planning,' A/8430, QSA; 'Correspondences regarding Town Planning on Mineside and Townside, 1930–1935,' A/8465, QSA; Kirkman, *Mount Isa*, 9–15, 21–2.
42 R. Cilento to J. Mullan, 29 August 1938, 48/2309 Health and Home Affairs/2, QSA.
43 L. Landy to police commissioner, Brisbane, 18 August 1930, A/64261, QSA; G. Gray to L. Landy, 8 January 1930, A/64261, QSA; H.J. Reinke to L. Landy, 7 January 1930, A/64261, QSA.
44 Kirkman, *Mount Isa*, 31; MIM Community Department, 'Description of Mount Isa, 1935,' 3; *Mount Isa Mines Magazine*, August 1959, 14; *Mount Isa Standard*, 20 January 1949, 3.
45 Kirkman, *Mount Isa*, 84.
46 Registrar of Firms, volumes 1–4, QSA SRS55194-1-1 to SRS55194-1-4, QSA.
47 McCarthy to W.H. Ryan, 24 and 25 October 1929, and 3 and 8 January 1930; Gray to L. Landy, 8 January 1930, A/64261, QSA.
48 L. Landy to sub-inspector of police, Cloncurry, 7 January 1930, A/64261, QSA.
49 Kirkman, *Mount Isa*, 15–16, 36, 39–43, 48–59.
50 Kirkman, *Mount Isa*, 38–47; Penrose, 'Occupational Lead Poisoning,' 128; *Smith's Weekly* (Sydney), 24 December 1932, 11.

51 Kirkman, *Mount Isa*, 58–9.
52 Annual Assessment of Schools, Mount Isa, EDU/AB843, QSA; Cummings, 'Neighbourhood for Mount Isa,' 35–6, 38–9, 45; Kirkman, *Mount Isa*, 45–6, 87; Kleinschmidt, 'Socio-Educational Study,' 13–15, 38, 46, 48–51; Sellwood, 'Report on Accommodation.'
53 A.J. Smith to W. Power, 18 February 1957, TR1873/1, QSA; 'Licensing Commission: Re: Application for Liquor License, Mount Isa Workers' Club'; Quinn to Cooke, 30 June 1959, A/64307, QSA.
54 Cummings, 'Neighbourhood for Mount Isa,' 39.
55 Anonymous to Licensing Commission, 19 March 1961; Anonymous to Licensing Commission 29 June 1962; K. Morgan to Licensing Commission, 16 September 1962; A. MacDonald to Licensing Commission, 1 March 1963; Licensing Commission to Workers' Club, 18 March 1963, TR1873/1, QSA; 'Licensing Commission: Re: Application for Liquor License, Workers' Club.'
56 Lears, 'Concept of Cultural Hegemony,' 575.
57 Mount Isa Shire Council, 'Explanation for the Proposals'; *Mount Isa Mines Magazine*, August 1959, 14–15, and June 1969, 19–20; *Courier-Mail* (Brisbane), 5 September 1972, 4; *Australian* (Sydney), 29 December 1973, 11, and 3 July 1978, 10.
58 Blainey, *Mines in the Spinifex*, 232–5; Kirkman, *Mount Isa*, 107–9.

Chapter 6

1 Lears, 'Concept of Cultural Hegemony,' 591.
2 Williams, *Marxism and Literature*, 132–4.
3 Norcliffe, *Global Game, Local Arena*, 170–3.
4 BOHP, tape B-22, side A; tape B-27, side A; tape J-8, side A.
5 Genovese, *Roll Jordan, Roll*; Kealey and Palmer, *Dreaming of What Might Be*; Palmer, *Working-Class Experience*; Thompson, *Customs In Common*; Thompson, *Making of the English Working Class*.
6 Government of Newfoundland, *Tenth Census of Newfoundland and Labrador, 1935*, 1:550–1; Government of Newfoundland, *Eleventh Census of Newfoundland and Labrador, 1945*, 1:12.
7 BOHP, tape S-41, side A; tape S-42, side A; tape B-2, side A; tape B-46, side A; tape J-3, side A; Government of Newfoundland, *Eleventh Census of Newfoundland, 1945* (Nominal).
8 Government of Newfoundland, *Eleventh Census of Newfoundland and Labrador, 1945*, 1:69; Government of Newfoundland, *Report of the Commission of Enquiry*, 7.

9 Department of Public Health and Welfare, *Tenth Census of Newfoundland and Labrador, 1935*, 2:65.
10 BOHP, tape B-1, side A; tape B-7-A, side A; tape B-46, side A; tape S-25, side B.
11 Government of Newfoundland, *Eleventh Census of Newfoundland and Labrador*, 1:229–31; Government of Newfoundland, *Report of the Commission of Enquiry*, 7.
12 BOHP, tape B-6, side A; tape B-22, side A; tape B-46, side A; tape S-22, side A; tape S-26, side A; tape S-34, side B; tape S-38, side B; tape S-42, side A.
13 Ogden, *Ballads of Corner Brook*, 18, 24, 44.
14 BOHP, tape B-11, side A; tape B-42, side A.
15 *Western Star* (Corner Brook), 23 September 1925, 2; 21 April 1926, 2; 7 July 1926, 2; BOHP, tape B-11-B, side A; tape S-6, side A; Ogden, *Ballads of Corner Brook*, 18, 24, 44, and 46.
16 BOHP, tape B-11-B, side A; tape B-42-A, side A; Horwood, *Corner Brook*, 51–2.
17 BOHP, tape B-42-A, side A; tape B-11-B, side A; tape B-42-A, side A; tape J-3, side A; tape S-41, side A; tape S-46, side A.
18 Horwood, *Corner Brook*, 54–5.
19 Magistrate's Bench Books, Corner Brook 1933–52, box 443, GN5/3/G/12, Rooms, and box 548, GN5/3/G/17; BOHP, tape S-46, side A; *Western Star* (Corner Brook), 1 May, 1; and 2 May 1931, 1.
20 Lears, 'Concept of Cultural Hegemony,' 574.
21 Perkins, *Outback Insights*, 19.
22 Interview with Julius Kruttschnitt, 2.
23 Ibid., 6.
24 *Mount Isa Mines Magazine*, June 1959, 15, and August 1959, 14; *Cloncurry Advocate*, 5 September 1931, 1–2; Kirkman, *Mount Isa*, 19, 31; National Trust of Queensland, *Study of a Tent House*, 1, 4; Waldegrave, *Ya Gotta Be Jokin'!'* 35.
25 Kirkman, *Mount Isa*, 2; MIM Community Department, 'Description of Mount Isa, 1935,' 1.
26 Department of Education, Correspondences re: Mount Isa schools and Mount Isa school yearbooks, EDU/AB843 and EDU/AB1067, QSA; Perkins, *Outback Insights*, 52.
27 Northern Australia Development Committee, 'Co-ordinator General's Department: Northern Australia Nutritional Survey, 1947–1948,' A/11, QSA; *Mount Isa Standard*, 22 January 1948, 1.
28 Kirkman, *Mount Isa*, 5–6;
29 Cahir, 'Women in North Queensland,' 111.

30 Kleinschmidt, 'Socio-Educational Study of Mount Isa,' 18. Statistics for married and single men and women in Mount Isa during this period are sketchy. Figures come from a variety of scattered sources including company files and academic and media reports. Regular and reliable census data were not available.
31 *Australian* (Sydney), 29 December 1973, 11.
32 Ibid.; Kirkman, *Mount Isa*, 65.
33 Perkins, *Outback Insights*, 81.
34 Coroner's inquest, JUS/N1006/36/64, QSA; Perkins, *Outback Insights*, 113.
35 Ryan, 'Growth and Development of Mount Isa,' 12.
36 *Mount Isa Mines Magazine*, September–October 1956, 3.
37 'Our Neighbour' section in *Mount Isa Mines Magazine* (1952–3).
38 Interview with Julius Kruttschnitt Interview, 9; Kirkman, *Mount Isa*, 20, 34–5.
39 Correspondences regarding Squatters and Town Planning, A/8430; JUS/N1095/41/88; JUS/N917/30/760; A/64261, QSA; Perkins, *Outback Insights*, 43, 81; *Mount Isa Standard*, 4 March 1948, 1; *Australian* (Sydney), 29 December 1973, 11.
40 *Mount Isa Standard*, 13 May 1948, 2; 1 July 1948, 3; 3 December 1948, 1; 10 February 1949, 3.
41 Bench Record and Summons Book, Mount Isa, 1924–31, no. 28, SRS5325, QSA; McCarthy to W.H. Ryan, 3 January 1930, A/64261, QSA; Blainey, *Mines in the Spinifex*, 157.
42 *Cloncurry Advocate*, 3 October 1931, 1; *Mount Isa Mail*, 4 February 1955, 1; 21 July 1955, 1; Perkins, *Outback Insights*, 86; *North-West Star* (Mount Isa), 21 June 1973, 6; *Mount Isa Standard*, 3 December 1948, 1; 17 December 1948, 1 and 3.
43 Coroner's inquest, JUS/N923/31/112; Denning to police commissioner, 22 January 1948, A/64292, QSA.
44 Julius Kruttschnitt to G.B. O'Malley, 22 April 1949, pigeonhole 63: Lead Poisoning Report, 46/702c-49/592, A/8446, QSA; *Worker* (Sydney), 9 August 1933, 8; James V. Duhig, 'Reports of Enquiry into Lead Poisoning and Its Incidence at Mount Isa, Queensland, May 1933,' pigeonhole 63, 46/702c-49/592, A/8446, QSA; Mount Isa Mines Limited, 'Safety Instructions for Underground Employees at Mount Isa Mines Limited, January 1955,' 22, Box 17, MIM Collection, MICCL.
45 Kerry to Howard, 13 June 1935, A/64273, QSA.
46 DeLacey, *Blood Stains the Wattle*, 228.
47 See the Bench Records and Summons Books for Mount Isa, SRS5325, QSA, and JUS/N inquest files for regular charges of drinking in public, obscen-

ity charges, drinking after-hours, and cases in which alcoholism emerges as a common causal factor of death.

48 Court Records, SRS5325, QSA; *Cloncurry Advocate*, 4 July 1931; 3 October 1931; *Mount Isa Standard*, 4 March 1948, 1; 17 June 1948, 1–2; 15 July, 1; 22 October 1948, 1; 3 December 1948, 3; 13 January 1949, 1; 25 March, 1; *Mount Isa Mail*, 8 March 1955, 3; 5 May 1955, 3; 21 July, 1; *Mount Isa Mines Magazine*, May 1952, 1; Perkins, *Outback Insights*, 79, 113–15; JUS/N107/39/682, QSA; coroner's inquest, JUS/N921/31/30, QSA; Kleinschmidt, 'Socio-Educational Study of Mount Isa,' 38; *North-West Star* (Mount Isa), 19 June 1973, 6.

49 *Mount Isa Mines Magazine*, February 1957, 8–10, 23; August 1959, 14; *Courier-Mail* (Brisbane), 5 September 1972, 4; *Australian* (Sydney), 29 December 1973, 11; 3 July 1978, 9, 13; Blainey, *Mines in the Spinifex*, 200, 233.

50 *Australian* (Sydney), 29 December 1973, 11.

51 Lucas, *Minetown, Milltown, Railtown*, 407.

Conclusion

1 *Brisbane Times*, 19 August 2008; 'Australian Plea for Ugly Women,' BBC; 'Mt Isa Mayor Picks Up "Sexist" Ernie,' BBC.

Bibliography

Primary Sources

Corner Brook

'The Labour Movement.' In *Corner Brook's 50th Anniversary Souvenir Booklet.* Corner Brook: Western Star, 1975.

Adams, Thomas. *The Design of Residential Areas: Basic Considerations, Principles, and Methods.* New York: Arno, 1976. First published in 1934.

– *Outline of Town and City Planning: A Review of Past Effects and Modern Aims.* New York: Russell Sage Foundation, 1936.

– *Recent Advances in Town Planning.* New York: MacMillan, 1932.

Adams, Thomas, and F. Longstreth Thompson. 'Preliminary Sketch for the Town of Corner Brook, c. 1923.' Box 56 (Corner Brook Material box 1), MG17, The Rooms Archives [hereafter Rooms], St John's.

Armstrong, Whitworth, and Company, Ltd. 'Property Map of Corner Brook, c. 1922.' TR081(c), series 2, Olga Eastman Collection A999-033, CBMA.

Bland, John, and Harold Spence-Sales. *The Urban Development of Greater Corner Brook, Newfoundland.* Montreal: n.p., 1951.

Bowater Contract. File 5, box S2-3-2, GN38, Rooms.

Bowater Newfoundland Limited. 'Bowater's News and Views,' 15 February 1967. File 7 (1-B-7), A999-052, CBMA.

Bowater Newfoundland Pulp and Paper Mills Limited. *A Report on Existing Conditions and Recommended Improvements for West Corner Brook.* Corner Brook: Bowater, 1 November 1939. File 1, box S6-1-6, GN38, Rooms.

Bowater Oral History Project. 1980–3. A series of tape-recorded oral interviews. See the endnotes throughout for citations of specific tapes. Ferriss Hodgett Library, Sir Wilfred Grenfell College, Corner Brook.

Bowater World (New York) 6 (Autumn 1962). File 27 (4-A-27), box 2C, A001-027, CBMA.

Colonial Secretary's Office. *Census of Newfoundland and Labrador, 1921*. Vol. 1, *Population, Sex, Condition, Denomination, Profession, etc.* St John's: Government of Newfoundland, 1923.

Corner Brook Co-operative Society Limited. *Silver Anniversary, August 1st, 1963*. Corner Brook: Western Star, 1963.

Corner Brook Co-operative Society Limited. 'Golden Anniversary, August 1st, 1938–1988.' File 13 (1-C-13), PM220, A000-037, CBMA.

Corner Brook Housing Corporation. 'Report of Operations: 1967.' Corner Brook: Housing Corporation, 1967.

'Corner Brook Labour Situation, March–April 1938.' File 4, box S5-6-1, GN38, Rooms.

Corner Brook Museum and Archives. *Corner Brook Architectural Inventory*. Uncatalogued accession at CBMA as of August 2005, researched February to June 2004.

Correspondence (various). File 182, MG8, Rooms; boxes 1, 2, 10, 56 (Corner Brook Material box 1), 57 (Corner Brook Material box 2), MG17, Rooms; file 7, box S2-3-2, GN8; file 7, box S6-1-6, GN38, Rooms.

Cross, Doris. Interviewer NA, 22 August 1997. File 24 (1-B-24), TR117(b), A000-013, CBMA.

Department of Justice. Justice Files, Re: Municipal Government for Corner Brook West, 1935–36. File 94, box 167, GN13/1/B, Rooms.

Department of Public Health and Welfare. *Tenth Census of Newfoundland and Labrador (Nominal)*. St John's: Queen's Printer for Newfoundland, 1935.

Department of Public Health and Welfare. *Tenth Census of Newfoundland and Labrador, 1935*. Vol. 1, *Population by Districts and Settlements*. St John's: Evening Telegram, 1937.

Department of Public Health and Welfare. *Tenth Census of Newfoundland and Labrador, 1935*. Vol. 2, *Families and Dwellings, Occupations and Earnings, Buildings*. St John's: Evening Telegram, 1937.

'Fisher Agreement, 1902.' File 27, box 2, MG17, Rooms.

Globe and Mail (Toronto). 3 June 1938–6 April 1953.

Goldenberg, H. Carl. *Report on Municipal Administration and Services in the Greater Corner Brook Area of Newfoundland*. April 1950. St John's.

Government of Newfoundland. Relief Division Comparative Expenditures, 1932–1935. GN38/S6-6-1/1, Rooms.

– *Eleventh Census of Newfoundland and Labrador, 1945*. Vol. 1. St John's: Colonial Secretary's Office, 1949.

– *Eleventh Census of Newfoundland, 1945 (Nominal)*. Microform. National Government publication, 1945.

– *1921 Nominal Census*. CNS, Queen Elizabeth II Library, Memorial University of Newfoundland.

– 'Population of Incorporated Cities, Towns, and Villages.' CNS, Queen Elizabeth Library, Memorial University of Newfoundland.

– *Report of the Commission of Enquiry into the Questions Relating to the Imposition of the School Tax at Corner Brook.* April 1956. File 2, series 2 (1-A-2), A999-002, CBMA.

Government of Newfoundland and Labrador. 'Population of Incorporated Cities, Towns, and Villages.' 1972. CNS, Queen Elizabeth II Library, Memorial University of Newfoundland.

Greenland, Gail, William Redden, and Graham Snow. *Survey of Recreation: City of Corner Brook.* St John's: Government of Newfoundland, 1968.

House of Assembly. *Journal of the House of Assembly of Newfoundland.* St John's: House of Assembly, 1920.

Institute of Local Government. *Single-Enterprise Communities in Canada: A Report to the Central Mortgage and Housing Corporation.* Kingston, ON: Queen's University Press, 1953.

International Paper Company. 'Survey of Expansion of International Paper Company during 1927.' 1 March 1938. Box 2C, PM405, A001-007, CBMA.

International Power and Paper Company of Newfoundland. *Regulations Covering Erection of Buildings in the Townsite of Corner Brook.* Corner Brook: Town Department, 1938. File 27 (1-B-27), A000-016, CBMA.

– 'Rules 1928.' CBMA Exhibit.

'Labour Agreement between Bowater's Newfoundland Pulp and Paper Mills Ltd and the International Brotherhood of Papermakers, June 1946.' CNS, Queen Elizabeth Library, Memorial University of Newfoundland.

'The Labour Movement.' In *Corner Brook's 50th Anniversary Souvenir Booklet.* Corner Brook: Western Star, 1975.

Newfoundland Design Associates Limited. *Corner Brook Housing Area Study.* St John's: Newfoundland Design Associates Limited, 1968.

Newfoundland Power and Paper Company Limited, Board of Directors Meeting, 18 June 1924, 29 September 1925, 27 November 1925, 27 October 1926. File 306, box 15, MG17, Rooms.

– *Corner Brook Development for Messrs Sir W.G. Armstrong, Whitworth and Company Ltd: House Type 2, Andrew R. Cobb Architect.* 1924. Box 56 (Corner Brook Material box 1), MG17, Rooms.

– Inter-Office Correspondence, 31 March 1925. File 30 (1-B-30), A000-0191, CBMA.

– *Specification and General Conditions for Type 3, 4 and 5 Houses for the Newfoundland Power and Paper Utilities Corporation Ltd at Corner Brook, Newfoundland.* July 1925. Box 56 (Corner Brook Material box 1), MG17, Rooms.

Newfoundland Register of Trade Unions, 1938. Box 1, GN22-1, Rooms.

Newfoundland Royal Commission. *Report. Presented by the Secretary of State for Dominion Affairs to Parliament by Command of His Majesty, November, 1933.* London: His Majesty's Stationery Office, 1933.

Ogden, H.G. *Ballads of Corner Brook.* St John's: Dicks, 1925. File 59 (6-F-59), A003-068, CBMA.

Peat, Marwick, Mitchell and Company. *Local Government in Corner Brook: A Progress Report.* St John's: Government of Newfoundland and Labrador, 1966.

Pickett, Stanley H., and J.T. Allston. 'Planning for Corner Brook: Canada's Newest Planning Legislation in Action.' *Community Planning Review* part 1, 8.1 (1958): 177–82, Part II: 8, 2 (1958): 19–25.

Province of Newfoundland. *Report of the Royal Commission on Forestry, 1955.* St John's: David R. Thistle, Printer to the Queen's Most Excellent Majesty, 1955.

Provisional Board of Directors Meeting, 31 October 1922, 17 November 1922, 29 December 1922, 1 February 1923, 27 February 1923, 19 April 1923, and 8 June 1923. Box 56 (Corner Brook Material box 1), MG17, Rooms.

'Reid vs. NP&P, NP&P Utilities, and Armstrong's, 1926.' Box 57 (Corner Brook Material box 2), MG17, Rooms

Sir W.G. Armstrong, Whitworth and Company, Ltd Agreement, 5 July 1922. File 26, box 2, MG17, Rooms.

Times (London). 10 December 1904–1 November 1940.

'Trust Deed for Securing $10,000,000 5½ Per Cent "B" Mortgage Debenture Stock (Newfoundland Products Corporation), 1922.' File 150, box 15, GN8, Rooms.

Western Star (Curling and Corner Brook). 16 May 1922–13 February 1971.

William Monroe Papers. Correspondence on the Corner Brook Strike, 1924. File 226, box 22, and file 237, box 24, GN8, Rooms

William Warren Papers. Files 202 and 206 (Humber Strike), box 20, GN8, Rooms.

Mount Isa

Australian (Sydney). 3 July 1978, 29 December 1973, 3 July 1978.

'Australian Plea for Ugly Women.' 18 August 2008. BBC, http://news.bbc.co.uk/2/hi/asia-pacific/7567239.stm.

Bench Record and Summons Book, Mount Isa, 1924–1931. No. 28, SRS5325, QSA.

Brisbane Courier. 24 April 1927, 23 August 1929.

Brisbane Times. 19 August 2008.

Cloncurry Advocate. 24 January 1931–22 December 1950.

'Correspondences regarding Squatters and Town Planning, 1948.' A/8430, QSA.

Correspondence (various). QSA. See endnotes for specific references.

Courier-Mail (Brisbane). 1930s–1970s.

Department of Education. 'Annual Assessment of Schools, Mount Isa.' EDU/AB843 and EDU/AB1067, QSA.

Dwyer, D.J., and Associates. *A Proposal for the Development of an Irrigated Garden Suburb at Fisher, City of Mount Isa*. Brisbane: Hooker Regional Developments, 1970. John Oxley Library, Brisbane.

Financial Times. 18 December 1931.

Fisher, G.R. 'Staff Reports on Overseas Trips, 1937.' Box 19, MIM Collection, Mount Isa City Council Library (MICCL).

Foots, James W. 'Businessmen's Seminar Speech, June 1979.' Box 1, MIM Collection, MICCL.

Foots, James W. 'The Current State and Future Prospects of Australia.' Australian Institute of Management Conference, 17 November 1982. Box 3, MIM Collection, MICCL.

Justice Department. 'American Military Misconduct at Mount Isa.' A/12030 and A/12031, QSA.

Kennedy, F.H. 'A General Report on Mount Isa Mines Limited, July 1946.' Box 7, MIM Collection, MICCL.

Kruttschnitt, Julius. Interview, 1972. Interviewer unknown. Box 7, MIM Collection, MICCL.

Langer, Karl. 'Plans for Mount Isa Mines Ltd Cooperative Housing Scheme, 1954.' Langer Collection 9-5, John Oxley Library.

Licensing Commission. 'Re: Application for Liquor License, Mount Isa Workers' Club.' TR1873/1, QSA.

Mackie, Pat, with Elizabeth Vassilieff. *Mount Isa: The Story of a Dispute*. Hawthorn, AUS: Hudson, 1989.

Mackie, Pat. *Many Ships to Mount Isa*. Adelaide: Seaview, 2002.

Mill, Geoffrey. *Report upon Population Growth, 1970–1990 in Respect of Urban Development in Mount Isa*. Mount Isa: City of Mount Isa, 1970. John Oxley Library.

Mining Trust. 'Plant Inventory, December 1929.' Shelf 4, MIM Collection, MICCL.

Mount Isa Mail. 11 February 1955–15 December 1964. Incorporates the *Cloncurry Advocate*.

Mount Isa Mines Community Department. 'Description of Mount Isa, 1935.' Box 19, MIM Collection, MICCL.

Mount Isa Mines Ltd. *Annual Report*. 1962–72. John Oxley Library.

Mount Isa Mines Ltd. 'Plant Inventory, December 1930.' Shelf 4, MIM Collection, MICCL.

Mount Isa Mines Magazine. December 1947–April 1964.

Mount Isa Shire Council. 'An Explanation of the Proposals Contained in the Town Planning Scheme for the Town of Mount Isa.' Mount Isa: Town Planning Committee, 1967.

Mount Isa Standard. 22 January 1948–26 August 1949.

'Mt Isa Mayor Picks Up "Sexist" Ernie,' 21 November 2008. ABC News. http://abc.net.au/news/stories/2008/11/21/2425663.htm.

North-West Star (Mount Isa). 19 and 21 June 1973.

Police Commissioner Queensland (various correspondences). 518, 522, 524, A/64268; A/64273; A/67562; A/8465; A/8645; A/64261; A/64292; A/64298; A/64307; A/64308; A/64309, QSA. See endnotes for specific references.

Queensland Department of Labor. Collected newspaper clippings covering the 1964–5 labour dispute at Mount Isa. File 45, TR1735/1, QSA.

Queensland Government Mining Journal. May 1924–June 1962.

Queensland Inquest Files. JUS/N series 1929–39. See endnotes for specific references.

Queensland Parliamentary Debates. Brisbane: Frederick Philips, 1930.

Queensland State Government. *1971 Census: Population and Dwelling Characteristics*. Brisbane: Government Printers, 1972.

Queensland Trades and Labor Congress. 'Hands off the Trade Unions: Slave Act Must Be Repealed.' Brisbane: Coronation, 1961. A/64308, QSA.

Registrar of Firms, Vols. 1–4. SRS55194-1-1 to SRS55194-1-4, QSA.

Sellwood, V.G. 'Report on Accommodation Available for Public Servants in Mount Isa.' Public Works Department. TR1158/4, QSA.

Smith's Weekly (Sydney). 24 December 1932.

Times (London). 14 June 1933–3 May 1965.

Truth (Melbourne). 1 October 1961.

Voice of the Rank and File. April 1961–February 1966.

Worker (Sydney). 9 August 1933–31 January 1934.

Other Sources

Adamson, Walter L. *Hegemony and Revolution: A Study of Antonio Gramsci's Political and Cultural Theory*. Berkeley: University of California Press, 1980.

Alexander, David. 'Newfoundland's Traditional Economy and Development to 1934.' *Acadiensis* 5 (Spring 1976): 56–78.

Anderson, Perry. 'The Antinomies of Antonio Gramsci.' *New Left Review* 100 (1976–7): 5–78.

Ankli, Robert E. 'The Canadian Newsprint Industry, 1900–1940.' In *Variations in Business and Economic History: Essays in Honor of Donald L. Kemmerer*, ed. Bruce Dalgaard and Richard K. Vedder, 1–30. London: Jai, 1982.

Armstrong, R.E.M. *The Kalkadoons: A Study of an Aboriginal Tribe on the Queensland Frontier*. Brisbane: William Brooks, 1977.

Aungles, Stan. 'Structural Conflicts between the State, Local Government and Monopoly Capital: The Case of Whyalla in South Australia.' *Australia and New Zealand Journal of Sociology* 15 (March 1979): 24–35.

Australian Government. Australian Mines Atlas. http://www.australianminesatlas.gov.au/?site=atlas.

Baker, Melvin. 'The Interplay of Private and Public Enterprise in the Production of Electricity on the Island of Newfoundland, 1883–1966.' In *Twentieth-Century Newfoundland: Explorations*, ed. James Hiller and Peter Neary, 273–96. St John's: Breakwater Books, 1994.

Bassler, Gerhard P. *Alfred Valdmanis and the Politics of Survival*. Toronto: University of Toronto Press, 2000.

Bell, Peter. 'Essay on North Queensland Mining Settlement.' In *Readings in North Queensland Mining History*, Vol. 2, ed. Kett Kennedy, 1–48. Townsville: James Cook University Press, 1982.

– 'Houses in North Queensland Mining Towns, 1864–1914.' In *Readings in North Queensland Mining History*, Vol. 1, ed. Kett Kennedy, 299–328. Townsville: James Cook University Press, 1980.

– 'International Investment in Early Mount Isa.' In *Readings in North Queensland Mining History*, Vol. 2, ed. Kett Kennedy, 275–306. Townsville: James Cook University Press, 1982.

Berkman, Don. *Making the Mount Isa Mine, 1923–1933*. Victoria: The Australasian Institute of Mining and Metallurgy, 1996.

Blackmur, Douglas. 'Arbitration, Legislation and Industrial Peace: Queensland in the Reconstruction Years.' *Labour History* 63 (1992): 115–34.

– *Strikes: Causes, Conduct and Consequences*. Sydney: Federation, 1993.

Blainey, Geoffrey. *Mines in the Spinifex: The Story of Mount Isa Mines*. Rev. ed. Sydney: Angus and Peterson, 1970.

– *The Rush That Never Ended: A History of Australian Mining*. 3rd ed. Melbourne: Melbourne University Press, 1978.

Bolton, Geoffrey. *Spoils and Spoilers: A History of Australians Shaping Their Environment*. 2nd ed. Sydney: Allen and Unwin, 1992.

Boothman, Barry E.C. 'High Finance / Low Strategy: Corporate Collapse in the Canadian Pulp and Paper Industry, 1919–1932.' *Business History Review* 74 (2000): 611–56.

Botting, Ingrid. 'Getting a Grand Falls Job: Migration, Labour Markets, and

Paid Domestic Work in the Pulp and Paper Mill Town of Grand Falls, Newfoundland, 1905–1939.' PhD diss., Memorial University of Newfoundland, 2000.

Bradbury, John H. 'Towards an Alternate Theory of Resource-Based Town Development in Canada.' *Economic Geography* 55 (April 1979): 147–66.

Braverman, Harry. *Labor and Monopoly Capital: The Degradation of Work in the Twentieth Century*. New York: Monthly Review, 1974.

Buder, Stanley. *Pullman: An Experiment in Industrial Order and Community Planning, 1880–1930*. New York: Oxford University Press, 1967.

– *Visionaries and Planners: The Garden City Movement and the Modern Community*. New York: Oxford University Press, 1990.

Bulmer, M.I.A. 'Sociological Models of the Mining Community.' *Sociological Review* 23 (February 1975): 61–92.

Burgmann, Verity. *Revolutionary Industrial Unionism: the Industrial Workers of the World in Australia*. Cambridge: Cambridge University Press, 1995.

Cadigan, Sean. 'Power and Agency in Newfoundland and Labrador's History.' *Labour / Le Travail* 54 (Fall 2004): 223–43.

Cahir, Pauline. 'Women in North Queensland.' In *Lectures on North Queensland History, Second Series*, 97–117. Townsville: James Cook University Press, 1975.

Carlson, Linda. *Company Towns of the Pacific Northwest*. Seattle: University of Washington Press, 2003.

Carthey, Bretta, and Bob Potter. *Mount Isa: The Great Queensland Strike*. London: Solidarity, 1966.

Chandler, Alfred D. *The Visible Hand: The Managerial Revolution in American Business*. Cambridge, MA: Belknap, 1978.

Chaput, Donald, and K.H. Kennedy. *The Man from ASARCO: A Life and Times of Julius Kruttschnitt*. Parkville, AUS: The Australasian Mineral Heritage Trust, 1992.

Collins, Betsy. *The Copper Crucible*. Brisbane: Jacaranda, 1966.

Collins, Margaret, and Gertrude Caines. 'The Development of Hospital Services in Corner Brook, Newfoundland, 1923–1976.' Undergraduate essay, Ferriss Hodgett Library, Sir Wilfred Grenfell College, Corner Brook.

Corner Brook Downtown Business Association. 'Historical Survey of Broadway Businesses.' File 14 (1-B-14), Broadway Collection, CBMA.

Crawford, Margaret. *Building the Workingman's Paradise: The Design of American Company Towns*. New York: Verso, 1995.

– 'The World in a Shopping Mall.' In *Variations on a Theme Park: The New American City and the End of Public Space*, ed. Michael Sorkin, 3–30. New York: Hill and Wang, 1992.

Cummings, Malcolm R. 'A Neighbourhood for Mount Isa.' MA diss., University of Queensland, 1960.

Curtis, R. Emerson. 'Civilization in the Spinifex: The Story of Mount Isa and Her Mine.' *Walkabout*, April 1947, 6–14.

DeLacey, Keith. *Blood Stains the Wattle*. Rockhampton: Central Queensland University Press, 2002.

Dougan, David. *The Great Gun-Maker: The Story of Lord Armstrong*. Newcastle: Frank Graham, 1970.

Drynan, M. 'The History of Mount Isa.' Unpublished manuscript, 1982, Mount Isa City Council Library, Mount Isa.

Eklund, Erik. '"Intelligently Directed Welfare Work"?: Labour Management Strategies in Local Context: Port Pirie, 1915–29.' *Labour History* 76 (1999): 125–48.

– 'Managers, Workers, and Industrial Welfarism: Management Strategies at ER&S and the Sulphide Corporation, 1895–1929.' *Australian Economic History Review* 37, no. 2 (1997): 137–57.

– 'The "Place" of Politics: Class and Localist Politics at Port Kembla, 1900–1930.' *Labour History* 78 (May 2000): 94–113.

– *Steel Town: The Making and Breaking of Port Kembla*. Melbourne: Melbourne University Press, 2002.

Ellem, Brandon, and John Shields. 'Making a "Union Town": Class, Gender and Consumption in Inter-War Broken Hill.' *Labour History* 78 (2000): 116–44.

Elliott, Rosemary M. 'Newfoundland Politics in the 1920s: The Genesis and Significance of the Hollis Walker Enquiry.' In *Newfoundland in The Nineteenth and Twentieth Centuries: Essays in Interpretation*, ed. James Hiller and Peter Neary, 181–204. Toronto: University of Toronto Press, 1980.

Elton, Kathy-Jane. 'Christopher Fisher.' In *Encyclopedia of Newfoundland and Labrador*, ed. Joseph R. Smallwood, 2:129. St John's: St John's Newfoundland Book Publishers.

Fairfield, John D. 'Scientific Management of Urban Space: Professional City Planning and the Legacy of Progressive Reform.' *Journal of Urban History* 20 (February 1994): 179–204.

Faue, Elizabeth. 'Community, Class, and Comparison in Labour History and Local History.' *Labour History* 78 (2000): 155–63.

Fishman, Robert. *Urban Utopias in the Twentieth Century: Ebenezer Howard, Frank Lloyd Wright, and Le Corbusier*. New York: Basic Books, 1977.

Fitzgerald, Ross. *A History of Queensland from 1915 to the 1980s*. London: University of Queensland Press, 1984.

Forster, Clive. *Australian Cities*. 3rd ed. London: Oxford University Press, 2004.

Frost, Lionel, and Tony Dingle. 'Sustaining Suburbia: An Historical Perspective on Australia's Urban Growth.' In *Australian Cites: Issues, Strategies and Policies for Urban Australia in the 1990s*, ed. Patrick Troy, 20–8. London: Cambridge University Press, 1995,

Garner, John S., ed. *The Company Town: Architecture and Society in the Early Industrial Age*. New York: Oxford University Press, 1992Genovese, Eugene D. *Roll Jordan Roll: The World the Slaves Made*. New York: Pantheon Books, 1974.

Geertz, Clifford. *After the Fact: Two Countries, Four Decades, One Anthropologist*. Cambridge, MA: Harvard University Press, 1995.

Gibson, Katherine D. and Ronald J. Horvath. 'Global Capital and the Restructuring Crisis in Australian Manufacturing.' *Economic Geography* 59, no. 2 (April 1983): 178–94.

Gillespie, Bill. *A Class Act: An Illustrated History of the Labour Movement in Newfoundland and Labrador*. St John's: Creative Printers and Publishers, 1986.

Greening, W.E. *Paper Makers in Canada: A History of the Paper Makers Union in Canada*. Cornwall, ON: International Brotherhood of Papermakers, 1952.

Griffiths, John. '"Give My Regards to Uncle Billy ... ": The Rites and Rituals of Company Life at Lever Brothers, c.1900–c.1990.' *Business History* 37 (1995): 25–45.

Harrison, Michael. *Bournville: Model Village to Garden Suburb*. West Sussex: Phillimore, 1999.

Hearn, Mark, and Harry Knowles. *One Big Union: A History of the Australian Workers Union 1886–1994*. Cambridge: Cambridge University Press, 1996.

Heinrich, Thomas. 'Product Diversification in the U.S. Pulp and Paper Industry: The Case of International Paper, 1898–1941.' *Business History Review* 75 (2001): 467–505.

Hiller, James K. 'The Origins of the Pulp and Paper Industry in Newfoundland.' *Acadiensis* 11 (Spring 1982): 46–68.

– 'The Politics of Newsprint: The Newfoundland Pulp and Paper Industry, 1915–1939.' *Acadiensis* 19 (Spring 1990): 3–39.

Hore-Lacy, Ian, ed. *Broken Hill to Mount Isa: The Mining Odyssey of W.H. Corbould*. Melbourne: Hyland House, 1981.

Horwood, Harold. *Corner Brook: A Social History of a Paper Town*. St John's: Breakwater Books, 1986.

Inglis, Fred. *Clifford Geertz: Culture, Custom, and Ethics*. Cambridge, UK: Polity, 2000.

Irving, R.J. 'New Industries for Old? Some Investment Decisions of Sir W.G. Armstrong, Whitworth & Co. Ltd, 1900–1914.' *Business History* 17 (1975): 150–75.

John, Richard R. 'Elaborations, Revisions, Dissents: Alfred Chandler Jr's *The*

Visible Hand after Twenty Years.' *Business History Review* 71 (Summer 1997): 151–200.

Kealey, Gregory S., and Bryan D. Palmer. *Dreaming of What Might Be: The Knights of Labor in Ontario.* Cambridge: Cambridge University Press, 1982.

Kennedy, K.H. 'Mining.' In *Labor in Power: The Labor Party and Government in Queensland, 1915–1957*, ed. D.J. Murphy, R.B. Joyce, and Colin A. Hughes, 282–311. Brisbane: University of Queensland Press, 1980.

– 'Mount Isa Mines: Corporate Leadership over Six Decades.' In *Shaping Queensland through History*, ed. Peter Griggs, 53–60. Brisbane: Royal Geographic Society, 1988.

– 'Mount Isa's Russian Connection.' *Royal Historical Society of Queensland Journal* 12 (date NA): 183–99.

Kennedy, K.H., and Noreen Kirkman. 'The Evolution of Company Welfare: Practices at Mount Isa, Queensland.' In *Towards a Social History of Mining in the Nineteenth and Twentieth Centuries: Papers Presented to the International Mining History Congress*, ed. Klaus Tenfelde, 1155–66. Bochum, Germany: C.H. Beck Munchen, 1989.

Kirkman, Noreen. *Mount Isa: Oasis of the Outback.* Townsville: James Cook University Press, 1998.

Kleinschmidt, Boyd N. 'A Socio-Educational Study of Mount Isa.' MA diss., University of Queensland, 1955.

Klemola, Kauno. 'Mount Isa Finnish Community: A Case Study.' Australian Council of Social Service Conference, 1968. Fryer Research Library, University of Queensland.

Lears, T.J. Jackson. 'The Concept of Cultural Hegemony: Problems and Possibilities.' *American Historical Review* 90 (June 1985): 567–93.

Letto, Doug. *Chocolate Bars and Rubber Boots: The Smallwood Industrialization Plan.* Paradise, NL: Blue Hill, 1998.

Lucas, Rex A. *Minetown, Milltown, Railtown: Life in Canadian Communities of Single Industry.* Toronto: University of Toronto Press, 1974.

Machlis, Gary E., and Jo Ellen Force. 'Community Stability and Timber-Dependent Communities.' *Rural Sociology* 53 (1988): 220–34.

MacIntyre, Stuart. *A Concise History of Australia.* Cambridge: Cambridge University Press, 2000.

MacKinnon, Richard. 'Company Housing in Wabana, Bell Island, Newfoundland.' *Material History Bulletin* 14 (Spring 1982): 67–71.

Macleod, Malcolm. 'A Death at Deer Lake: Catalyst of a Forgotten Work Stoppage.' *Labour / Le Travail* 16 (Fall 1985): 179–91.

Marcosson, Isaac F. *Metal Magic: The Story of the American Smelting and Refining Company.* New York: Farrar, Straus, 1949.

Marx, Karl, and Friedrich Engels. *The Communist Manifesto*. 3rd. ed. New York: Washington Square, 1964.

McCann, L.D. 'The Changing Internal Structure of Canadian Resource Towns.' In *Little Communities and Big Industries: Studies in the Social Impact of Canadian Resource Extraction*, ed. Roy T. Bowles, 61–81. Toronto: Butterworth, 1982.

McCrystal, P. 'The Metal Mining Industry of Mount Isa.' 1973. Fryer Research Library, University of Queensland.

McGowan, Barry. 'Class, Hegemony and Localism: The Southern Mining Region of New South Wales, 1850–1900.' *Labour History* 86 (2004): 93–113.

McIntyre, Stuart. *A Concise History of Australia*. Cambridge: Cambridge University Press, 2000.

Mill Basket, episode 2-17. Corner Brook public access television, second season, January 1997–June 1997. Air date: n/a.

Mouat, Jeremy. 'Industry and Community: A Comparison of Broken Hill (New South Wales), Waihi (New Zealand), and Rossland (British Columbia).' In *Sözialgeschichte der Bergarbeiterkommune im Vergliech*, ed. Roy A. Church, 267–83. Munich: Beck, 1992.

– *Roaring Days: Rossland's Mines and the History of British Columbia*. Vancouver: University of British Columbia Press, 1995.

National Trust of Queensland. *A Study of a Tent House at Fourth Avenue, Mount Isa*. Brisbane: National Trust, 1977.

Neary, Peter. 'The Bradley Report on Logging Operations in Newfoundland, 1934: A Suppressed Document.' *Labour / Le Travail* 16 (1985): 193–232.

– *Newfoundland in the North Atlantic World, 1929–1949*. Montreal and Kingston: McGill-Queen's University Press, 1988.

– 'Traditional and Modern Elements in the Social and Economic History of Bell Island and Conception Bay.' *The Canadian Historical Association: Historical Papers*. 1973.

Nelles, H.V. *The Politics of Development: Forest, Mines and Hydro-Electric Power in Ontario, 1849–1941*. Toronto: Macmillan, 1974.

Neufeld, Andrew, and Andrew Parnaby. *The IWA in Canada: The Life and Times of an Industrial Union*. Vancouver: IWA Canada / New Star Books, 2000.

Noel, S.J.R. *Politics in Newfoundland*. Toronto: University of Toronto Press, 1971.

Norcliffe, Glen. *Global Game, Local Arena: Restructuring in Corner Brook, Newfoundland*. St John's: Institute of Social and Economic Research, 2005.

Palmer, Bryan D. *Working-Class Experience: Rethinking the History of Canadian Labour, 1800–1991*. 2nd ed. Toronto: McClelland and Stewart, 1992.

Parr, Joy. *The Gender of Breadwinners: Women, Men, and Change in Two Industrial Towns, 1880–1950*. Toronto: University of Toronto Press, 1990.

Patmore, Greg. 'Working Lives in Regional Australia: Labour History and Local History.' *Labour History* 78 (2000): 1–6.

Penrose, Beris. 'Occupational Lead Poisoning at Mount Isa Mines in the 1930s.' *Labour History* 73 (November 1997): 123–41.

Perkins, Di. *Outback Insights: A Social History of Northwest Queensland, 1925–50*. Mount Isa: Mount Isa District Historical Society, 1996.

Radforth, Ian. *Bushworkers and Bosses: Logging in Northern Ontario, 1900–1980*. Toronto: University of Toronto Press, 1987.

Ravetz, Alison. *The Government of Space: Town Planning in Modern Society*. London: Faber and Faber, 1986.

Reader, W.J. *Bowater: A History*. Cambridge: Cambridge University Press, 1981.

Reid, David. *Townsite Heritage Conservation District Development Scheme*. Corner Brook: Development Control Department, 1983.

Rollwagen, Katherine. 'When Ghosts Hovered: Community and Crisis in a Company Town, Britannia Beach, British Columbia, 1957–1964.' *Urban History Review* 35, no. 2 (2007): 25–36.

Ryan, J.H. 'The Growth and Development of Mount Isa: Town and Region.' BA thesis, University of Melbourne, 1960.

Saarinen, Oiva. 'The City-Building Process in Canada.' In *Shaping the Urban Landscape: Aspects of the Canadian City-Building Process*, ed. Gilbert Stelter and Alan Artibise, 1–29. Ottawa: Carleton University Press, 1982.

– 'The Influence of Thomas Adams and the British New Towns Movement in the Planning of Canadian Resource Communities.' In *The Usable Past: Planning and Politics in the Modern Canadian City*, ed. Gilbert Stelter and Alan Artibise, 268–92. Toronto: MacMillan, 1979.

– 'Single-Sector Communities in Northern Ontario: The Creation and Planning of Dependent Towns.' In *Power and Place: Canadian Urban Development in the North American Context*, ed. Gilbert Stelter and Alan Artibise, 219–61. Vancouver: University of British Columbia Press, 1986.

Scott, J.D. *Vickers: A History*. London: Weidenfeld and Nicolson, 1962.

Sheldon, Gordon. *Industrial Siege: The Mount Isa Dispute*. Melbourne: F.W. Cheshire, 1965.

Sherlock, Shawn. '"Good-bye the State's Progress": State Enterprise and Labor's Plan for a North Queensland Steel Industry, 1915–1920.' *Labour History* 90 (2006): 61–75.

Shields, John. 'Lead Bonus Happy: Profit-Sharing, Productivity and Industrial Relations in the Broken Hill Mining Industry, 1925–1983.' *Australian Economic History Review* 37, no. 3 (November 1997): 222–3.

Silverstein, Ken. 'Shopping for Sweat: The Human Cost of a Two-Dollar T-Shirt.' *Harper's Magazine* (January 2010): 36–44.

Simpson, Michael. 'Thomas Adams in Canada, 1914–1930.' *Urban History Review* 11 (October 1982): 1–16.

– *Thomas Adams and the Modern Planning Movement: Britain, Canada, and the United States, 1900–1940.* London: Alexandrine, 1985.

Steinkamp, Harold. 'The Mining Town in the Social Environment, Mount Isa.' AMIC-Environmental Workshop, 1981. John Oxley Library, Brisbane.

Stelter, Gilbert A. 'The City-Building Process in Canada.' In *Shaping the Urban Landscape: Aspects of the Canadian City-Building Process*, ed. G. Stelter and A. Artibise, 413–34. Ottawa: Carleton University Press, 1982.

– 'A Sense of Time and Place: The Historian's Approach to Canada's Urban Past.' In *The Canadian City: Essays In Urban History*, ed. Gilbert Stelter, 420–41. Toronto: McClelland and Stewart, 1977.

Stelter, Gilbert A., and Alan F.J. Artibise. 'Canadian Resource Towns in Historical Perspective.' In *Shaping the Urban Landscape: Aspects of the Canadian City-Building Process*, ed. Gilbert Stelter and Alan Artibise, 413–34. Ottawa: Carleton University Press, 1982.

Sutherland, Dufferin. 'Newfoundland Loggers Respond to the Great Depression.' *Labour / Le Travail* 29 (1992): 83–115.

– 'We Are Only Loggers: Loggers and the Struggle for Development in Newfoundland, 1929–1959,' PhD diss., Simon Fraser University, 1995.

Symonds, Richard. *The Architecture and Planning of the Townsite Development, Corner Brook, 1923–1925.* St John's: Heritage Foundation of Newfoundland and Labrador, 2001.

Tanner, Alex. *The Long Road North.* Richmond, AU: Hyde Park, 1995.

Thomas, Pete. *Buried Treasure: What Everyone Should Know about Mount Isa Mines.* Brisbane: Queensland Guardian, 1964.

– *Storm in the Tropics: The Historic Mount Isa Struggle, 1964–1965.* Brisbane: Pete Thomas, 1965.

Thompson, Edward P. *The Making of the English Working Class.* London: Penguin Books, 1988. First published in London by Pelican Books, 1968.

Thompson, E.P. *Customs In Common.* Pontypool, Wales: Merlin, 1991.

Waldegrave, H.B. *'Ya Gotta Be Jokin'!'* Sussex: Book Guild, 1985.

Weir, Jean B. *Rich in Interest and Charm: The Architecture of Andrew Randall Cobb, 1876–1943.* Halifax: Art Gallery of Nova Scotia, 1990.

White, Neil. 'Creating Community: Industrial Paternalism and Town Planning in Corner Brook, Newfoundland, 1923–1955.' *Urban History Review* 32 (Spring 2004): 45–58.

– 'Global Industrial Enclaves: Company Towns and Export-Processing Zones Compared, 1900–200. In *Empires and Autonomy: Moments in the History of Globalization*, ed. Stephen M. Streeter, John C. Weaver, and William D. Coleman, 117–37. Vancouver: University of British Columbia Press, 2009.

Wikipedia: www.wikipedia.org.
Williams, C.W. *Yellow, Green, and Red*. Brisbane: The Worker Newspaper Proprietary, 1967.
Wonders, William C. 'Parasite Communities of Newfoundland.' *Community Planning Review* 2 (1953).
Zeiger, Robert H. *Rebuilding the Pulp and Paper Workers' Union, 1935–1941*. Knoxville: University of Tennessee Press, 1984.

Index